W9-CMP-460

**INTERVIEWS
AND OTHER
WRITINGS
1977–1984**

MICHEL FOUCAULT

POLITICS
PHILOSOPHY
CULTURE

INTERVIEWS
AND OTHER
WRITINGS
1977–1984

TRANSLATED BY ALAN SHERIDAN AND OTHERS

EDITED WITH AN INTRODUCTION BY
LAWRENCE D. KRITZMAN

ROUTLEDGE • NEW YORK AND LONDON

First published in 1988
Paperback published in 1990 by

Routledge
an imprint of
Routledge, Chapman & Hall, Inc.
29 West 35th Street
New York, NY 10001

Published in Great Britain by

Routledge
11 New Fetter Lane
London EC4P 4EE

Library of Congress Cataloging-in-Publication Data

Foucault, Michel.
 Politics, philosophy, culture.

 1. Foucault, Michel — Interviews. I. Kritzman,
Lawrence D. II. Title.
B2430.F722E5   1988   194   87–31243
ISBN 0–415–90082–4
ISBN 0-415-90149-9 (pb)

British Library Cataloguing in Publication Data

Foucault, Michel
 Politics, philosophy, culture: interviews
 and other writings of Michel Foucault,
 1977–1984.
 1. Philosophy
 I. Title II. Kritzman, Lawrence D.
 194   B2430.F722E5
 ISBN 0–415–90082–4
 ISBN 0-415-90149-9 (pb)

Contents

The Ethics of Sexuality

The Politics of Sexuality

Notes on the Power of Culture

Foreword

The late Michel Foucault left behind an impressive collection of interviews that demonstrate the breadth and diversity of his concerns and offer a unique opportunity to come to terms with the entire body of his work. The dialogic form of the interview enabled Foucault to engage intimately in a critical reflection on the crucial shifts in his philosophical, political, and cultural perspectives. No other European intellectual since Jean-Paul Sartre has been so committed to the interview as a cultural form. Foucault used it masterfully to gloss and supplement his theoretical works in an accessible and personal way and thereby assure it a central place within his *corpus*. In this volume I have compiled a rich selection of Foucault's interviews, most of which were previously unavailable in English, that elucidate the most compelling preoccupations of the last years of his critical production. I have chosen texts which clearly articulate Foucault's social and political vision, and the evolution of his theory of sexuality. I have also included a small number of other texts which "essay" some of the theoretical concerns sketched out in the interviews: politics and reason, the nature of modernity, the history of criminology, and the ethics of sexuality. *Politics, Philosophy, Culture* offers the most up to date guide to Foucault by Foucault and traces the self-portrait of an unpretentious intellectual in search of "politics as ethics."

I am pleased to thank those who helped me bring this manuscript into being: first and foremost my editor at Routledge, William P. Germano, who provided unwavering support, good humor, and keen critical acumen. I owe a special debt of gratitude to Cecelia Cancellaro whose superb administrative skills and intelligent suggestions helped bring this project to fruition. I would also like to thank the late Michel de Certeau, Dr. D. Dilldock, Marguerite Dobrenn, Jean-Pierre and Marie-Odile Faye, Pierre Nora, Gerald Prince, and Alan Sheridan for their assistance at various stages. Stephen Ferrell and Lynn Ware of Ohio State University helped in the proofreading of the final manuscript. Editions Gallimard and Paule Neuvéglise were generous enough to permit me to use the magnificent photographs of Foucault by Jacques Robert for the jacket design.

Lawrence D. Kritzman
New York and Columbus
June 1988

Foucault and the Politics of Experience

"Do not ask who I am and do not ask me to remain the same: leave it to our bureaucrats and our police to see that our papers are in order" [The Archeology of Knowledge].

Michel Foucault's death in 1984 at the age of fifty-eight created an enormous void in the French intellectual scene. No other thinker in recent history had so dynamically influenced the fields of history, philosophy, literature and literary theory, the social sciences, even medicine. As a thinker Foucault engaged in a series of provocative dialogues with his theoretical forefathers – Marx, Nietzsche, Freud, Sartre – in order to reconceptualize the notions of the human subject, marginality, the institutional, and the political within the context of power relations. His genealogical method uncovered the variety of discursive practices such as the technologies of normalization and control through which social relations take shape; it radically challenged Western political epistemology and thereby forged a new role for critical thought that is independent of utopian models. But ironically, the figure who opted for the anonymity of the "masked philosopher" simultaneously redefined, through penetrating critical activity, what it meant to be an intellectual in the postmodern world by attempting to transcend the constraints of established political doctrine.

The events of May 1968 ushered in a new era in French political thought that led to substantive reflections on the practice of cultural criticism: they created, according to Foucault, a consciousness of Marxism's "decline as a dogmatic framework" and its "powerlessness . . . to confront a whole series of questions that were not traditionally a part of its statutory domain (questions about women, about relations between sexes, about medicine, about mental illness, about the environment, about minorities, about delinquency)."[1] In the wake of the student demonstrations and general strike that failed to coalesce into a revolutionary force, an anti-Marxist reaction surged forth. It questioned the pertinence of historical materialism and the relevance of a reified political doctrine in assessing social reality. This reaction opposed the idea that man's social relationships and destiny are determined by the logic of history as articulated by the so-called unhappy consciousness of the universal intellectual. The failure of the proletariat, that mythological revolutionary vanguard, to support the student uprisings of 1968, along with the French Communist Party's series of expedient political compromises with de Gaulle, suggested, at least on the local level, that the myth of history could not eradicate repression and that there was no inextricable relationship between the human project and the quest for historical totality. The French Communist party was simply another repressive force.[2] It exploited Marxist doctrine and became what Sartre characterized in the 1970s as "this revolutionary party . . . determined not to make a revolution."[3] In short, the lesson derived from the events of May 1968 was that the oppression associated with power could not be located within a single socio-political apparatus; it was dispersed in complex networks of social

1. "The Minimalist Self," in this volume and "Polemics, Politics and Problematizations: An Interview with Paul Rabinow," in *The Foucault Reader* (New York: Pantheon, 1984), p. 386. In another perspective Frank Lentricchia in *Ariel and the Police* (Madison: University of Wisconsin Press, 1988), pp. 30–102, situates Foucault's discourse within a "Marxist horizon."

2. See Alan Sheridan, *Michel Foucault: The Will to Truth* (London: Tavistock, 1980); Régis Debray, *Teachers, Writers, Celebrities: The Intellectuals of Modern France* (London: Verso, 1981); Barry Smart, *Foucault, Marxism, and Critique* (London: Routledge and Kegan Paul, 1983); Mark Poster, "Sartre's Concept of the Intellectual," in *Notebooks for Cultural Analysis* (Durham: Duke University Press, 1984), pp. 39–52 and "Foucault and Sartre," in *Foucault, Marxism and History* (Cambridge: Polity Press, 1984); Pascal Ory and Jean-François Sirinelli, *Les intellectuels en France, de l'Affaire Dreyfus à nos jours* (Paris: Armand Colin, 1986); Jeannine Verdès-Leroux, *Le réveil des somnambules: le parti communiste, les intellectuels et la culture (1965–1985)* (Paris: Fayard/Minuit, 1987); Keith A. Reader, *Intellectuals and the Left in France since 1968* (London: St. Martin's Press, 1987).

3. Jean-Paul Sartre, *On a raison de se révolter*, discussions with Philippe Gavi and Pierre Victor (Paris: Gallimard, 1974), p. 38.

control that encompassed the bureaucracy of an ossified revolutionary party.

On a more global level, however, the leading intellectuals of the period became increasingly aware of contradictions that had been developing since the late 1950s. History, it was realized, could not bring salvation to man through traditional revolutionary praxis. The Soviet invasions of Hungary in 1956 and Czechoslovakia in 1968, and the increased stalinization of a French communist party which followed a more nationalistic line on the Algerian question, exacerbated this situation. To be sure, reason was attacked by some as a weapon to reinforce mastery, and the apocalyptic vision of history was regarded as a "played out idea." Intellectuals such as Michel Foucault, Gilles Deleuze, Edgar Morin, and André Glucksmann, to name but a few, saw the Gulag, the system of Soviet prisons and places of exile, and the repression of the Solidarity trade union movement in Poland, as one of the excesses of Marxism and the result of the very rationalism of theoretical mastery.[4]

After their long Marxist experience, most French intellectuals, have moved on, now dissociating Marxism from democratic development. As Edgar Morin maintains in *Pour sortir du XXe siècle* we have indeed crossed over into a post-totalitaraian age, one in which anticolonial and antifascist imperatives converge in an anti-Marxist ethic.[5] In 1936, when the France of the Popular Front exemplified the ideals of democracy and Socialism, their cultural gods were Malraux, Aragon, Picasso and Gide – supporters of the government or of various ideologies. However, even in the early 1980s with the Socialists in power in France there were no longer any "symbolic" intellectuals of the Left, offering their transcendental reputations both as artists and militants to a political cause that proclaims freedom as being inextricably linked to something whole and universal. In effect, we live in a period in which there is a general suspicion and delegitimization of political ideologies. Caution is exercised in terms of the

---

4. Jürgen Habermas, in *Lectures on the Discourse of Modernity* (Cambridge: Harvard University Press, 1985), considers Foucault, Deleuze, and Lyotard neo-conservative thinkers since their theoretical gestures do not offer an alternative to the capitalist mode.

5. Edgar Morin, *Pour sortir du XXe siècle* (Paris: Nathan, 1981).

classical Marxist solutions for the infelicities of socio-economic reality. Without denying its unquestionable influence on the elaboration of his thought, Foucault cites Marxism's failure to function as a heuristic tool to "satisfy our desire for understanding this enigmatic thing we call power."[6] In this context, figures such as Foucault and Deleuze have revised the intellectual's role in militant practice. The intellectual is no longer commissioned to play the role of advisor to the masses and critic of ideological content, but rather to become one capable of providing instruments of analysis. We are through with the intellectual who functions as master of truth and justice by lending his or her voice to an oppressed consciousness: "For us the intellectual theorist," claims Deleuze in a discussion with Foucault, "has ceased to be a subject, a representing and representative consciousness . . . there is no longer any representation, there is only action, theory's action, the action of practice in the relationships of networks".[7]

More recently, in *Tombeau de l'Intellectuel*, Jean-François Lyotard takes this position even a step further by adamantly declaring the death of those intellectuals whose aim it is to speak on behalf of humanity in the name of an abstract and moralistic truth.[8] Here Lyotard puts to rest the doctrines of natural rights and universal reason, positions originating in the Enlightenment and culminating in Hegel's identification of truth with totality. For Lyotard, there is no universal subject capable of putting forth a new conception of the world: "An artist, a writer, a philosopher . . . experiments. He does not need to identify himself with a universal subject and to take in charge the responsibility of the human community in order to assume those of creation."[9]

By 1968 existential marxism and the politics of engagement

6. Michel Foucault, "Les intellectuels et le pouvoir," [a discussion with Gilles Deleuze] *L'Arc* 49 (1972), p. 6. English translation as "Intellectuals and Power" in *Language, Counter-Memory, Practice: Selected Essays and Interviews by Michel Foucault*, edited with an introduction by Donald F. Bouchard, translated by Donald F. Bouchard and Sherry Simon (Ithaca: Cornell University Press, 1977), p. 213.

7. Gilles Deleuze, "Intellectuals and Power," in *Language, Counter-Memory, Practice*, pp. 206–7.

8. Jean-François Lyotard, *Tombeau de l'Intellectuel* (Paris: Galilée, 1984).

9. Lyotard, pp. 15–16.

had already become passé. (Sartre's appearance before the students occupying the Sorbonne was greeted with cries of "Let Papa speak!"). The intellectually committed writer, a vestige of nineteenth-century bourgeois ideology, was no longer a viable possibility but merely a historical anachronism. Sartre declared that the classical intellectual in the tradition of Voltaire, Zola, and Péguy remains an enemy of the people who is yet to attain a popular status. Nevertheless, he worked at fashioning a *persona*, one struggling to demystify traditional left-wing rhetoric through the development of a cultural hermeneutics attuned to the institutional sclerosis of the Communist party. Sartre "moralized" the politics of contemporary life and acceded to what Hegel termed the dignity of effective reality. "An intellectual exists in order to draw attention to the principles of revolution."[10]

But the experience of 1968 taught Sartre that the intellectual must suppress himself as intellectual in order to put his skills at the services of the masses. In a taped interview of 1974 with Herbert Marcuse, Sartre made a definitive break with the idealized conceptualization of the committed intellectual whose over-estimation of self-value isolated him from the "apprenticeship of democracy in a milieu of revolt." The choice to invert his role as intellectual reveals a long-felt sense of class guilt as well as the desire to eradicate his bourgeois self-image. Sartre's argument, as he develops it, aims to revise his function as intellectual through concrete political action. He insists in his discussion with Herbert Marcuse that the intellectual will effect politics by putting his status at the service of the oppressed; the risk of ideological warfare was inappropriate without the risk of the body.

MARCUSE: The intellectual can always formulate or elaborate the goal of the progressive movement and the demands of the workers.

10. *Sartre* [transcript of the film *Sartre par lui-même* by Alexandre Astruc et Michel Contat (1976)] (Paris: Gallimard, 1977), p. 121. See Germaine Brée, *Camus and Sartre* (New York: Pantheon, 1972); Mark Poster, *Existential Marxism in Post-War France: From Sartre to Althusser* (Princeton: Princeton University Press, 1975); Ronald Aronson, *Sartre: Philosophy in the World* (London: Verso, 1980); Simone de Beauvoir, *La Cérémonie des adieux* (Paris: Gallimard, 1981); Annie Cohen-Solal, *Sartre* (Paris: Gallimard, 1985); *Sartre* (New York: Simon and Schuster, 1987).

SARTRE: Yes! He can do it! But the workers can also do it! And they can do it better for themselves than the intellectuals.

MARCUSE: By themselves?

SARTRE: And for themselves! They can better express what they feel, what they think . . . the intellectual, not always, but most of the time, is not the best one to formulate . . . I want to change all that. Personally I feel myself still an old intellectual . . . I do not have a bad conscience. For me, the classical intellectual is an intellectual who ought to disappear.[11]

Sartre's anti-elitist exigencies impelled him to take to the streets and dismantle, so he would claim, the prestige of the petit bourgeois intelligentsia. In its place he would call for the creation of a proletarianized intellectual with a mass audience to whom he would owe his knowledge and from whom he would derive his praxis. Sartre gave theoretical expression to the marginal power of collective experience and its potential to build a more radicalized form of socialism based on direct participation. Nevertheless this preference for the unadulterated struggle of the group ostensibly did not challenge the need for the intellectual to represent the universal by serving a public and a myth which historical circumstances have engendered. To the very end, Sartre believed that knowledge was power and truth and that in effect ideas shape reality.

However, if any one figure is responsible for breaking with the totalizing ambition of the universal intellectual it was Michel Foucault, who invented what he termed the "specific intellectual": one who no longer speaks as master of truth and justice and is content, nevertheless, to simply discover the truth of power and privileges. To be sure, for Foucault the intellectual enterprise is no longer a task external to one's work as intellectual. The specific intellectual is cognizant of the discursive operations of the institution that he or she analyzes without aspiring to guru status. The role of theory is therefore not to formulate a global analysis of the ideologically coded, but rather to analyze the specificity of the mechanisms of power and to build, little by little, "strategic knowledge." "What we have to present are instruments and tools that

11. See the review article of Douglas Kellner, *Telos* 22 (1974–75), 195–96. This is a translation of a conversation between Sartre and Marcuse that originally appeared in *Liberation* (June 7, 1974).

people might find useful. By forming groups specifically to make these analyses, to wage these struggles, by using these instruments or others: this is how, in the end, possibilities open up."[12] Foucault undertakes a topological and geological survey of those institutions where theory emerges from practice: for example, the mental institution with its physicians; the social security system with its bureaucrats; the school with its administrators. Foucault ostensibly shifts emphasis away from the messianic Sartrean discourse on revolution and global transformation to those technologies of control that constitute the fabric of all social institutions and form the basis of our modern political warfare. If power is dispersed in a multiplicity of networks, resistance can only be realized through a series of localized strategies. "The overthrow of these micro-powers does not obey the law of all or nothing."[13]

Unlike Sartre, for instance, who supported the Maoist concept of popular justice through the institution of revolutionary courts, Foucault expressed an unquestionable distrust for such a system since it "reintroduced the ideology of the penal system into popular practice."[14] Instead of opting for revolutionary justice as a panacea for social ills, Foucault regarded it as but one more example of the social reification derived from the bourgeois inspired penal system. Foucault's innate distrust of this revolutionary idealism stems from his attempt to situate the "alternative courts" within the parameters of that humanist myth which subscribes to the belief that popular inquiry can produce objective truth. Accordingly, he sees his function here too as one of problematizing the presuppositions of utopian dreams by liberating the power of truth from the forms of hegemony that imprison it.

In Foucault's praxis the intellectual does not act upon the general will to bring about the creation of an "open society." Gone is the utopian dream of an idyllic, rational, democratic

12. "Confinement, Psychiatry, Prison," in this volume.

13. Michel Foucault, *Power, Truth, Strategy*, ed. Meaghan Morris and Paul Patton (Sydney: Feral, 1979), p. 126.

14. *Power/Knowledge: Selected Interviews and Other Writings 1972–1977*, edited by Colin Gordon (New York: Pantheon, 1980) p. 16. For a negative interpretation of the antijudicial principle in Foucault's writing see Luc Ferry and Alain Renaut, *La Pensée 68* (Paris: Gallimard, 1985), p. 163.

state in which alienation disappears; gone too is the so-called ideal continuity of history and with it a destiny that is controlled by a regulatory teleological movement. In essence Foucault's critical vision portrays a new kind of intellectual for whom the transcendent laws of political ideologies are greeted with increased scepticism. He argues, in effect, that we must no longer analyze modern politics as a congealed and essentialized conflict between master and rebel, but rather as a dispersed and indefinite field of power relations or strategies of domination.

Foucault is as John Rajchman terms him, a "postrevolutionary" figure because he defends the necessity of revolt as a particular form of struggle appropriate to specific technologies of control.[15] Foucault inverts the Sartrean ideological imperative founded on an essentialized notion of power, concentrating instead on uncovering the particularities and contingencies of our knowledge and discursive practices as political technologies. "All the forms of liberty, acquired or claimed, all the rights which⁴ one values, even those involving the least important of matters, doubtlessly find in revolt a last point on which to anchor themselves, one that is more solid and near than natural rights."[16] In essence, the role of the intellectual is not to shape and determine the collective political will from a metacritical perspective. Foucault puts it most poignantly in a last interview where he claims that he is competent to speak only of what he knows: "the role of an intellectual," he says, "is not to tell others what they have to do. By what right would he do so? . . . The work of an intellectual is not to shape others' political will; it is, through the analyses that he carries out in his own field, to question over and over again what is postulated as self-evident, to disturb people's mental habits, the way they do and think things, to dissipate what is familiar and accepted, to reexamine rules and institutions . . . to participate in the formation of a political will."[17] Foucault thus opens up the whole question of the relationship of

15. John Rajchman, *Michel Foucault: The Freedom of Philosophy* (New York: Columbia University Press, 1985), pp. 61–67. "[Foucault] . . . attempted to defend the specificity of revolt . . . [he] would claim that we need to devise forms of struggle appropriate to the specific "technologies" which confront us. . . " (p. 73, n.5).

16. Michel Foucault, "Inutile de se soulever?," *Le Monde* (11-12 May 1979), 1–2.

17. See "The Concern for Truth," in this volume.

theory to practice, a phenomenon from which a new ethic is put forth, one based not on the lifting of censorship and prohibition but rather on a more limited ethic that invents new forms of life independent from reified political and social structures. Foucault articulates an unquestionable suspicion toward any order through which knowledge is transformed into power and vice versa.

If the intellectual, as Foucault conceives of him, is to engage in political action, he can only do so by transcending the forms of power that transform him into a discursive instrument of truth within which "theory" is just another form of oppression.

> I believe precisely that the forms of totalization offered by politics are always . . . very limited. I am attempting . . . apart from any *totalization* – which would be at once *abstract* and *limiting* – to *open up* problems that are as *concrete* and *general* as possible, problems that approach politics from behind and cut across societies on the diagonal.[18]

It is therefore difficult to situate Foucault's political practice within a single perspective. His refusal to become an ideologue not only challenges the traditional notion of the institution of the intellectual in France, but it also reveals an uneasiness in articulating a general and yet formulaic political project:

> I think I have in fact been situated in most of the squares of the political checkerboard, one after another and sometimes simultaneously: as anarchist, leftist, ostentatious or disguised Marxist, nihilist, explicit or secret anti-Marxist, technocrat in the service of Gaullism, new liberal, etc. . . . None of these descriptions is important by itself; taken together, on the other hand, they mean something. And I must admit that I rather like what they mean.[19]

Foucault therefore conceives of himself as a protean being whose quasi-Nietzschean stance is derived from the refusal to let thought coagulate into systematic doctrine and become the

18. "Politics and Ethics: An Interview with Paul Rabinow, Charles Taylor, Martin Jay, Richard Rorty, and Leo Lowenthal," in *The Foucault Reader*, Paul Rabinow, editor (New York: Pantheon, 1984), pp. 375–76.

19. "Polemics, Politics, and Problematizations: An Interview with Michel Foucault," in *The Foucault Reader*, pp. 383–84.

vehicle of some moralistic truth. His "experimental" attitude – which is one of testing out his ideas – is derived not only from the historical and critical analysis of the power/knowledge matrix, but from the Kantian problematic of the present in which philosophy, no longer an object of pure speculation, is regarded as integrally linked to the destiny of the political community. In essence, Foucault practices the politics of experience as an analytics of truth that delineates an ontology of the present. "My aim is not to write the social history of a prohibition but the political history of the production of 'truth'."[20]

Foucault's project is a genealogical analysis of the forms of rationality and the microphysics of power that incarnate the history of the present. It enables him to opt for a politics of experience that is qualitatively different from the comforting security of political militancy. Foucault was concerned, above all else, with the idea of experience. This he defines as three modes of objectification (fields of knowledge with concepts; dividing practices or rules; the relationship to oneself) through which individuals become subjects.[21] Foucault's battlefield was at the same time the world of archives and manuscripts and the concrete political imperatives of the day. Like Sartre, in a way, Foucault became the leading French intellectual of his time to identify with various socio-political causes: his intervention on behalf of prisoners and prison reform; his concern for those who have been socially marginalized such as immigrants, mental patients, homosexuals; his sympathy for the plight of conscripted soldiers; and his unwavering support for Eastern European dissidents and the Solidarity Union in Poland. But the goal of his quest was not based on an abstract moral imperative; it was less a question of speaking on behalf of the downtrodden than of carrying out documentary investigation. Thus rejecting what he termed the "indignity of speaking for others," Foucault engaged in a new form of social activism – the analysis of political technologies – in which the intellectual works inside of institutions and

20. See "Power and Sex," in this volume.

21. Michel Foucault, "Why Study Power: The Question of the Subject," an afterword to Hubert L. Dreyfus and Paul Rabinow, *Michel Foucault: Beyond Structuralism and Hermeneutics* (Chicago: University of Chicago Press, 1982), p. 208.

attempts to constitute a new political ethic by challenging the institutional regime of the production of truth. Political activism therefore becomes the critical analysis of the conflicts within specific sectors of society without allowing the intellectual to engage in the charade of ideological hermeneutics. In terms of concrete political activity, from the early 1970s onward, Foucault actively participated with Jean-Marie Domenach and Pierre Vidal-Naquet in the Prison Information Group (GIP) whose goal was to create a situation in which prisoners could articulate their own needs independent of intellectual pontification.[22] The support of the prisoners' strife included demonstrations that brought attention and publicity to the agitated climate within the prisons. Foucault's participation in this group and subsequent activity in the Association for the Defense of Prisoners' Rights and the Prisoners' Action Group demonstrated how the intellectual's engagement in local struggles both challenges and disrupts the clandestine discourse of the prison. This activity eventually enabled Foucault to delineate the political technology of prison life as a regime of truth owing its very existence to the secrecy of punishment. Instead of using theory in a positivistic way, prioritizing it at the expense of its object of study, Foucault engages in a critical activity in which theory is derived from the analysis of the discursive production of prison life and thereby becomes practice: " . . . theory does not express, translate, or serve to apply practice: it is practice."[23] Accordingly, the four brochures published in the collection *Intolérable*, under the auspices of the GIP, contain many of the *topoi* subsequently developed by Foucault in *Discipline and Punish*.

Transcending his initial hypothesis that prisons generate delinquency through the management of unlawfulness, Foucault uncovers, in a series of journalistic essays, the abuse of prisoners' rights in the punitive practices laid down by prison administrations.[24] In response to prisoners' rights movements at Fresnes, Fleury, and Bois d'Arcy in the summer

---

22. Se Marc Kravetz, "Qu'est-ce que le GIP?," *Magazine Littéraire* 101 (1975) and Daniel Defert and Jacques Donzelot, "La charnière des prison," *Magazine Littéraire* 112–13 (1976).

23. "Intellectuals and Power," pp. 207–8.

24. Michel Foucault, "Du bon usage criminel," *Le Nouvel observateur* 722 (11

of 1981 Foucault proposed that the law and the prison must be thought out anew. The change from a conservative political regime to a more moderate one (i.e. the election of the Socialists in May 1981) did not necessarily eliminate all abuses of rights in the application of the law; the reform of the penal code merely modifies the principles of sentencing and not the reality of the punishment, its nature, its conditions of application, its effects, and how it can be supervised. If, as Foucault declares, the idea of incarceration is regarded as a poor form of punishment, it must also be accepted that both punishment and security mechanisms are inadequate preventative measures. In this context, Foucault challenges us to rethink the concept of the punishable in society and the relations between public power, the right to punish, and its application.

In response to the Mitterrand administration's proposed abolition of the death penalty, Foucault used the opportunity as pretext to "essay" the roots of the problem: the right to kill and its ethical implications – the relations between individuals' liberty and their death – as it has been practiced by the State. Regarded as an exercise of sovereignty, the practice of justice has, since the nineteenth century, claimed the right to correct and punish. Instead of emerging in a radical way from a penal practice that maintains it is intended to correct, the replacement of the death penalty by life sentences affirms nevertheless that certain individuals are "incorrigible." Foucault went so far as to suggest that one needs to put a time limit on every sentence in order to transcend the immobility and schlerosis of our penal institutions. Foucault beckons us to remain alert, "to make penalty a subject of constant reflection, of research, of *experiment*, of transformation."[25] Having embarked on this

24 *cont.*

September 1978), 40–42; "Manières de justice," *Le Nouvel observateur* 743 (1979), 20–21; "La stratégie du pourtour," *Le Nouvel observateur* 757 (1979); "Toujours les prisons," *Esprit* 1 (1980), 184–86; "De la necessité de mettre fin à toute peine," *Libération* (18 September 1981), p. 5; "Il faut tout repenser, la loi et la prison," *Libération* (6 April 1981), p. 2. These texts reveal a significant transformation of attitude in relation to an earlier interview on prison life: "Michel Foucault on Attica: an Interview," *Telos* 19 (1974), 154–61.

25. "De la nécessité de mettre fin à toute peine," p. 5. Translation by Alan Sheridan.

non-idealist inquiry into the consequences of the abolition of the death penalty, Foucault warns that the power that exercises the right to punish must itself become the object of endless vigilance lest it resurface as just another technology of control.

As early as the publication of *Madness and Civilization* (1961) Foucault suggests that the incarceration of the insane through institutions of our own making enables us to distinguish between truth and madness and the marginal and the normal. If psychiatrists possessed the authority to cure, it was derived in large measure from performative acts whose power was less a question of knowledge than of moral authority. The doctor was best described as "Father and Judge, Family and Law – his medical practice being for a long time no more than a complement to the old rites of Order, Authority, and Punishment."[26] But this behavior created a factory for illness which ostensibly became the generative force of the knowledge that it produced. Foucault's interest in the science of psychiatry therefore stemmed from the way in which it implicated a political structure and moral practice.

From the mid to late 1970s, Foucault transposed this critique of the institution of psychiatry to a more pointed analysis of the psychiatric confinement of Soviet dissidents, characterizing it as a function of the social order. Underlying this practice is the notion of the dangerous individual, a concept theorized in late nineteenth-century psychiatry and criminology, and which is described in the modern Soviet penal code as an offense. Without attempting to universalize the internment metaphor as an emblem of all forms of oppression, Foucault denounces the Gulag archipelago of the Soviet system as one shaped by the collaborative efforts of a judicial process and a medical science functioning in the service of "public hygiene." Foucault's analyses uncovered the function of discipline in Eastern Europe as a phenomenon adhering to a standard of "normalization" that segretated the sane or healthy from the medically ill.

For Foucault, the activity of dissidents is one of insurrection against subjected knowledge. But ironically he neglects

26.   Michel Foucault, *Madness and Civilization: A History of Insanity in the Age of Reason* trans. Richard Howard (London: Tavistock, 1977), p.272.

the relationship between subjectivity and the idea of justice since "rights," as he envisages them, are fatally entrapped within structures of power from which they cannot be extricated. Edward Said best elucidates Foucault's heuristic practice of "showing how discourse is not only that which translates struggle or systems of domination, but that for which struggles are conducted."[27]

Yet in the case of Iran the intense desire for radical change appeared to transcend what might appear as the "prison house of discourse." If the Iranian revolution initially attracted Foucault it was because it offered an exemplary case of a spiritual politics that would radically transform the nature of the state.[28] Beyond the utopian framework evoked by the revolutionaries, the Shi'ite opposition to the Shah embodied a political will in which religion and revolt joined forces. Ironically, Foucault claimed that the Islamic religion inherently possessed the ability to realize what Marx suggested that all religion could create: the spirit of a world without spirit. The "political spirituality" in question here facilitates entry into a realm beyond the laws and discursive constraints that societies maintain; it radically transforms subjectivity through the experience of an absolutely collective will.

Through his many articles and interviews Foucault supported, although never quite militantly, the imperatives of the gay movement which, like other experiences such as drugs and communes, situated the individual on the threshold of other forms of consciousness and inscribed him in the "culture of the self".[29] "If scientific socialism emerged from

27. Edward Said, "Foucault and the Imagination of Power," in *Foucault: A Critical Reader*, edited by David Couzens Hoy (New York: Basil Blackwell, 1986), p. 153. On this notion see Michel Foucault, "Orders of Discourse," *Social Science Information* 10 (1972).

28. Michel Foucault, "A quoi rêvent les Iraniens?" *Le Nouvel observateur* 726 (16 October 1978), 48–49; "L'Iran ai militari, ultima carta dello Scia: sfida all'opposizione," *Corriere della sera* (7 November 1978), 1–2; "Ordine all'Iran: 'Bloccato il petrolio, siate pronti a distruggere gli impianti': il mitico capa della rivolta," *Corriere della sera* (26 November 1978), 1–2; "Lettre ouverte à Mehdi Bazargan," *Le Nouvel observateur* 753 (14 April 1979), 46; "Inutile de se soulever?" *Le Monde* (11 May 1979), 1–2; "L'esprit d'un monde sans esprit," in *Iran: la révolution au nom de Dieu*, ed. Claire Brière and Pierre Blanchet (Paris: Seuil, 1979, pp. 225–41). Translated in this volume as "Iran: The Spirit of a World without Spirit."

29. "La loi de la pudeur," debate with Jean Danet et Guy Hocquenghem [Dialogues of *France-Culture* April 4, 1978], in *Fous d'enfance, Recherches* 37 (1979), 69–82

the *Utopias* of the nineteenth century," claimed Foucault, "it is possible that a real socialization will emerge in the twentieth century from *experiences.*"[30] Yet this possibility does not arise from the lifting of the repressive hypothesis proposed by neo-Freudians such as Reich and others, but rather from the constitution of subjectivity as an object to know. Gay sexuality is to be thought of as a dynamic mode in which the refusal of a more traditional lifestyle emanates from a sexual choice that transforms one's own mode of being; sexuality should be used to experiment, to invent new relations in which desire is problematized in a world of polymorphous perversions. For according to Foucault the ideology of sexual liberation is just another disciplinary technique for transforming sex into discourse and the homosexual into a species with a particular mode of life. "One should not be a homosexual," affirms Foucault, "but one who clings passionately to the idea of being gay."[31] The transgressive behavior in question here can only be realized through the exuberant delights of Nietzschean free play.

Foucault's intellectual project thus defines itself as a "genealogy of the modern subject as a historical and cultural reality."[32] The question that arises is whether or not a radical Foucauldian politics can exist given what activists such as Nicos Polantzas have characterized as his pessimistic hypothesis concerning the possibilities of massive social reform.[33] Is Foucault's (failed) attempt to establish a more sytematic political philosophy coupled with his desire to replace it by a critical epistemology of social practices any less a sign of

[translated in this volume by Alan Sheridan as "Sexual Morality and the Law"]; "Un plaisir si simple," *Gai pied* 1 (1979); "De l'amitié comme mode de vie," interview with R. de Ceccatty, J. Dante and J. Le Bitoux, *Le Gai Pied* 25 (1981), 38–39; "Sexuality and Solitude: an interview with Richard Sennett," *London Review of Books*, (21 May–3 June 1981), 3–7; "L'homosexualité dans l'antiquité," interview with J.P. Joecker, A. Sanzio and M. Ouerd, *Masques* 13 (1982), 15–24; "Sexual Choice, Sexual Act: An Interview with James O'Higgins," *Salmagundi* 58–59 (1982), 10–24 [reprinted in this volume]; "Non aux compromis" interview with R. Surzur, *Gai Pied* 43 (1982), p. 9; "Des caresses d'homme considerées comme un art," *Liberation* (June 1, 1982), p. 27.

30. *Language, Counter-Memory, Practice*, p. 231.

31. "L'homosexualité dans l'antiquité," p. 24.

32. Michel Foucault and Richard Sennett, "Sexuality and Solitude," in *Humanities in Review* 1 (1982), p. 9. See Lawrence Kritzman, "Foucault and the Ethics of Sexuality," *L'Esprit créateur* 25 (1985), 86–96.

political activism? Can't one conceive of social commitment beyond the myths of individual autonomy, the politics of freedom, and the existence of revolution? Within this context it would be incorrect to assume that the failure of Foucault's theory to propose an ideal reason reveals an unmitigated lack of hope. On the contrary, the technique of the self is inextricably linked to the moral formation of an individual for whom the process of subjectivization is an ontological as well as a social question; and it is *experience* which results in the constitution of this subject. Deleuze suggests that Foucault's legacy to what some have characterized in an unflattering way as "la pensée 68," is to have asked the question: What is the nature of truth in today's world and how is it modulated by power and the ability to *resist* it? I myself would ask, isn't the emergence of new types of political struggles linked to the birth of new subjectivities that require more strategically located forms of critical analysis? There are not only multiple truths but multiple ways of articulating them. If Foucault evokes the possibility of the "end of politics" it is because he wishes to replace it by a critical history of the present functioning as a new politics of truth.

Foucault's *révolution douce* thus challenges us to decipher truth and through that process to discenter dramatically thought. "To think is to experience, to problematize. Knowledge, power, and the self are the triple foundation of thought."[34] Despite critiques by some that Foucault's late works are somewhat reactionary because of their failure to advance radically the cause of critical theory, one can nevertheless extrapolate a political metaphor from the Foucauldian call to self-government advocated in the last two volumes of *The History of Sexuality*. Perhaps the quintessential challenge

33. Nicos Poulantzas, *State, Power and Socialism* (London: New Left Books, 1978). Jean Baudrillard in *Oublier Foucault* (Paris: Callimard, 1977) tries wrongly, I believe, to demonstrate that Foucault's discourse allows no place for the real since his theory is regarded as a mere reflection of the power that it seeks to describe and therefore transforms it into a reified object that cannot be resisted. Also see Gillian Rose, *Dialectic of Nihililsm* (Oxford: Blackwell, 1984), p. 207: "Neither positive nor negative . . . affirmation is without determination or characteristic; it does not represent an encounter with the power of another but an ecstasy of blinding tears, which . . . is simply that old familiar despair."

34. Gilles Deleuze, *Foucault* (Paris: Editions de Minuit, 1986), p. 124.

in the post-Sartrean age is to invent new forms of life based on an ethical stance endlessly disengaging itself from all forms of discourse based on the familiar and accepted. In the end, Foucault's politics of experience elicits new hope by problematizing the rules and institutions that have reified the substance of daily life. But Foucault is now gone. France suffers from the passivity of its intellectuals and faces a horizon of despair.[35] If hope is in the offing it may only be in the more recent Foucauldian admonition to self-government and the aesthetics of existence that it implies. It may only be realized by refusing to acquiesce to the ultimate sovereignty of any one system of thought.

35.   Alain Finkielkraut in *La défaite de la pensée* (Paris: Gallimard, 1987) sees the current malaise of the French cultural scene as a phenomenon emanating from the attempt to prioritize the consumption and publicity of a more "democratized" mass culture, to the detriment of rigorous intellectual thought.

Self-Portraits

1

The Minimalist Self

Michel Foucault rarely talked about himself. In fact he scorned the discourse that has come to be known as intellectual biography. Nevertheless this discussion with Stephen Riggins offers some insight into the philosopher who found his personal life "uninteresting" and preferred to remain anonymous. From anecdotal remarks concerning the quest for monastic austerity and a cultural ethos of silence to the transformation of the self through one's own knowledge, Foucault's self-portrait approximates a minimalist aesthetic experience. The interview was recorded in English and published in the Canadian journal Ethos *in the Autumn of 1983.*

S.R.   One of the many things that a reader can unexpectedly learn from your work is to appreciate silence. You write about the freedom it makes possible, its multiple causes and meanings. For instance, you say in your last book that there is not one but many silences. Would it be correct to infer that there is a strongly autobiographical element in this?

FOUCAULT   I think that any child who has been educated in a Catholic milieu just before or during the Second World War had the experience that there were many different ways of speaking as well as many forms of silence. There were some kinds of silence which implied very sharp hostility and others which meant deep friendship, emotional admiration, even love. I remember very well that when I met the filmmaker Daniel Schmidt who visited me, I don't know for what purpose, we discovered after a few minutes that we really had nothing to say to each other. So we stayed together from about three o'clock in the afternoon to midnight. We drank, we smoked hash, we had dinner. And I don't think we spoke more than twenty minutes during those ten hours. From that moment a rather long friendship started. It was for me the first time that a friendship originated in strictly silent behavior.

Maybe another feature of this appreciation of silence is related to the obligation of speaking. I lived as a child in a petit bourgeois, provincial milieu in France and the obligation of speaking, of making conversation with visitors, was for me something both very strange and very boring. I often wondered why people had to speak. Silence may be a much more interesting way of having a relationship with people.

S.R. There is in North-American Indian culture a much greater appreciation of silence than in English-speaking societies and I suppose in French-speaking societies as well.

FOUCAULT Yes, you see, I think silence is one of those things that has unfortunately been dropped from our culture. We don't have a culture of silence; we don't have a culture of suicide either. The Japanese do, I think. Young Romans or young Greeks were taught to keep silent in very different ways according to the people with whom they were interacting. Silence was then a specific form of experiencing a relationship with others. This is something that I believe is really worthwhile cultivating. I'm in favor of developing silence as a cultural ethos.

S.R. You seem to have a fascination with other cultures and not only from the past; for the first ten years of your career you lived in Sweden, West Germany and Poland. This would seem a very atypical career for a French academic. Can you explain why you left France and why, when you returned in about 1961, from what I have heard, you would have preferred to live in Japan?

FOUCAULT There is a snobbism about anti-chauvinism in France now. I hope what I say is not associated with those kinds of people. Maybe if I were an American or a Canadian I would suffer from some features of North-American culture. Anyway, I have suffered and I still suffer from a lot of things in French social and cultural life. That was the reason why I left France in 1955. Incidentally, in 1966 and 1968 I also spent two years in Tunisia for purely personal reasons.

S.R. Could you give some examples of the aspects of French society that you suffered from?

FOUCAULT Well, I think that, at the moment when I left France, freedom for personal life was very sharply restricted there. At this time Sweden was supposed to be a much freer country. And there I had the experience that a certain kind of freedom may have, not exactly the same effects, but as many restrictive effects as a directly restrictive society. That was an important experience for me. Then I had the opportunity of spending one year in Poland where, of course, the restrictions and oppressive power of the Communist party are really something quite different. In a rather short period of time I had the experience of an old traditional society, as France was in the late 1940s and early 1950s, and the new free society which was Sweden. I won't say I had the total experience of all the political possibilities but I had a sample of what the possibilities of Western societies were at that moment. That was a good experience.

S.R. Hundreds of Americans went to Paris in the '20s and '30s for exactly the same reasons you left in the '50s.

FOUCAULT Yes. But now I don't think they come to Paris any longer for freedom. They come to have a taste of an old traditional culture. They come to France as painters went to Italy in the 17th century to see a dying civilization. Anyway, you see, we very often have the experience of much more freedom in foreign countries than in our own. As foreigners we can ignore all those implicit obligations which are not in the law but in the general way of behaving. Secondly, merely changing your obligations is felt or experienced as a kind of freedom.

S.R. If you don't mind, let us return for a while to your early years in Paris. I understand that you worked as a psychologist at the Hôpital Ste. Anne in Paris.

FOUCAULT Yes, I worked there a little more than two years, I believe.

S.R. And you have remarked that you identified more with the patients than the staff. Surely that's a very atypical experience for anyone who is a psychologist or psychiatrist. Why did you feel, partly from that experience, the necessity of radically questioning psychiatry when so many other people were content to try to refine the concepts which were already prevalent?

FOUCAULT   Actually, I was not officially appointed. I was studying psychology in the Hôpital Ste. Anne. It was the early '50s. There was no clear professional status for psychologists in a mental hospital. So as a student in psychology (I studied first philosophy and then psychology) I had a very strange status there. The "chef de service" was very kind to me and let me do anything I wanted. But nobody worried about what I should be doing; I was free to do anything. I was actually in a position between the staff and the patients, and it wasn't my merit, it wasn't because I had a special attitude, it was the consequence of this ambiguity in my status which forced me to maintain a distance from the staff. I am sure it was not my personal merit because I felt all that at the time as a kind of malaise. It was only a few years later when I started writing a book on the history of psychiatry that this malaise, this personal experience, took the form of an historical criticism or a structural analysis.

S.R.   Was there anything unusual about the Hôpital Ste. Anne? Would it have given an employee a particularly negative impression of psychiatry?

FOUCAULT   Oh no. It was as typical a large hospital as you could imagine and I must say it was better than most of the large hospitals in provincial towns that I visited afterwards. It was one of the best in Paris. No, it was not terrible. That was precisely the thing that was important. Maybe if I had been doing this kind of work in a small provincial hospital I would have believed its failures were the result of its location or its particular inadequacies.

S.R.   As you have just mentioned the French provinces, which is where you were born, in a sort of derogatory way, do you, nevertheless, have fond memories of growing up in Poitiers in the 1930s and '40s?

FOUCAULT   Oh yes. My memories are rather, one could not exactly say strange, but what strikes me now when I try to recall those impressions is that nearly all the great emotional memories I have are related to the political situation. I remember very well that I experienced one of my first great frights when Chancellor Dollfuss was assassinated by the Nazis in, I think, 1934. It is something very far from us now. Very few people remember the murder of Dollfuss. I remember very well that I was really scared by that. I think it was my first strong fright about death. I also remember refugees from Spain arriving in Poitiers. I remember fighting in school with my classmates about the Ethiopian War. I think that boys and girls of this generation had their childhood formed by these great historical events. The menace of war was our background, our framework of existence. Then the war arrived. Much more than the activities of family life, it was these events concerning the world which are the substance of our memory. I say "our" because I am nearly sure that most boys and girls in France at this moment had the same experience. Our private life was really threatened. Maybe that is the reason why I am fascinated by history and the relationship between personal experience and those events of which we are a part. I think that is the nucleus of my theoretical desires. [*Laughter*]

S.R. You remain fascinated by the period even though you don't write about it.

FOUCAULT Yes, sure.

S.R. What was the origin of your decision to become a philosopher?

FOUCAULT You see, I don't think I ever had the project of becoming a philosopher. I had not known what to do with my life. And I think that is also something rather typical for people of my generation. We did not know when I was ten or eleven years old, whether we would become German or remain French. We did not know whether we would die or not in the bombing and so on. When I was sixteen or seventeen I knew only one thing: school life was an environment protected from exterior menaces, from politics. And I have always been fascinated by living protected in a scholarly environment, in an intellectual milieu. Knowledge is for me that which must function as a protection of individual existence and as a comprehension of the exterior world. I think that's it. Knowledge as a means of surviving by understanding.

S.R. Could you tell me a bit about your studies in Paris?

Is there anyone who had a special influence upon the work that you do today or any professors you are grateful to for personal reasons?

FOUCAULT No, I was a pupil of Althusser, and at that time the main philosophical currents in France were Marxism, Hegelianism and phenomenology. I must say I have studied these but what gave me for the first time the desire of doing personal work was reading Nietzsche.

S.R. An audience that is non-French is likely to have a very poor understanding of the aftermath of the May Rebellion of '68 and you have sometimes said that it resulted in people being more responsive to your work. Can you explain why?

FOUCAULT I think that before '68, at least in France, you had to be as a philosopher a Marxist, or a phenomenologist or a structuralist and I adhered to none of these dogmas. The second point is that at this time in France studying psychiatry or the history of medicine had no real status in the political field. Nobody was interested in that. The first thing that happened after '68 was that Marxism as a dogmatic frame-work declined and new political, new cultural interests concerning personal life appeared. That's why I think my work had nearly no echo, with the exception of a very small circle, before '68.

S.R. Some of the works you refer to in the first volume of *The History of Sexuality*, such as the Victorian book *My Secret Life*, are filled with sexual fantasies. It is often impossible to distinguish between fact and fantasy. Would there be a value in your focusing explicitly upon sexual fantasies and creating an archaeology of them rather than one of sexuality?

FOUCAULT [*Laughter*] No, I don't try to write an archaeol-ogy of sexual fantasies. I try to make an archaeology of discourse about sexuality which is really the relationship between what we do, what we are obliged to do, what we are allowed to do, what we are forbidden to do in the field of sexuality and what we are allowed, forbidden, or obliged to say about our sexual behavior. That's the point. It's not a problem of fantasy; it's a problem of verbalization.

S.R. Could you explain how you arrived at the idea that the sexual repression that characterized 18th and 19th century

Europe and North America, and which seemed so well-documented historically, was in fact ambiguous and that there were beneath it forces working in the opposite direction?

FOUCAULT   Indeed, it is not a question of denying the existence of repression. It's one of showing that repression is always a part of a much more complex political strategy regarding sexuality. Things are not merely repressed. There is about sexuality a lot of defective regulations in which the negative effects of inhibition are counterbalanced by the positive effects of stimulation. The way in which sexuality in the 19th century was both repressed but also put in light, underlined, analyzed through techniques like psychology and psychiatry shows very well that it was not simply a question of repression. It was much more a change in the economics of sexual behavior in our society.

S.R.   In your opinion what are some of the most striking examples which support your hypothesis?

FOUCAULT   One of them is children's masturbation. Another is hysteria and all the fuss about hysterical women. These two examples show, of course, repression, prohibition, interdiction and so on. But the fact that the sexuality of children became a real problem for the parents, an issue, a source of anxiety, had a lot of effects upon the children and upon the parents. To take care of the sexuality of their children was not only a question of morality for the parents but also a question of pleasure.

S.R.   A pleasure in what sense?

FOUCAULT   Sexual excitement and sexual satisfaction.

S.R.   For the parents themselves?

FOUCAULT   Yes. Call it rape, if you like. There are texts which are very close to a systemization of rape. Rape by the parents of the sexual activity of their children. To intervene in this personal, secret activity, which masturbation was, does not represent something neutral for the parents. It is not only a matter of power, or authority, or ethics; it's also a pleasure. Don't you agree with that? Yes, there is enjoyment in intervening. The fact that masturbation was so strictly forbidden for children was naturally the cause of anxiety. It was also a reason for the intensification of this activity, for mutual masturbation and for the pleasure of secret communication between children about this theme. All this has given a certain shape to family life, to the relationship between children and parents, and to the relations between children. All that has, as a result, not only repression but an intensification both of anxieties and of pleasures. I don't want to say that the pleasure of the parents was the same as that of the children or that there was no repression. I tried to find the roots of this absurd prohibition.

One of the reasons why this stupid interdiction of masturbation was maintained for such a long time was because of this pleasure and anxiety and all the emotional network around it. Everyone knows very well that it's impossible to prevent a child from masturbating. There is no scientific evidence that it harms anybody. One can be sure that it is at least [*Laughter*] the only pleasure that really harms nobody. Why has it been forbidden for such a long time then? To the best of my knowledge, you cannot find more than two or three references in all the Greco-Latin literature about masturbation. It was not relevant. It was supposed to be, in Greek and Latin civilization, an activity either for slaves or for satyrs. [*Laughter*] It was not relevant to speak about it for free citizens.

S.R. We live at a point in time when there is great uncertainty about the future. One sees apocalyptic visions of the future reflected widely in popular culture. Louis Malle's *My Dinner with André*, for example. Isn't it typical that in such a climate sex and reproduction come to be a preoccupation and thus writing a history of sexuality would by symptomatic of the time?

FOUCAULT No, I don't think I would agree with that. First, the preoccupation with the relationship between sexuality and reproduction seems to have been stronger, for instance, in the Greek and Roman societies and in the bourgeois society of the 18th and 19th centuries. No. What strikes me is the fact that now sexuality seems to be a question without direct relation with reproduction. It is your sexuality as your personal behavior which is the problem.

Take homosexuality, for instance. I think that one of the reasons why homosexual behavior was not an important issue in the 18th century was due to the view that if a man had children, what he did besides that had little importance. During the 19th century you begin to see that sexual behavior was important for a definition of the individual self. And that is something new. It is very interesting to see that before the 19th century forbidden behavior, even if it was very severely judged, was always considered to be an excess, a "libertinage", as something too much. Homosexual behavior was only considered to be a kind of excess of natural behavior, an instinct that is difficult to keep within certain limits. From the 19th century on you see that behavior like homosexuality came to be considered an abnormality. When I say that it was libertinage I don't say that it was tolerated.

I think that the idea of characterizing individuals through their sexual behavior or desire is not to be found, or very rarely, before the 19th century. "Tell me your desires, I'll tell you who you are." This question is typical of the 19th century.

S.R.   It would not seem any longer that sex could be called *the* secret of life. Has anything replaced it in this respect?

FOUCAULT   Of course it is not *the* secret of life now, since people can show at least certain general forms of their sexual preferences without being plagued or condemned. But I think that people still consider, and are invited to consider, that sexual desire is able to reveal what is their deep identity. Sexuality is not *the* secret but it is still a symptom, a manifestation of what is the most secret in our individuality.

S.R.   The next question I would like to ask may at first seem odd and if it does I'll explain why I thought it was worth asking. Does beauty have special meaning for you?

FOUCAULT   I think it does for everyone. [*Laughter*] I am near-sighted but not blind to the point that it has no meaning for me. Why do you ask? I'm afraid I have given you proof that I am not insensitive to beauty.

S.R.   One of the things about you which is very impressive is the sort of monachal austerity in which you live. Your apartment in Paris is almost completely white; you also avoid all the "objets d'art" that decorate so many French homes. While in Toronto during the past month you have on several occasions worn clothes as simple as white pants, a white Tshirt and a black leather jacket. You suggested that perhaps the reason you like the color white so much is that in Poitiers during the '30s and '40s it was impossible for the exterior of houses to be genuinely white. You are staying here in a house whose white walls are decorated with black cut-out sculptures and you remarked that you especially appreciated the straightforwardness and strength of pure black and white. There is also a noteworthy phrase in *The History of Sexuality*: "that austere monarchy of sex". You do not fit the image of the sophisticated Frenchman who makes an art out of living well. Also, you are the only French person I know who has told me he prefers American food.

FOUCAULT   Yes. Sure. [*Laughter*] A good club sandwich with a coke. That's my pleasure. It's true. With ice cream. That's true.

Actually, I think I have real difficulty in experiencing pleasure. I think that pleasure is a very difficult behavior. It's not as simple as that [*Laughter*] to enjoy one's self. And I must say that's my dream. I would like and I hope I'll die of an overdose [*Laughter*] of pleasure of any kind. Because I think it's really difficult and I always have the feeling that I do not feel *the* pleasure, the complete total pleasure and, for me, it's related to death.

S.R.   Why would you say that?

FOUCAULT   Because I think that the kind of pleasure I would consider as *the* real pleasure would be so deep, so intense, so overwhelming that I couldn't survive it. I would die. I'll give you a clearer and simpler example. Once I was struck by a car in the street. I was walking. And for maybe two seconds I had the impression that I was dying and it was really a very, very intense pleasure. The weather was wonderful. It was 7 o'clock during the summer. The sun was descending. The sky was very wonderful and blue and so on. It was, it still is now, one of my best memories. [*Laughter*]

There is also the fact that some drugs are really important for me because they are the mediation to those incredibly intense joys that I am looking for and that I am not able to experience, to afford by myself. It's true that a glass of wine, of good wine, old and so on, may be enjoyable but it's not for me. A pleasure must be something incredibly intense. But I think I am not the only one like that.

I'm not able to give myself and others those middle range pleasures that make up everyday life. Such pleasures are nothing for me and I am not able to organize my life in order to make place for them. That's the reason why I'm not a social being, why I'm not really a cultural being, why I'm so boring in my everyday life. [*Laughter*] It's a bore to live with me. [*Laughter*]

S.R.   A frequently quoted remark of Romain Rolland is that the French Romantic writers were "'visuels'" for whom music was only a noise. Despite the remark being an obvious exaggeration, most recent scholarship tends to support it. Many references to paintings occur in some of your books but few to music. Are you also representative of this characteristic of French culture that Rolland called attention to?

FOUCAULT   Yes, sure. Of course French culture gives no place to music, or nearly no place. But it's a fact that in my personal life music played a great role. The first friend I had when I was twenty was a musician. Then afterwards I had another friend who was a composer and who is dead now. Through him I know all the generation of Boulez. It has been a very important experience for me. First, because I had contact with the kind of art which was, for me, really enigmatic. I was not competent at all in this domain; I'm still not. But I felt beauty in something which was quite enigmatic for me. There are some pieces by Bach and Webern which I enjoy but what is, for me, real beauty is a "phrase musicale, un morceau de musique", that I cannot understand, something I cannot say anything about. I have the opinion, maybe it's quite arrogant or presumptuous, that I could say something about any of the most wonderful paintings in the world. For this reason they are not absolutely beautiful. Anyway, I have written something about Boulez. What has been for me the influence of living with a musician for several months. Why it was important even in my intellectual life.

S.R.   If I understand correctly, artists and writers responded to your work more positively at first than philosophers, sociologists, or other academics.

FOUCAULT   Yes, that's right.

S.R.   Is there a special kinship between your kind of philosophy and the arts in general?

FOUCAULT   Well, I think I am not in a position to answer. You see, I hate to say it, but it's true that I am not a really good academic. For me intellectual work is related to what you could call aestheticism, meaning transforming yourself. I believe my problem is this strange relationship between knowledge, scholarship, theory, and real history. I know very well, and I think I knew it from the moment when I was a child, that knowledge can do nothing for transforming the world. Maybe I am wrong. And I am sure I am wrong from a theoretical point of view for I know very well that knowledge has transformed the world.

But if I refer to my own personal experience I have the feeling knowledge can't do anything for us and that political power may destroy us. All the knowledge in the world can't do anything against that. All this is related not to what I think theoretically (I know that's wrong) but I speak from my personal experience. I know that knowledge can transform us, that truth is not only a way of deciphering the world (and maybe what we call truth doesn't decipher anything) but that if I know the truth I will be changed. And maybe I will be saved. Or maybe I'll die but I think that is the same anyway for me. [*Laughter*]

You see, that's why I really work like a dog and I worked like a dog all my life. I am not interested in the academic status of what I am doing because my problem is my own transformation. That's the reason also why, when people say, "Well, you thought this a few years ago and now you say something else," my answer is, [*Laughter*] "Well, do you think I have worked like that all those years to say the same thing and not to be changed?" This transformation of one's self by one's own knowledge is, I think, something rather close to the aesthetic experience. Why should a painter work if he is not transformed by his own painting?

S.R.   Beyond the historical dimension is there an ethical concern implied in *The History of Sexuality*? Are you not in some ways telling us how to act?

FOUCAULT   No. If you mean by ethics a code which would tell us how to act, then of course *The History of Sexuality* is not an ethics. But if by ethics you mean the relationship you have to yourself when you act, then I would say that it intends to be an ethics, or at least to show what could be an ethics of sexual behavior. It would be one which would not be dominated by the problem of the deep truth of the reality of our sex life. The relationship that I think we need to have with ourselves when we have sex is an ethics of pleasure, of intensification of pleasure.

S.R.   Many people look at you as someone who is able to tell them the deep truth about the world and about themselves. How do you experience this responsibility? As an intellectual, do you feel responsible toward this function of seer, of shaper of mentalities?

FOUCAULT   I am sure I am not able to provide these people with what they expect. [*Laughter*] I never behave like a prophet. My books don't tell people what to do. And they often reproach me for not doing so (and maybe they are right) and at the same time they reproach me for behaving like a prophet. I have written a book about the history of psychiatry from the 17th century to the very beginning of the 19th. In this book I said nearly nothing about the contemporary situation but people still have read it as an anti-psychiatry position. Once, I was invited to Montreal to attend a symposium about psychiatry. At first I refused to go there since I am not a psychiatrist, even if I have some experience, a very short experience as I told you earlier. But they assured me that they were inviting me only as a historian of psychiatry to give an introductory speech. Since I like Quebec I went. And I was really trapped because I was presented by the president as *the* representative in France of anti-psychiatry. Of course there were nice people there who had never read a line of what I had written and they were convinced that I was an anti-psychiatrist.

I have done nothing other than write the history of psychiatry to the beginning of the 19th century. Why should so many people, including psychiatrists, believe that I am an anti-psychiatrist? It's because they are not able to accept the real history of their institutions which is, of course, a sign of psychiatry being a pseudo-science. A real science is able to accept even the shameful, dirty stories of its beginning. [*Laughter*]

So you see, there really is a call for prophetism. I think we have to get rid of that. People have to build their own ethics, taking as a point of departure the historical analysis, sociological analysis and so on, one can provide for them. I don't think that people who try to decipher the truth should have to provide ethical principles or practical advice at the same moment, in the same book and the same analysis. All this prescriptive network has to be elaborated and transformed by people themselves.

S.R.   For a philosopher to have made the pages of *Time* magazine, as you did in November 1981 is an indication of a certain kind of popular status. How do you feel about that?

FOUCAULT   When newsmen ask me for information about my work I consider that I have to accept. You see, we are paid by society, by the taxpayers [*Laughter*] to work. And really I think that most of us try to do our work the best we can. I think it is quite normal that this work, as far as it is possible, is presented and made accessible to everybody. Naturally, a part of our work cannot be accessible to anybody because it is too difficult. The institution which I belong to in France (I don't belong to the university but to the Collège de France) obliges its members to make public lectures, open to anyone who wants to attend, in which we have to explain our work. We are both researchers and people who have to explain publicly our research. I think there is in this very old institution — it dates from the 16th century — something very interesting. The deep meaning is, I believe, very important. When a newsman comes and asks for information about my work I try to provide it in the clearest way I can.

Anyway, my personal life is not at all interesting. If somebody thinks that my work cannot be understood without reference to such and such a part of my life, I accept to consider the question. [*Laughter*] I am ready to answer if I agree. As far as my personal life is uninteresting, it is not worthwhile making a secret of it. [*Laughter*] By the same token, it may not be worthwhile publicizing it.

2

Critical Theory/Intellectual History

In the following interview Foucault situates himself in relation to the pantheon of modern European intellectual thought — Marx, Nietzsche, Freud — and addresses the issues surrounding the myths associated with history and politics. Foucault explains the direction his critical activity has taken him as a response to a certain dissatisfaction with the phenomenological theory of the subject. In its place he opts for an analysis of the historical conditions and forms of rationality in which the human subject positions itself as an object of knowledge. In asking the question what is the nature of the present, Foucault concludes by describing a new kind of Left thought and articulating his reaction to the decline of Marxism in contemporary France. The interview was conducted by Gérard Raulet and published as "Structuralism and Post-Structuralism: An Interview with Michel Foucault," in Telos 55 (Spring 1983), 195–211. The translation is by Jeremy Harding.

G.R.   How should we begin? I have had two questions in mind. First, what is the origin of this global term, "post-structuralism"?

FOUCAULT   First, none of the protagonists in the structuralist movement — and none of those who, willingly or otherwise, were dubbed structuralists — knew very clearly what it was all about. Certainly, those who were applying structural methods in very precise disciplines such as linguistics and comparative mythology knew what was structuralism, but as soon as one strayed from these very precise disciplines, nobody knew exactly what it was. I am not sure how interesting it would be to attempt a redefinition of what was known, at the time, as structuralism. It would be interesting, though, to study formal thought and the different kinds of formalism that ran through Western culture during the 20th century. When we consider the extraordinary destiny of formalism in painting or formal research in music, or the importance of formalism in the analysis of folklore and legend, in architecture, or its application to theoretical thought, it is clear that formalism in general has probably been one of the strongest and at the same time one of the most varied currents in 20th century Europe. And it is worth pointing out that formalism has very often been associated with political situations and even political movements. It would certainly be worth examining more closely the relation of Russian formalism to the Russian Revolution. The role of formalist art and formalist thought at the beginning of the 20th century, their ideological value, their links with different political movements — all of this would be very interesting. I am struck by how far the structuralist movement in France and Western Europe during the sixties echoed the efforts of certain Eastern countries — notably Czechoslovakia — to free themselves of dogmatic Marxism, and towards the mid-fifties and early sixties, while countries like Czechoslovakia were seeing a renaissance of the old tradition of pre-war European formalism, we also witnessed the birth in Western Europe of what was known as structuralism — which is to say, I suppose, a new modality of this formalist thought and investigation. That is how I would situate the structuralist phenomenon: by relocating it within the broad current of formal thought.

G.R. In Western Europe, Germany was particularly inclined to conceive the student movement, which began earlier there than it did in France (from '64 or '65, there was definite agitation in the universities), in terms of Critical Theory.

FOUCAULT Yes.

G.R. Clearly, there is no necessary relation between Critical Theory and the student movement. If anything, the student movement instrumentalized Critical Theory, or made use of it. In the same way, there is not direct connection either between structuralism and '68.

FOUCAULT   That is correct.

G.R.   But were you not saying, in a way, that structuralism was a necessary preamble?

FOUCAULT   No. There is nothing necessary in this order of ideas. But to put it very, very crudely, formalist culture, thought and art in the first third of the 20th century were generally associated with Left political movements — or critiques — and even with certain revolutionary instances; and Marxism concealed all that. It was fiercely critical of formalism in art and theory, most clearly from the '30s onwards. Thirty years later, you saw people in certain Eastern bloc countries and even in France beginning to unsettle Marxist dogmatism with types of analysis obviously inspired by formalism. What happened in France in 1968, and in other countries as well, is at once extremely interesting and highly ambiguous — and interesting because of its ambiguity. It is a case of movements which, very often, have endowed themselves with a strong reference to Marxism and which, at the same time, have insisted on a violent critique *vis-à-vis* the dogmatic Marxism of parties and institutions. Indeed, the range of interplay between a certain kind of non-Marxist thinking and these Marxist references was the space in which the student movements developed — movements that sometimes carried revolutionary Marxist discourse to the height of exaggeration, but which were often inspired at the same time by an anti-dogmatic violence that ran counter to this type of discourse.

G.R.   An anti-dogmatic violence in search of references . . .

FOUCAULT   And looking for them, on occasion, in an exasperated dogmatism.

G.R.   Via Freud or via structuralism.

FOUCAULT   Correct. So, once again, I would like to reassess the history of formalism and relocate this minor structuralist episode in France — relatively short, with diffuse forms — within the larger phenomenon of formalism in 20th century, as important in its way as romanticism or even positivism was during the 19th century.

G.R.   We will return later to positivism. For now, I want to follow the thread of this French evolution which you are almost retracing: a thread of references (both very dogmatic and inspired by a will to anti-dogmatism) to Marx, Freud and structuralism, in the hope of discovering in people like Lacan a figure who would put an end to syncretism and would manage to unify all these strands. This approach, moreover, drew a magisterial response from Lacan to the Students at Vincennes, running roughly as follows: "You want to combine Marx and Freud. Psychoanalysis can teach you that you are looking for a master; and you will have this master"[1] — an extremely violent kind of disengagement from this attempt at a combination. I read in Vincent Descombes' book, *Le même et l'autre*, with which you are no doubt familiar . . . [2]

FOUCAULT   No, I know it exists but I have not read it.

G.R.   . . . that fundamentally, it was necessary to wait until 1972 in order to emerge from this vain effort to combine Marxism and Freudianism; and that its emergence was achieved by Deleuze and Guattari, who came from the Lacanian school. Somewhere, I took the liberty of writing that we had certainly emerged from this fruitless attempt at a combination, but in a way that Hegel would have criticized. In other words, we went in pursuit of the third man — Nietzsche — to bring him into the site of the impossible synthesis, referring to him rather than to the impossible combination of Marx and Freud. In any case, according to Descombes, it seems that this tendency to resort to Nietzsche began in 1972. What do you think?

FOUCAULT   No, I do not think that is quite right. First, you know how I am. I am always a bit suspicious of these forms of synthesis which present French thought as Freudian-Marxist at one stage and then as having discovered Nietzsche at another. Since 1945, for a whole range of political and cultural reasons, Marxism in France was a kind of horizon

1. The exact quotation can be found in transcript of the proceedings at Vincennes, December 1969, published in *Le Magazine Litéraire*, No. 121, February 1977. "What you as a revolutionary aspire to is a master. You will have one." (Translator's note).

2. Vincent Descombes, *Le Même et l'autre: quarante-cinq ans de philosophie française* (Paris: Editions de Minuit, 1979); *Modern French Philosophy* translated by L. Scott-Fox (New York: Cambridge University Press, 1980) [L.D.K.].

which Sartre thought for a time was impossible to surpass. At that time, it was definitely a very closed horizon, and a very imposing one. Also, we should not forget that throughout the period from 1945 to 1955 in France, the entire French university — the young French university, as opposed to what had been the traditional university — was very much preoccupied with the task of building something which was not Freudian-Marxist but Husserlian-Marxist: the phenomenology-Marxism relation. That is what was at stake in the debates and efforts of a whole series of people. Merleau-Ponty and Sartre, in moving from phenomenology to Marxism, were definitely operating on that axis. Desanti too . . .

G.R.   Dufrenne, even Lyotard.

FOUCAULT   And Ricoeur, who was certainly not a Marxist, but a phenomenologist in no way oblivious to Marxism . . . So, at first they tried to wed Marxism and phenomenology; and it was later, once a certain kind of structural thinking — structural method — had begun to develop, that we saw structuralism replace phenomenology and become coupled with Marxism. It was a movement from phenomenology towards Marxism and essentially it concerned the problem of language. That, I think was a fairly critical point: Merleau-Ponty's encounter with language. And, as you know, Merleau-Ponty's later efforts addressed that question. I remember clearly some lectures in which Merleau-Ponty began speaking of Saussure who, even if he had been dead for fifty years, was quite unknown, not so much to French linguists and philologists, but to the cultured public. So the problem of language appeared and it was clear that phenomenology was no match for structural analysis in accounting for the effects of meaning that could be produced by a structure of the linguistic type, in which the subject (in the phenomenological sense) did not intervene to confer meaning. And quite naturally, with the phenomenological spouse finding herself disqualified by her inability to address language, structuralism became the new bride. That is how I would look at it. Even so, psychoanalysis — in large part under the influence of Lacan — also raised a problem which, though very different, was not analogous. For the unconscious could not feature in any discussion of a phenomenological kind; of which the most conclusive proof, as the French saw it anyhow, was the fact that Sartre and Merleau-Ponty — I am not talking about the others — were always trying to break down what they saw as positivism, or mechanism, or Freudian "*chosisme*" in order to affirm a constituting subject. And when Lacan, around the time that questions of language were beginning to be posed, remarked, "Whatever you do, the unconscious as such can never be reduced to the effects of a conferral of meaning to which the phenomenological subject is susceptible," he was posing a problem absolutely symmetrical with that of the linguists. Once again, the phenomenological subject was disqualified by psychoanalysis, as it had been by linguistic theory. And it is quite understandable at that point that Lacan could say the unconscious was structured like a language. For one and all, it was the same type of problem. So we had a Freudian-structuralist-Marxism: and with phenomenology disqualified for the reasons I have just outlined, there was simply a succession of fiancées, each flirting with Marx in turn. Only all was not exactly going well. Of course, I am describing it as though I were talking about a very general movement. What I describe did undoubtedly take place and it involved a certain number of individuals; but there were also people who did not follow the movement. I am thinking of those who were interested in the history of science — an important tradition in France, probably since the time of Comte. Particularly around Canguilhem, an extremely influential figure in the French University — the young French University.[3] Many of his students were neither Marxists nor Freudians, nor structuralists. And here I am speaking of myself.

G.R.   You were one of those people, then?

FOUCAULT   I have never been a Freudian, I have never been a Marxist and I have never been a structuralist.

G.R.   Yes, here too, as a formality and just so the American reader is under no misapprehensions, we only need to look at the dates. You began . . .

---

3.   Georges Canguilhem (1904–   ). Specialist in epistemology and the history of science. Studies the relationship between science and ideology, the specificity of the biological sciences, and the question of normality. Supervisor of Foucault's *doctorat d'état* on *Histoire de la folie* [L.D.K.].

FOUCAULT   My first book was written towards the end of my student days. It was *Madness and Civilization*, written between '55 and '60. This book is neither Freudian nor Marxist nor structuralist. Now, as it happened, I had read Nietzsche in '53 and, curious as it may seem, from a perspective of inquiry into the history of knowledge — the history of reason: how does one elaborate a history of rationality? This was the problem of the 19th century.

G.R.   Knowledge, reason, rationality.

FOUCAULT   Knowledge, reason, rationality, the possibility of elaborating a history of rationality . . . I would say that here again, we run across phenomenology, in someone like Koyré, a historian of science, with his German background, who came to France between 1930 and '33,[4] I believe, and developed a historical analysis of the forms of rationality and knowledge in a phenomenological perspective. For me, the problem was framed in terms not unlike those we mentioned earlier. Is the phenomenological, transhistorical subject able to provide an account of the historicity of reason? Here, reading Nietzsche was the point of rupture for me. There is a history of the subject just as there is a history of reason; but we can never demand that the history of reason unfold at a first and founding act of the rationalist subject. I read Nietzsche by chance, and I was surprised to see that Canguilhem, the most influential historian of science in France at the time, was also very interested in Nietzsche and was thoroughly receptive to what I was trying to do.

G.R.   On the other hand, there are no perceptible traces of Nietzsche in his work . . .

FOUCAULT   But there are; and they are very clear. There are even explicit references; more explicit in his later texts than in his earlier ones. The relation of the French to Nietzsche and even the relation of all 20th century thought to Nietzsche was difficult, for understandable reasons . . . But I

---

4.   Alexandre Koyré (1892–1964). Professor and academic philosopher. He was responsible along with Jean Hippolyte for the introduction of Hegelian dialectics into French thought. It was his course "Introduction à la lecture de Hegel" given from 1934 to 1939 and published in 1947 that generated a philosophical debate for Marxist intellectuals in the immediate post-war period [L.D.K.].

am talking about myself. We should also talk about Deleuze.[5] Deleuze wrote his book on Nietzsche around 1960. The book must have appeared in '65. He was interested in empiricism, in Hume, and again in the question: is the theory of the subject which we have in phenomenology a satisfactory one? He could elude this question by means of the bias of Hume's empiricism. I am convinced that he encountered Nietzsche under the same conditions. So I would say that everything which took place in the sixties arose from a dissatisfaction with the phenomenological theory of the subject, and involved different escapades, subterfuges, break-throughs, according to whether we use a negative or a positive term, in the direction of linguistics, psychoanalysis or Nietzsche.

G.R.   At any rate, Nietzsche represented a determining experience for the abolition of the founding act of the subject.

FOUCAULT   Exactly. And this is where French writers like Bataille and Blanchot were important for us.[6] I said earlier that I wondered why I had read Nietzsche. But I know very well. I read him because of Bataille, and Bataille because of Blanchot. So, it is not at all true that Nietzsche appeared in 1972. He appeared in 1972 for people who were Marxists during the '60s and who emerged from Marxism by way of Nietzsche. But the first people who had recourse to Nietzsche were not looking for a way out of Marxism. They wanted a way out of phenomenology.

G.R.   You have spoken about historians of science, of writing a history of knowledge, a history of rationality and a history of reason. Before returning to Nietzsche, could we briefly define the four terms, which might well be taken — in the light of what you have said — to be synonymous?

FOUCAULT   No, no. I was describing a movement which

5.   Gilles Deleuze (1925–). French philosopher in the Nietzschean tradition and professor at the University of Paris VII. One of the first to theorize the philosophy of difference. Deleuze formulates with Felix Guattari the anti-Oedipus theory (1974). Author of an important study on Foucault (1986) [L.D.K.].

6.   Georges Bataille (1897–1962). Early French surrealist and founder of the Collège de Sociologie in 1936–37. Recognized by the literary avant-garde in the late sixties (i.e. the *Tel quel* group) as the creator of a violently erotic writing whose transgressive force is the expression of a mystical quest for the absolute.
    Maurice Blanchot (1907–). Novelist and critic known for his contribution to the new critical movement in France [L.D.K.].

involved many factors and many different problems. I am not saying that these problems are identical. I am speaking about the kinship between the lines of inquiry and the proximity of those who undertook them.

G.R.   All the same, could we try to specify the relation? It is true that this can definitely be found in your books, particularly, *The Archaeology of Knowledge*. Nonetheless, could we try to specify these relations between science, knowledge and reason?

FOUCAULT   It is not very easy in an interview. I would say that the history of science has played an important role in philosophy in France. I would say that perhaps if modern philosophy (that of the 19th and 20th centuries) derives in great part from the Kantian question, "Was ist Aufklärung?" or, in other words, if we admit that one of the main functions of modern philosophy has been an inquiry into the historical point at which reason could appear in its "adult" form, "unchaperoned," then the function of 19th century philosophy consisted in asking, "What is this moment when reason accedes to autonomy? What is the meaning of a history of reason and what value can be ascribed to the ascendancy of reason in the modern world, through these three great forms: scientific thought, technical apparatus and political organization?" I think one of philosophy's great functions was to inquire into these three domains, in some sense to take stock of things or smuggle an anxious question into the rule of reason. To continue then . . . to pursue the Kantian question, "Was ist Aufklärung?" This reprise, this reiteration of the Kantian question in France assumed a precise and perhaps, moreover, an inadequate form: "What is the history of science?" What happened, between Greek mathematics and modern physics, as this universe of science was built? From Comte right through the 1960s, I think the philosophical function of the history of science has been to pursue this question. Now in Germany this question "What is the history of reason, of rational forms in Europe?" did not appear so much in the history of science but in the current of thought which runs from Max Weber to Critical Theory.

G.R.   Yes, the meditation on norms, on values.

FOUCAULT   From Max Weber to Habermas. And the same

question arises here. How do matters stand with the history of reason, with the ascendancy of reason, and with the different forms in which this ascendancy operates? Now, the striking thing is that France knew absolutely nothing — or only vaguely, only very indirectly — about the current of Weberian thought. Critical Theory was hardly known in France and the Frankfurt School was practically unheard of. This, by the way, raises a minor historical problem which fascinates me and which I have not been able to resolve at all. It is common knowledge that many representatives of the Frankfurt School came to Paris in 1935, seeking refuge, and left very hastily, sickened presumably — some even said as much — but saddened anyhow not to have found more of an echo. Then came 1940, but they had already left for England and the U.S., where they were actually much better received. The understanding that might have been established between the Frankfurt School and French philosophical thought — by way of the history of science and therefore the question of the history of rationality — never occurred. And when I was a student, I can assure you that I never once heard the name of the Frankfurt School mentioned by any of my professors.

G.R.   It is really quite astonishing.

FOUCAULT   Now, obviously, if I had been familiar with the Frankfurt School, if I had been aware of it at the time, I would not have said a number of stupid things that I did say and I would have avoided many of the detours which I made while trying to pursue my own humble path — when, meanwhile, avenues had been opened up by the Frankfurt School. It is a strange case of non-penetration between two very similar types of thinking which is explained, perhaps, by that very similarity. Nothing hides the fact of a problem in common better than two similar ways of approaching it.

G.R.   What you have just said about the Frankfurt School (about Critical Theory, if you like) which might, under different circumstances, have spared you some fumblings, is even more interesting in view of the fact that one finds a Negt or a Habermas doffing his hat to you. In an interview I did with Habermas, he praised your "masterly description of the bifurcation of reason" — the bifurcation of reason at a given moment. But I have still wondered whether you would agree with this bifurcation of reason as conceived by Critical Theory — with the dialectic of reason, in other words, whereby reason becomes perverse under the effects of its own strength, transformed and reduced to instrumental knowledge. The prevailing idea in Critical Theory is the dialectical continuity of reason, and of a perversion that completely transformed it at a certain stage — which it now becomes a question of rectifying. That is what seemed to be at issue in the struggle for emancipation. Basically, to judge from your work, the will to knowledge has never ceased to bifurcate in some way or another — bifurcating hundreds of times in the course of history. Perhaps "bifurcate" is not even the right word . . . Reason has split knowledge again and again.

FOUCAULT   Yes, yes. I think that the blackmail which has very often been at work in every critique of reason or every critical inquiry into the history of rationality (either you accept rationality or you fall prey to the irrational) operates as though a rational critique of rationality were impossible, or as though a rational history of all the ramifications and all the bifurcations, a contingent history of reason, were impossible . . . I think, that since Max Weber, in the Frankfurt School and anyhow for many historians of science such as Canguilhem, it was a question of isolating the form of rationality presented as dominant, and endowed with the status of the one-and-only reason, in order to show that it is only *one* possible form among others. In this French history of science — I consider it quite important — the role of Bachelard, whom I have not mentioned so far, is also crucial.

G.R.   Even so, this praise from Habermas is a little barbed. According to Habermas, you provided a masterly description of the "moment reason bifurcated." This bifurcation was unique. It happened once. At a certain point, reason took a turn which led it towards an instrumental rationality, an auto-reduction, a self-limitation. This bifurcation, if it is also a division, happened once and once only in history, separating the two realms with which we have been acquainted since Kant. This analysis of bifurcation is Kantian. There is the knowledge of understanding and the knowledge of reason, there is instrumental reason and there is moral reason. To assess this bifurcation, we clearly situate ourselves at the vantage point of practical reason, or moral-practical reason. Whence a unique bifurcation, a separation of technique and practice which continues to dominate the entire German history of ideas. And as you said earlier, this tradition arises from the question, "Was ist Aufklärung?" Now, in my view, this praise reduces your own approach to the history of ideas.

FOUCAULT   True, I would not speak about *one* bifurcation of reason but more about an endless, multiple bifurcation — a kind of abundant ramification. I do not address the point at which reason became instrumental. At present, for example, I am studying the problem of techniques of the self in Greek and Roman antiquity; how man, human life and the self were all objects of a certain number of *technai* which, with their exacting rationality, could well be compared to any technique of production.

G.R.   Without comprising the whole of society.

FOUCAULT   Right. And what led the *techne* of self can very well be analysed, I think, and situated as a historical phenomenon — which does not constitute *the* bifurcation of reason. In this abundance of branchings, ramifications, breaks and ruptures, it was an important event, or episode; it had considerable consequences, but it was not a *unique* phenomenon.

G.R.   But directly we cease to view the self-perversion of reason as a unique phenomenon, occurring only once in history at a moment that reason loses something essential, something substantial — as we would have to say after Weber — would you not agree that your work aims to rehabilitate a fuller version of reason? Can we find, for example, another conception of reason implicit in your approach; a project of rationality that differs from the one we have nowadays?

FOUCAULT   Yes, but here, once more, I would try to take my distance from phenomenology, which was my point of departure. I do not believe in a kind of founding act whereby reason, in its essence, was discovered or established and from which it was subsequently diverted by such and such an event. I think, in fact, that reason is self-created, which is why I have tried to analyse forms of rationality: different foundations, different creations, different modifications in which rationalities engender one another, oppose and pursue one another. Even so, you cannot assign a point at which reason would have lost sight of its fundamental project, or even a point at which the rational becomes the irrational. During the 1960s, I wanted to begin as much with the phenomenological account (with its foundation and essential project of reason, from which we have shifted away on account of some forgetfulness and to which we must return) as with the Marxist account, or the account of Lukács. A rationality existed, and it was the form *par excellence* of Reason itself, but a certain number of social conditions (capitalism, or rather, the shift from one form of capitalism to another) precipitated this rationality into a crisis, i.e., a forgetting of reason, a fall into the irrational. I tried to take my bearings in relation to these two major models, presented very schematically and unfairly.

G.R.   In these models, we see either a unique bifurcation or a forgetfulness, at a given moment, following the confiscation of reason by a class. Thus the movement across history towards emancipation consists not only in reappropriating what was confiscated (to confiscate it again) but — on the contrary — in giving reason back its truth, intact, investing it with the status of an absolutely universal science. For you, clearly — you have made it plain in your writing — there is no project of a new science, of a broader science.

FOUCAULT   Definitely not.

G.R.   But you show that each time a type of rationality asserts itself, it does so by a kind of cut-out — by exclusion or by self-demarcation, drawing a boundary between self and other. Does your project include any effort to rehabilitate this other? Do you think, for example, in the silence of the mad person you might discover a language that would have much to say about the conditions in which works are brought into existence?

FOUCAULT   Yes, what interested me, starting out from the general frame of reference we mentioned earlier, were precisely the forms of rationality applied by the human subject to itself. While historians of science in France were interested essentially in the problem of how a scientific object is constituted, the question I asked myself was this: how is it that the human subject took itself as the object of possible knowledge? Through what forms of rationality and historical conditions? And finally at what price? This is my question: at what price can subjects speak the truth about themselves? At what price can subjects speak the truth about themselves as mad persons? At the price of constituting the mad person as absolutely other, paying not only the theoretical price but also an institutional and even an economic price, as determined by the organization of psychiatry. An ensemble of complex, staggered elements where you find that institutional game-playing, class relations, professional conflicts, modalities of knowledge and, lastly, a whole history of the subject of reason are involved. That is what I have tried to piece back together. Perhaps the project is utterly mad, very complex — and I have only brought a few moments to light, a few specific points such as the problem of the mad subject and what it is. How can the truth of the sick subject ever be told? That is the substance of my first two books. *The Order of Things* asked the price of problematizing and analyzing the speaking subject, the working subject the living subject. Which is why I attempted to analyse the birth of grammar, general grammar, natural history and economics. I went on to pose the same kind of question in the case of the criminal and systems of punishment: how to state the truth of oneself, insofar as one might be a criminal subject. I will be doing the same thing with sexuality, only going back much further: how does the subject speak truthfully about itself, inasmuch as it is the subject of sexual pleasure? And at what price?

G.R. According to the relation of subjects to whatever they are, in each case, through the constitution of language or knowledge.

FOUCAULT It is an analysis of the relation between forms of reflexivity — a relation of self to self — and, hence, of relations between forms of reflexivity and the discourse of truth, forms of rationality and effects of knowledge.

G.R. In any event, it is not a case of exhuming some prehistorical "archaic" by means of archaeology. (You shall see why I ask this question. It directly concerns certain readings of the so-called French Nietzschean current in Germany.)

FOUCAULT No, absolutely not. I meant this word "archaeology," which I no longer use, to suggest that the kind of analysis I was using was out-of-phase, not in terms of time but by virtue of the level at which it was situated. Studying the history of ideas, as they evolve, is not my problem so much as trying to discern beneath them how one or another object could take shape as a possible object of knowledge. Why, for instance did madness become, at a given moment, an object of knowledge corresponding to a certain type of knowledge? By using the word "archaeology" rather than "history," I tried to designate this desynchronisation between ideas about madness and the constitution of madness as an object.

G.R. I asked this question because nowadays there is a tendency — its pretext being the appropriation of Nietzsche by the new German Right — to lump everything together; to imagine that French Nietzscheanism — if it exists at all — is in the same vein. All these elements are associated in order to recreate what are fundamentally the fronts of theoretical class struggle, so hard to find nowadays.

FOUCAULT I do not believe there is a single Nietzscheanism. There are no grounds for believing that there is a true Nietzscheanism, or that ours is any truer than others. But those who found in Nietzsche, more than thirty-five years ago, a means of displacing themselves in terms of a philosophical horizon dominated by phenomenology and Marxism have nothing to do with those who use Nietzsche nowadays. In any case, even if Deleuze has written a superb book about Nietzsche, and although the presence of Nietzsche in his other works is clearly apparent, there is no deafening reference to Nietzsche, nor any attempt to wave the Nietzschean flag for rhetorical or political ends. It is striking that someone like Deleuze has simply taken Nietzsche seriously, which indeed he has. That is what I wanted to do. What serious use can Nietzsche be put to? I have lectured on Nietzsche but written very little about him. The only rather extravagant homage I have rendered Nietzsche was to call the first volume of my *History of Sexuality* "The Will to Knowledge."

G.R.   Certainly, as regards the will to knowledge, I think we have been able to see in what you have just said that it was always a *relation*. I suppose you will detest this word with its Hegelian ring. Perhaps we should say "evaluation" as Nietzsche would; a way of evaluating truth. At any rate, a way in which force, neither an archaic instance nor an originary or original resource, is actualized; and so too, a relation of forces and perhaps already a relation of power in the constituting act of all knowledge.

FOUCAULT   I would not say so. That is too involved. My problem is the relation of self to self and of telling the truth. My relation to Nietzsche, or what I owe Nietzsche, derives mostly from the texts of around 1880, where the question of truth, the history of truth and the will to truth were central to his work. Did you know that Sartre's first text — written when he was a young student — was Nietzschean? "The History of Truth," a little paper first published in a *Lycée* review around 1925. He began with the same problem. And it is very odd that his approach should have shifted from the history of truth to phenomenology, while for the next generation — ours — the reverse was true.

G.R.   I think we are now in the process of clarifying what you mean by "will to knowledge" — this reference to Nietzsche. You concede a certain kinship with Deleuze but only up to a point. Would this kinship extend as far as the Deleuzian notion of desire?

FOUCAULT   No, definitely not.

G.R.   I am asking this question because Deleuzian desire — productive desire — becomes precisely this kind of originary resource which then begins to generate forms.

FOUCAULT   I do not want to take up a position on this, or say what Deleuze may have had in mind. The moment a kind of thought is constituted, fixed or identified within a cultural tradition, it is quite normal that this cultural tradition should take hold of it, make what it wants of it and have it say what it did not mean, by implying that this is merely another form of what it was actually trying to say. Which is all a part of cultural play. But my relation to Deleuze is evidently not that;

so I will not say what I think he meant. All the same, I think his task was, at least for a long time, to formulate the problem of desire. And evidently the effects of the relation to Nietzsche are visible in his theory of desire, whereas my own problem has always been the question of truth, of telling the truth, the *wahr-sagen* — what it is to tell the truth — and the relation between "telling the truth" and forms of reflexivity, of self upon self.

G.R. Yes, but I think Nietzsche makes no fundamental distinction between will to knowledge and will to power.

FOUCAULT I think there is a perceptible displacement in Nietzsche's texts between those which are broadly preoccupied with the question of will to knowledge and those which are preoccupied with will to power. But I do not want to get into this argument for the very simple reason that it is years since I have read Nietzsche.

G.R. It is important to try to clarify this point, I think, precisely because of the hold-all approach which characterizes the way this question is received abroad, and in France for that matter.

FOUCAULT I would say, in any case, that my relation to Nietzsche has not been historical. The actual history of Nietzsche's thought interests me less than the kind of challenge I felt one day, a long time ago, reading Nietzsche for the first time. When you open *The Gay Science* after you have been trained in the great, time-honored university traditions — Descartes, Kant, Hegel, Husserl — and you come across these rather strange, witty, graceful texts, you say: Well I won't do what my contemporaries, colleagues or professors are doing; I won't just dismiss this. What is the maximum of philosophical intensity and what are the current philosophical effects to be found in these texts? That, for me, was the challenge of Nietzsche.

G.R. In the way all this is received at the moment, I think there is a second hold-all concept, i.e., post-modernity, which quite a few people refer to and which also plays a role in Germany, since Habermas has taken up the term in order to criticize this trend in all its aspects . . .

FOUCAULT What are we calling post-modernity? I'm not up to date.

G.R.   . . . the current of North American sociology (Bell) as much as what is known as post-modernity in art, which would require another definition (perhaps a return to a certain formalism). Anyway, Habermas attributes the term post-modernity to the French current, the tradition, as he says in his text on post-modernity, "running from Bataille to Derrida by way of Foucault." This is an important question in Germany, because reflections on modernity have existed for a long time — ever since Weber. What is post-modernity, as regards the aspect which interests us here? Mainly it is the idea of modernity, of reason, we find in Lyotard: a "grand narrative" from which we have finally been freed by a kind of salutary awakening. Post-modernity is a breaking apart of reason; Deleuzian schizophrenia. Post-modernity reveals, at least, that reason has only been one narrative among others in history; a grand narrative, certainly, but one of many, which can now be followed by other narratives. In your vocabulary, reason was *one* form of will to knowledge. Would you agree that this has to do with a certain current? Do you situate yourself within this current; and, if so, how?

FOUCAULT   I must say that I have trouble answering this. First, because I've never clearly understood what was meant in France by the word "modernity." In the case of Baudelaire, yes, but thereafter I think the sense begins to get lost. I do not know what Germans mean by modernity. The Americans were planning a kind of seminar with Habermas and myself. Habermas had suggested the theme of "modernity" for the seminar. I feel troubled here because I do not grasp clearly what that might mean, though the word itself is unimportant; we can always use any arbitrary label. But neither do I grasp the kind of problems intended by this term — or how they would be common to people thought of as being "post-modern." While I see clearly that behind what was known as structuralism, there was a certain problem — broadly speaking, that of the subject and the recasting of the subject — I do not understand what kind of problem is common to the people we call post-modern or post-structuralist.

G.R.   Obviously, reference or opposition to modernity is not only ambiguous, it actually confines modernity. Modernity also has several definitions: the historian's definition, Weber's definition, Adorno's definition and Benjamin's of

Baudelaire, as you've mentioned. So there are at least some references. Habermas, in opposition to Adorno, seems to privilege the tradition of reason, i.e., the Weberian definition of modernity. It is in relation to this that he sees in post-modernity the crumbling away or the break-up of reason and allows himself to declare that one of the forms of post-modernity — the one which is in relation with the Weberian definition — is the current that envisages reason as *one* form among others of will to knowledge — a grand narrative, but *one* narrative among others.

FOUCAULT That is not my problem, insofar as I am not prepared to identify reason entirely with the totality of rational forms which have come to dominate — at any given moment, in our own era and even very recently — in types of knowledge, forms of technique and modalities of government or domination: realms where we can see all the major applications of rationality. I am leaving the problem of art to one side. It is complicated. For me, no given form of rationality is actually reason. So I do not see how we can say that the forms of rationality which have been dominant in the three sectors I have mentioned are in the process of collapsing and disappearing. I cannot see any disappearance of that kind. I can see multiple transformations, but I cannot see why we should call this transformation a collapse of reason. Other forms of rationality are created endlessly. So there is no sense at all to the proposition that reason is a long narrative which is now finished, and that another narrative is under way.

G.R. Let us just say that the field is open to many forms of narrative.

FOUCAULT Here, I think, we are touching on one of the forms — perhaps we should call them habits — one of the most harmful habits in contemporary thought, in modern thought even; at any rate, in post-Hegelian thought: the analysis of the present as being precisely, in history, a present of rupture, or of high point, or of completion or of a returning dawn, etc. The solemnity with which everyone who engages in philosophical discourse reflects on his own time strikes me as a flaw. I can say so all the more firmly since it is something I have done myself; and since, in someone like Nietzsche, we find this incessantly — or, at least, insistently enough. I think we should have the modesty to say to ourselves that, on the one hand, the time we live in is not *the* unique or fundamental or irruptive point in history where everything is completed and begun again. We must also have the modesty to say, on the other hand, that — even without this solemnity — the time we live in is very interesting; it needs to be analyzed and broken down, and that we would do well to ask ourselves, "What is the nature of our present?" I wonder if one of the great roles of philosophical thought since the Kantian "Was ist Aufklärung?" might not be characterized by saying that the task of philosophy is to describe the nature of the present, and of "ourselves in the present." With the proviso that we do not allow ourselves the facile, rather theatrical declaration that this moment in which we exist is one of total perdition, in the abyss of darkness, or a triumphant daybreak, etc. It is a time like any other, or rather, a time which is never quite like any other.

G.R.   This poses dozens of questions; ones that you have posed yourself in any case. What is the nature of the present? Is the era characterized more than others, in spite of everything, by a greater fragmentation, by "deterritorialization" and "schizophrenia" — no need to take a position on these terms?

FOUCAULT   I would like to say something about the function of any diagnosis concerning the nature of the present. It does not consist in a simple characterization of what we are but, instead — by following lines of fragility in the present — in managing to grasp why and how that-which-is might no longer be that-which-is. In this sense, any description must always be made in accordance with these kinds of virtual fracture which open up the space of freedom understood as a space of concrete freedom, i.e., of possible transformation.

G.R.   Is it here, along the fractures, that the work of the intellectual — practical work, quite clearly — is situated?

FOUCAULT   That is my own belief. I would say also, about the work of the intellectual, that it is fruitful in a certain way to describe that-which-is by making it appear as something that might not be, or that might not be as it is. Which is why this designation or description of the real never has a prescriptive value of the kind, "because this is, that will be." It is also why, in my opinion, recourse to history — one of the great facts in French philosophical thought for at least twenty years — is meaningful to the extent that history serves to show how that-which-is has not always been; i.e., that the things which seem most evident to us are always formed in the confluence of encounters and chances, during the course of a precarious and fragile history. What reason perceives as *its* necessity, or rather, what different forms of rationality offer as their necessary being, can perfectly well be shown to have a history; and the network of contingencies from which it emerges can be traced. Which is not to say, however, that these forms of rationality were irrational. It means that they reside on a base of human practice and human history; and that since these things have been made, they can be unmade, as long as we know how it was that they were made.

G.R.   This work on the fractures, both descriptive and practical, is field work.

FOUCAULT   Perhaps it is field work and perhaps it is a work which can go further back in terms of historical analysis, starting with questions posed in the field.

G.R.   Would you describe the work on these fracture areas, work in the field, as the microphysics of power, the analytics of power?

FOUCAULT   Yes, it is something like that. It has struck me that these forms of rationality — put to work in the process of domination — deserve analysis in themselves, provided we recognize from the outset that they are not foreign to other forms of power which are put to work, for instance, in knowledge or technique. On the contrary, there is exchange; there are transmissions, transferences, interferences. But I wish to emphasize that I do not think it is possible to point to a unique form of rationality in these three realms. We come across the same types, but displaced. At the same time, there is multiple, compact interconnection, but no isomorphism.

G.R.   In all eras or specifically?

FOUCAULT   There is no general law indicating the types of relation between rationalities and the procedures of domination which are put to work.

G.R.   I ask this question because there is a scheme at work in a certain number of criticisms made about you. Baudrillard's criticism, for instance, is that you speak at a very precise moment and conceive a moment in which power has become "unidentifiable" through dissemination.[7] This unidentifiable dissemination, this necessary multiplication, is reflected in the microphysical approach. Or, again, in the opinion of Alexander Schubert,[8] you address a point where capitalism has dissolved the subject in a way which makes it possible to admit that the subject has only ever been a multiplicity of positions.

FOUCAULT   I would like to return to this question in a moment, because I had already begun to talk about two or three things. The first is that in studying the rationality of dominations, I try to establish interconnections which are not isomorphisms. Secondly, when I speak of power relations, of the forms of rationality which can rule and regulate them, I am not referring to Power — with a capital P — dominating and imposing its rationality upon the totality of the social body. In fact, there are power relations. They are multiple; they have different forms, they can be in play in family relations, or within an institution, or an administration — or between a dominating and a dominated class power relations having specific forms of rationality, forms which are common to them, etc. It is a field of analysis and not at all a reference to any unique instance. Thirdly, in studying these power relations, I in no way construct a theory of Power. But I wish to know how the reflexivity of the subject and the discourse of truth are linked — "How can the subject tell the truth about itself?" — and I think that relations of power exerting themselves upon one another constitute one of the determining elements in this relation I am trying to analyze. This is clear, for example, in the first case I examined, that of madness. It was indeed through a certain mode of domination exercised by certain people upon certain other people, that the

---

7.   Jean Baudrillard (1929–   ). Professor of Sociology at the University of Paris–X (Nanterre). His critical texts examine the question of modernity and the difficulty of deciphering the plethora of signs that the individual encounters in perceiving them. Author of *Oublier Foucault* (1977) [L.D.K.].

8.   *Die Decodierung des Menschen* (Focus Verlag, 1981).

subject could undertake to tell the truth about its madness, presented in the form of the other. Thus, I am far from being a theoretician of power. At the limit, I would say that power, as an autonomous question, does not interest me. In many instances, I have been led to address the question of power only to the extent that the political analysis of power which was offered did not seem to me to account for the finer, more detailed phenomena I wish to evoke when I pose the question of telling the truth about oneself. If I tell the truth about myself, as I am now doing, it is in part that I am constituted as a subject across a number of power relations which are exerted over me and which I exert over others. I say this in order to situate what for me is the question of power. To return to the question you raised earlier, I must admit that I see no grounds for the objection. I am not developing a theory of power. I am working on the history, at a given moment, of the way reflexivity of self upon self is established, and the discourse of truth that is linked to it. When I speak about institutions of confinement in the 18th century, I am speaking about power relations as they existed at the time. So I fail utterly to see the objection, unless one imputes to me a project altogether different from my own: either that of developing a general theory of power or, again, that of developing an analysis of power as it exists now. Not at all! I take psychiatry, of course, as it is now. In it, I look at the appearance of certain problems, in the very workings of the institution, which refer us, in my view, to a history — and a relatively long one, involving several centuries. I try to work on the history or archaeology, if you like, of the way people undertook to speak truthfully about madness in the 17th and 18th centuries. And I would like to bring it to light as it existed at the time. On the subject of criminals, for example, and the system of punishment established in the 18th century, which characterises our own penal system, I have not gone into detail on *all* kinds of power exercised in the 18th century. Instead, I have examined, in a certain number of model 18th century institutions, the forms of power that were exercised and how they were put into play. So I can see no relevance whatever in saying that power is no longer what it used to be.

G.R.   Two more rather disconnected questions, which nonetheless strike me as important. Let us begin with the status of the intellectual. We have broadly defined how you conceive the work, the practice even, of the intellectual. Would you be prepared to discuss here the philosophical situation in France along the following general lines? The function of the intellectual is no longer either to oppose the state with a universal reason or to provide it with its legitimation. Is there a connection with this rather strange, disconcerting situation we see today: a tacit kind of consensus among intellectuals with regard to the Left, and at the same time, the complete silence of thought on the Left — something one is tempted to see as forcing the powers of the Left to invoke very archaic themes of legitimation; the Socialist Party Congress at Valence with its rhetorical excesses, the class struggle . . .

FOUCAULT   The recent remarks of the President of the National Assembly to the effect that we must replace the egoist, individualist, bourgeois cultural model with a new cultural model of solidarity and sacrifice . . . I was not very old when Pétain came to power in France, but this year I recognized in the words of this socialist the very tones which lulled my childhood.

G.R.   Yes. Basically, we are witnessing the astonishing spectacle of a power, divested of intellectual logistics, invoking pretty obsolete themes of legitimation. As for intellectual logistics, it seems that as soon as the Left comes to power, no one on the Left has anything to say.

FOUCAULT   It is a good question. First, we should remember that if the Left exists in France — the Left in a general sense — and if there are people who have the sentiment of being on the Left, people who vote Left, and if there can be a substantial party of the Left (as the Socialist Party has become), I think an important factor has been the existence of a Left thought and a Left reflection, of an analysis, a multiplicity of analyses, developed on the Left, of political choices made on the Left since at least 1960, which have been made outside the parties. No thanks to the Communist Party, though, or to the old S.F.I.O. — which was not dead until '72 (it took a long time to die) — that the Left is alive and well in France.[9] It is because, through the Algerian war for example, in a whole sector of intellectual life also, in sectors dealing with the problems of daily life, sectors like those of political and economic analysis, there was an extraordinarily lively Left thought. And it did not die at the very moment the parties of the Left became disqualified for different reasons. On the contrary.

G.R.   No, at the time, certainly not.

FOUCAULT   And we can say that the Left survived for fifteen years — the first fifteen years of Gaullism and then the regime which followed — because of that effort. Secondly, it should be noted that the Socialist Party was greeted so responsively in large part because it was reasonably open to these new attitudes, new questions and new problems. It was open to questions concerning daily life, sexual life, couples, women's issues. It was sensitive to the problem of self-management, for example. All these are themes of Left thought — a Left thought which is not encrusted in the political parties and which is not traditional in its approach to Marxism. New problems, new thinking — these have been crucial. I think that one day, when we look back at this episode in French history, we will see in it the growth of a new kind of Left thought which — in multiple and non-unified forms (perhaps one of its positive aspects) — has completely transformed the horizon of contemporary Left movements. We might well imagine this particular form of Left culture as being allergic to any party organization, incapable of finding its real expression in anything but *groupuscules* and individualities. But apparently not. Finally, there has been — as I said earlier — a kind of symbiosis which has meant that the new Socialist Party is now fairly saturated with these ideas. In any case — something worthy of note — we have seen a number of intellectuals keeping company with the Socialist Party. Of course, the Socialist Party's very astute political tactics and strategy — and this is not pejorative — account for their coming to power. But here again, the

9.   S.F.I.O. The official name of the French socialist party formed in 1905 from Guesdist and Jauresist factions as the *Section Française de l'Internationale Ouvrière*. The party split in 1920 following the Congress of Tours when a majority of its members formed the first French communist party [L.D.K.].

Socialist Party came to power after having absorbed a certain number of Left cultural forms. However, since the Congress of Metz, and *a fortiori*, the Congress of Valence — where we heard things such as we discussed earlier — it is clear that this Left thought is asking itself questions.

G.R. Does this thought itself exist any more?

FOUCAULT I do not know. We have to bear several complex factors in mind. We have to see, for example, that in the Socialist Party, this new Left thought was most active in the circle of someone like Rocard — that the light of Rocard and his group, and of the Rocard current in the Socialist Party, is now hidden under a bushel, has had a major effect[10]. The situation is very complex. But I think that the rather wooden pronouncements of many Socialist Party leaders at present are a betrayal of the earlier hopes expressed by a large part of this Left thought. They also betray the recent history of the Socialist Party and they silence, in a fairly authoritarian manner, certain currents which exist within the party itself. Undoubtedly, confronted with this phenomenon, intellectuals are tending to keep quiet. (I say tending, because it is a journalistic obsession to say that the intellectuals are keeping quiet). Personally, I know several intellectuals who have reacted, who have given their opinion on some measure or on some problem. And I think that if we drew up an exact balance sheet of interventions by intellectuals over the last few months, there would certainly not be any less than before. Anyway, for my part, I have never written as many articles in the press as I have since word went out that I was keeping quiet. Still, let's not worry about me personally. It is true that these reactions are not a kind of assertive choice. They are finely nuanced interventions — hesitant, slightly doubtful, slightly encouraging, etc. But they correspond to the present state of affairs and instead of complaining about the silence of intellectuals, we should recognize much more clearly their thoughtful reserve in response to a recent event, a recent process, whose outcome we do not yet know for certain.

G.R. No necessary relation, then, between *this* political situation, *this* type of discourse and the thesis, nonetheless

10. Michel Rocard (1930–). Moderate Socialist leader aspiring to the French presidency. He bases his highly "technocratic" politics on socioeconomic reform. Named Prime Minister by Mitterrand in May 1988 [L.D.K.].

very widespread, that reason is power and so we are to divest ourselves of the one and the other?

FOUCAULT No. You must understand that is part of the destiny common to all problems once they are posed: they degenerate into slogans. Nobody has said, "Reason is power." I do not think anyone has said knowledge is a kind of power.

G.R. It has been said.

FOUCAULT It has been said but you have to understand that when I read — and I know it has been attributed to me — the thesis, "Knowledge is power," or "Power is knowledge," I begin to laugh, since studying their *relation* is precisely my problem. If they were identical, I would not have to study them and I would be spared a lot of fatigue as a result. The very fact that I pose the question of their relation proves clearly that I do not *identify* them.

G.R. Last question. The view that Marxism is doing rather badly today because it drank from the springs of the Enlightenment, has dominated·thought, whether we like it or not, since the '70s, if only because a number of individuals — intellectuals — known as the New Philosophers have vulgarized the theme. So, Marxism, we are told, is doing fairly badly.

FOUCAULT I do not know if it is doing well or badly. It is an idea that has dominated thought, or philosophy; that is the formula I stop at, if you like. I think you are quite right to put the question, and to put it in that way. I would be inclined to say — I nearly stopped you there — that this view has not dominated thought so much as the "lower depths" of thought. But that would be facile. Uselessly polemical. And it is not really fair. I think we should recognize that in France, towards the '50s, there were two circuits of thought which, if not foreign to one another, were practically independent of one another. There was what I would call the university circuit — a circuit of scholarly thought — and then there was the circuit of open thought, or mainstream thought. When I say "mainstream," I do not necessarily mean poor quality. But a university book, a thesis, a course, etc., were things you found in the academic presses, available to university readers. They had scarcely any influence, except in universities. There was the special case of Bergson. That was exceptional. But

from the end of the war onwards — and no doubt
Existentialism played a part in this — we have seen ideas of
profoundly academic origins, or roots (and the roots of Sartre,
after all, are Husserl and Heidegger, who were hardly public
dancers) addressed to a much broader public than that of the
universities. Now, even though there is nobody of Sartre's
stature to continue it, this phenomenon has become democratized. Only Sartre — or perhaps Sartre and Merleau-Ponty
— could do it. But then it tended to become something within
everybody's range, more or less. And for a certain number of
reasons. First, there was the dislocation of the university, the
growing number of students and professors, etc., who came
to constitute a kind of social mass; the dislocation of internal
structures and a broadening of the university public; also the
diffusion of culture (by no means a negative thing). The
public's cultural level, on average, has really risen considerably and, whatever one says, television has played a major
role. People come to see that there is a new history, etc. Add
to this all the political phenomena — the groups and
movements half-inside and half-outside the universities. It all
gave university activity an echo which reverberated widely
beyond academic institutions or even groups of specialist,
professional intellectuals. One remarkable phenomenon in
France at the moment is the almost complete absence of
specialized philosophy journals. Or they are more or less
worthless. So when you want to write something, where do
you publish? Where *can* you publish? In the end, you can only
manage to slip something into one of the wide-circulation
weeklies and general interest magazines. That is very
significant. And so what happens — and what is fatal in such
situations — is that a fairly evolved discourse, instead of being
relayed by additional work which perfects it (either with
criticism or amplification), rendering it more difficult and even
finer, nowadays undergoes a process of amplification from the
bottom up. Little by little, from the book to the review, to the
newspaper article, and from the newspaper article to television, we come to summarize a work, or a problem, in terms of
slogans. This passage of the philosophical question into the
realm of the slogan, this transformation of the Marxist
question, which becomes "Marxism is dead," is not the
responsibility of any one person in particular, but we can see

the slide whereby philosophical thought, or a philosophical issue, becomes a consumer item. In the past, there were two different circuits. Even if it could not avoid all the pitfalls, the institutional circuit, which had its drawbacks — it was closed, dogmatic, academic — nevertheless managed to sustain less heavy losses. The tendency to entropy was less, while nowadays entropy sets in at an alarming rate. I could give personal examples. It took fifteen years to convert my book about madness into a slogan: all mad people were confined in the 18th century. But it did not even take 15 months — it only took three weeks — to convert my book on will to knowledge into the slogan "Sexuality has never been repressed." In my own experience, I have seen this entropy accelerate in a detestable way for philosophical thought. But it should be remembered that this means added responsibility for people who write.

G.R.   I was tempted for a moment to say in conclusion — in the form of a question — not wanting to substitute one slogan for another : is Marxism not finished then? In the sense you use in *The Archaeology of Knowledge* that a "non-falsified Marxism would help us to formulate a general theory of discontinuity, series, limits, unities, specific orders, autonomies and differentiated dependencies."

FOUCAULT   Yes. I am reluctant to make assessments about the type of culture that may be in store. Everything is present, you see, at least as a virtual object, inside a given culture. Or everything that has already featured once. The problem of objects that have never featured in the culture is another matter. But it is part of the function of memory and culture to be able to reactualize any objects whatever that have already featured. Repetition is always possible; repetition with application, transformation. God knows in 1945 Nietzsche appeared to be completely disqualified . . . It is clear, even if one admits that Marx will disappear for now, that he will reappear one day. What I desire — and it is here that my formulation has changed in relation to the one you cited — is not so much the defalsification and restitution of a true Marx, but the unburdening and liberation of Marx in relation to party dogma, which has constrained it, touted it and brandished it for so long. The phrase "Marx is dead" can be given a conjunctural sense. One can say it is relatively true, but to say that Marx will disappear like that . . .

G.R. But does this reference in *The Archaeology of Knowledge* mean that, in a certain way, Marx is at work in your own methodology?

FOUCAULT Yes, absolutely. You see, given the period in which I wrote those books, it was good form (in order to be viewed favorably by the institutional Left) to cite Marx in the footnotes. So I was careful to steer clear of that.

3

An Aesthetics of Existence

The theorist who put forth the now classical post-modern topos on the death of man in the 1960s reveals here a certain nostalgia for the subject. Redefining in part the scope of his intellectual activity in the 1980s as constituting a new genealogy of morals, Foucault now centers his research on a subject who turns his life into an exemplary work of art. The question of truth in politics is one which must be addressed by an intellectual whose parrhesia (free speech) functions in the name of knowledge and experience. Originally given on April 25, 1984 to Alessandro Fontana (a collaborator with Foucault on I, Pierre Rivière) for the Italian weekly Panorama this discussion subsequently reappeared in Le Monde on July 15–16, 1984. The translation is by Alan Sheridan.

A.F.   Several years have gone by since *La Volonté de savoir*. I know that your latest books have presented you with a number of problems and difficulties. I would like you to talk to me about those difficulties and about this voyage into the Greco-Roman world, which was, though not unknown to you, at least unfamiliar.

FOUCAULT   The difficulties derived from the project itself, which was intended precisely to avoid them. By programming my work over several volumes according to a plan laid down in advance, I was telling myself that the time had now come when I could write them without difficulty, and simply unwind what was in my head, confirming it by empirical research.

I very nearly died of boredom writing those books: they were too much like the earlier ones. For some people, writing a book is always a risk — the risk, for instance, of not pulling it off. When you know in advance where you're going to end up there's a whole dimension of experience lacking, namely, the risk attached to writing a book that may not come off. So I changed the general plan: instead of studying sexuality on the borders of knowledge and power, I have tried to go further back, to find out how, for the subject himself, the experience of his sexuality as desire had been constituted. In trying to disentangle this problematic, I was led to examine certain very ancient Latin and Greek texts. This required a lot of preparation, a lot of effort, and left me right up to the end with a lot of uncertainties and hesitations.

A.F. There is always a certain "intentionality" in your works that often eludes the reader. *Histoire de la folie* was really the history of the constitution of that branch of knowledge known as psychology; *Les Mots et les choses* was the archaeology of the human sciences; *Surveiller et punir* was about the installation of the disciplines of the body and soul. It would seem that what is at the center of your recent works is what you call "truth games."

FOUCAULT I don't think there is a great difference between these books and the earlier ones. When you write books like these, you want very much to change what you think entirely and to find yourself at the end of it quite different from what you were at the beginning. Then you come to see that really you've changed relatively little. You may have changed your point of view, you've gone round and round the problem, which is still the same, namely, the relations between the subject, truth, and the constitution of experience. I have tried to analyze how areas such as madness, sexuality, and delinquency may enter into a certain play of the truth, and also how, through this insertion of human practice, of behavior, in the play of truth, the subject himself is affected. That was the problem of the history of madness, of sexuality.

A.F. Doesn't this really amount to a new genealogy of morals?

FOUCAULT Not withstanding the solemnity of the title and the grandiose mark that Nietzsche has left on it, I'd say yes.

A.F. In a piece that appeared in *Le Débat* in November 1983, you speak, in relation to Antiquity, of moralities turned towards ethics and of moralities turned towards codes.[1] Is this the same distinction as that between Greco-Roman moralities and those that emerge with Christianity?

FOUCAULT With Christianity, there occurred a slow, gradual shift in relation to the moralities of Antiquity, which were essentially a practice, a style of liberty. Of course, there had also been certain norms of behavior that governed each individual's behavior. But the will to be a moral subject and the search for an ethics of existence were, in Antiquity, mainly an attempt to affirm one's liberty and to give to one's own life a certain form in which one could recognize oneself, be recognized by others, and which even posterity might take as an example.

This elaboration of one's own life as a personal work of art, even if it obeyed certain collective canons, was at the centre, it seems to me, of moral experience, of the will to morality in Antiquity, whereas in Christianity, with the religion of the text, the idea of the will of God, the principle of obedience, morality took on increasingly the form of a code of rules (only certain ascetic practices were more bound up with the exercise of personal liberty).

From Antiquity to Christianity, we pass from a morality that was essentially the search for a personal ethics to a morality as obedience to a system of rules. And if I was interested in Antiquity it was because, for a whole series of reasons, the idea of a morality as obedience to a code of rules is now disappearing, has already disappeared. And to this absence of morality corresponds, must correspond, the search for an aesthetics of existence.

A.F. Has all the knowledge accumulated in recent years about the body, sexuality, the disciplines improved our relationship with others, our being in the world?

FOUCAULT I can't help but think that discussion around a whole series of things, even independently of political choices, around certain forms of existence, rules of behavior,

---

1. "Usage des plaisirs et techniques de soi," *Le Débat* 27 (November 1983), 46–72 [L.D.K.].

etc., has been profoundly beneficial — the relation with the body, between man and woman, with sexuality.

A.F. So this knowledge has helped us to live better.

FOUCAULT The change hasn't just been in what people thought about and talked about, but also in philosophical discourse, in theory and critique: indeed, in most of these analyses, people are not told what they ought to be, what they ought to do, what they ought to believe and think. What they do rather is to bring out how up till now social mechanisms had been able to operate, how the forms of repression and constraint had acted, and then, it seems to me, people were left to make up their own minds, to choose, in the light of all this, their own existence.

A.F. Five years ago, in your seminar at the Collège de France, we started to read Hayek and Von Mises.[2] People then said: Through a reflection on liberalism, Foucault is going to give us a book on politics. Liberalism also seemed to be a detour in order to rediscover the individual beyond the mechanisms of power. Your opposition to the phenomeno-logical subject and the psychological subject is well known. At that time, people began to talk about a subject of practices, and the rereading of liberalism took place to some extent with that in view. It will come as a surprise to nobody that people said several times: there is no subject in Foucault's work. The subjects are always subjected, they are the point of application of normative techniques and disciplines, but they are never sovereign subjects.

FOUCAULT A distinction must be made here. In the first place, I do indeed believe that there is no sovereign, founding subject, a universal form of subject to be found everywhere. I am very sceptical of this view of the subject and very hostile to it. I believe, on the contrary, that the subject is constituted through practices of subjection, or, in a more autonomous way, through practices of liberation, of liberty, as in Antiquity,

2. Friedrich August von Hayek (1899–). Austrian political economist who examined the relationship between individual values and economic controls.
   Richard von Mises (1883–1953). German mathematician and philosopher. Specialist in aerodynamics and hydrodynamics who set out to develop a frequency of probability theory based on an empirical method [L.D.K.].

on the basis, of course, of a number of rules, styles, inventions to be found in the cultural environment.

A.F. This brings us to contemporary politics. Times are hard: on the international plane, we are seeing the blackmail of Yalta and the confrontation of the two power blocs. At home, we have the specter of the economic crisis. In relation to all this, little remains between the Left and the Right but a difference of style. So how, given this reality and its dictates, is one to decide whether there is any possible alternative?

FOUCAULT It seems to me that your question is both right and somewhat narrow. It should be broken down into two kinds of question: in the first place, do we have to accept or not accept? secondly, if we do not accept, what can be done? For the first question, one must reply quite unambiguously: we must not accept, either the after-effects of the war, or the prolongation of a certain strategic situation in Europe, or the fact that half of Europe is enslaved.

Then we ask the other question: "What can be done against a power like that of the Soviet Union, in relation to our own government and with the peoples who, on both sides of the Iron Curtain, are determined to question the division as it has been established?" In relation to the Soviet Union, there is not a great deal to be done, except to assist as effectively as possible those who are struggling out there. As for the other two tasks, we have a lot to accomplish.

A.F. So we must not assume what might be called a Hegelian attitude and accept reality as it is, as it is presented to us. But there is still another question: "Is there a truth in politics?"

FOUCAULT I believe too much in truth not to suppose that there are different truths and different ways of speaking the truth. Of course, one can't expect the government to tell the truth, the whole truth, and nothing but the truth. On the other hand, we can demand of those who govern us a certain truth as to their ultimate aims, the general choices of their tactics, and a number of particular points in their programs: this is the *parrhesia* (free speech) of the governed, who can and must question those who govern them, in the name of the knowledge, the experience they have, by virtue of being citizens, of what those who govern do, of the meaning of their action, of the decisions they have taken.

However, one must avoid a trap in which those who govern try to catch intellectuals and into which they often fall: "Put yourselves in our place and tell us what you would do." It is not a question one has to answer. To make a decision on some question implies a knowledge of evidence that is refused us, an analysis of the situation that we have not been able to make. This is a trap. Nevertheless, as governed, we have a perfect right to ask questions about the truth: "What are you doing, for example, when you are hostile to Euromissiles, or when, on the contrary, you support them, when you restructure the Lorraine steel industry, when you open up the question of private education."

A.F.   In that descent into hell that a long meditation, a long search represents — a descent in which one sets off in a sense in search of a truth — what type of reader would you like to meet and tell this truth to? It is a fact that, although there may still be good authors, there are fewer and fewer good readers.

FOUCAULT   Never mind "good" readers — I'd say fewer and fewer readers. And it's true one isn't read anymore. One's first book is read, because one isn't known, because people don't know who one is, and it is read in disorder and confusion, which suits me fine. There is no reason why one should write not only the book, but also lay down the law as to how it should be read. The only such law is that of all possible readings. It doesn't bother me particularly if a book, given that it is read, is read in different ways. What is serious is that, as one goes on writing books, one is no longer read at all, and from distortion to distortion, reading out of others' readings, one ends up with an absolutely grotesque image of the book.

This does indeed pose a problem: is one to involve oneself in polemics and reply to each of these distortions and, consequently, lay down the law to readers, which I find repugnant, or leave the book to be distorted to the point at which it becomes a caricature of itself, which I find equally repugnant?

There is a solution, however: the only law on the press, the only law on books, that I would like to see brought in, would be a prohibition to use an author's name twice, together with a right to anonymity and to pseudonyms so that each book might be read for itself. There are books for which a knowledge of the author is a key to its intelligibility. But apart from a few great authors, this knowledge, in the case of most of the others, serves absolutely no purpose. It acts only as a barrier. For someone like me — I am not a great author, but only someone who writes books — it would be better if my books were read for themselves, with whatever faults and qualities they may have.

Theories of the Political:
History, Power and the Law

4

Politics and Reason

On October 10 and 16, 1979, Foucault was
invited to deliver at Stanford University the Tanner
Lectures on Human Values. "Omnes et Singulatim:
Towards a Criticism of Political Reason" reproduces
in its entirety those two lectures. Here Foucault
investigates the rapport between rationalization
and the excesses of power. He suggests a
transformation in relationships such as those
emanating from the notion of "individualizing
power," a phenomenon that he calls pastorship. In
his analysis of this modality of power Foucault
demonstrates how pastoral technology challenged
the structure of ancient Greek society and ultimately coalesces with the State in the modern
sense of the term. Foucault argues that early
Christianity further implemented the concept of
pastoral influences while functioning as a "game,"
one dealing with individual control and enacted
by the experience/knowledge/power triad. The
reason of the state in early modern Europe is
designated as an art of government which
presupposes a particular kind of knowledge and is
reflective of the very nature of the state itself. To
enable the state to consolidate and exercise this
power, the role of the police (Polizeiwissenschaft)
as individualizing and totalizing agent must be
augmented. Yet if political rationality is criticized
here by Foucault no alternative is offered other
than the radical questioning of its very roots. He
thus forecloses the possibility of other institutions
taking its place.

These lectures were first published in English
in The Tanner Lectures on Human Values, Sterling
M. McMurrin, editor, volume 2 (Raymond Aron,

Brian Barry, Jonathan Bennett, Robert Coles, George T. Stigler, Wallace Stegner and Michel Foucault), Salt Lake City: University of Utah Press and Cambridge: Cambridge University Press, 1981. The French version appeared in Le Débat *in the fall of 1986.*

I

The title sounds pretentious, I know. But the reason for that is precisely its own excuse. Since the nineteenth century, Western thought has never stopped laboring at the task of critizing the role of reason — or the lack of reason — in political structures. It's therefore perfectly unfitting to undertake such a vast project once again. However, so many previous attempts are a warrant that every new venture will be just about as successful as the former ones — and in any case, probably just as fortunate.

Under such a banner, mine is the embarrassment of one who has only sketches and uncompletable drafts to propose. Philosophy gave up trying to offset the impotence of scientific reason long ago; it no longer tries to complete its edifice.

One of the Enlightenment's tasks was to multiply reason's political powers. But the men of the nineteenth century soon started wondering whether reason weren't getting too powerful in our societies. They began to worry about a relationship they confusedly suspected between a rationalization-prone society and certain threats to the individual and his liberties, to the species and its survival.

In other words, since Kant, the role of philosophy has been to prevent reason going beyond the limits of what is given in experience; but from the same moment — that is, from the development of modern states and political management of society — the role of philosophy has also been to keep watch over the excessive powers of political rationality — which is rather a promising life expectancy.

Everybody is aware of such banal facts. But that they are banal does not mean they don't exist. What we have to do with banal facts is to discover — or try to discover — which specific and perhaps original problems are connected with them.

The relationship between rationalization and the excesses of political power is evident. And we should not need to wait for bureaucracy or concentration camps to recognize the existence of such relations. But the problem is: what to do with such an evident fact?

Shall we "try" reason? To my mind, nothing would be more sterile. First, because the field has nothing to do with guilt or innocence. Second, because it's senseless to refer to "reason" as the contrary entity to non-reason. Last, because such a trial would trap us into playing the arbitrary and boring part of either the rationalist or the irrationalist.

Shall we investigate this kind of rationalism which seems to be specific to our modern culture and which originates in Enlightenment? I think that that was the way of some of the members of the Frankfurter Schule. My purpose is not to begin a discussion of their works — they are most important and valuable. I would suggest another way of investigating the links between rationalization and power:

1. It may be wise not to take as a whole the rationalization of society or of culture, but to analyze this process in several fields, each of them grounded in a fundamental experience: madness, illness, death, crime, sexuality, etc.

2. I think that the word "rationalization" is a dangerous one. The main problem when people try to rationalize something is not to investigate whether or not they conform to principles of rationality, but to discover which kind of rationality they are using.

3. Even if the Enlightenment has been a very important phase in our history, and in the development of political technology, I think we have to refer to much more remote processes if we want to understand how we have been trapped in our own history.

This was my "ligne de conduite" in my previous work: analyze the relations between experiences like madness, death, crime, sexuality, and several technologies of power. What I am working on now is the problem of individuality — or, I should say, self-identity as referred to the problem of "individualizing power."

Everyone knows that in European societies political power has evolved towards more and more centralized forms. Historians have been studying this organization of the state, with its administration and bureaucracy, for dozens of years.

I'd like to suggest in these two lectures the possibility of analyzing another kind of transformation in such power relationships. This transformation is, perhaps, less celebrated. But I think that it is also important, mainly for modern societies. Apparently this evolution seems antagonistic to the evolution towards a centralized state. What I mean in fact is the development of power techniques oriented towards individuals and intended to rule them in a continuous and permanent way. If the state is the political form of a centralized and centralizing power, let us call pastorship the individualizing power.

My purpose this evening is to outline the origin of this pastoral modality of power, or at least some aspects of its ancient history. And in the next lecture, I'll try to show how this pastorship happened to combine with its opposite, the state.

The idea of the deity, or the king, or the leader, as a shepherd followed by a flock of sheep wasn't familiar to the Greeks and Romans. There were exceptions, I know — early ones in Homeric literature, later ones in certain texts of the Lower Empire. I'll come back to them later. Roughly speaking, we can say that the metaphor of the flock didn't occur in great Greek or Roman political literature.

This is not the case in ancient Oriental societies: Egypt, Assyria, Judaea. Pharaoh was an Egyptian shepherd. Indeed, he ritually received the herdsman's crook on his coronation day; and the term "shepherd of men" was one of the Babylonian monarch's titles. But God was also a shepherd leading men to their grazing ground and ensuring them food. An Egyptian hymn invoked Ra this way: "O Ra that keepest watch when all men sleep, Thou who seekest what is good for thy cattle . . . ." The association between God and King is easily made, since both assume the same role: the flock they watch over is the same; the shepherd-king is entrusted with the great divine shepherd's creatures. An Assyrian invocation to the king ran like this: "Illustrious companion of pastures,

Thou who carest for thy land and feedest it, shepherd of all abundance."

But, as we know, it was the Hebrews who developed and intensified the pastoral theme — with nevertheless a highly peculiar characteristic: God, and God only, is his people's shepherd. With just one positive exception: David, as the founder of the monarchy, is the only one to be referred to as a shepherd. God gave him the task of assembling a flock.

There are negative exceptions, too: wicked kings are consistently compared to bad shepherds; they disperse the flock, let it die of thirst, shear it solely for profit's sake. Jahweh is the one and only true shepherd. He guides his own people in person, aided only by his prophets. As the Psalms say: "Like a flock/hast Thou led Thy people, by Moses' and by Aaron's hand." Of course I can treat neither the historical problems pertaining to the origin of this comparison nor its evolution throughout Jewish thought. I just want to show a few themes typical of pastoral power. I'd like to point out the contrast with Greek political thought, and to show how important these themes became in Christian thought and institutions later on.

1. The shepherd wields power over a flock rather than over a land. It's probably much more complex than that, but, broadly speaking, the relation between the diety, the land, and men differs from that of the Greeks. Their gods owned the land, and this primary possession determined the relationship between men and gods. On the contrary, it's the Shepherd-God's relationship with his flock that is primary and fundamental here. God gives, or promises, his flock a land.

2. The shepherd gathers together, guides, and leads his flock. The idea that the political leader was to quiet any hostilities within the city and make unity reign over conflict is undoubtedly present in Greek thought. But what the shepherd gathers together is dispersed individuals. They gather together on hearing his voice: "I'll whistle and will gather them together." Conversely, the shepherd only has to disappear for the flock to be scattered. In other words, the shepherd's immediate presence and direct action cause the flock to exist. Once the good Greek lawgiver, like Solon, has resolved any conflicts, what he leaves behind him is a strong

city with laws enabling it to endure without him.

3. The shepherd's role is to ensure the salvation of his flock. The Greeks said also that the deity saved the city; they never stopped declaring that the competent leader is a helmsman warding his ship away from the rocks. But the way the shepherd saves his flock is quite different. It's not only a matter of saving them all, all together, when danger comes nigh. It's a matter of constant, individualized, and final kindness. Constant kindness, for the shepherd ensures his flock's food; every day he attends to their thirst and hunger. The Greek god was asked to provide a fruitful land and abundant crops. He wasn't asked to foster a flock day by day. And individualized kindness, too, for the shepherd sees that all the sheep, each and every one of them, is fed and saved. Later Hebrew literature, especially, laid the emphasis on such individually kindly power: a rabbinical commentary on Exodus explains why Jahweh chose Moses to shepherd his people: he had left his flock to go and search for one lost sheep.

Last and not least, it's final kindness. The shepherd has a target for his flock. It must either be led to good grazing ground or brought back to the fold.

4. Yet another difference lies in the idea that wielding power is a "duty." The Greek leader had naturally to make decisions in the interest of all; he would have been a bad leader had he preferred his personal interest. But his duty was a glorious one: even if in war he had to give up his life, such a sacrifice was offset by something extremely precious: immortality. He never lost. By way of contrast, shepherdly kindness is much closer to "devotedness." Everything the shepherd does is geared to the good of his flock. That's his constant concern. When they sleep, *he* keeps watch.

The theme of keeping watch is important. It brings out two aspects of the shepherd's devotedness. First, he acts, he works, he puts himself out, for those he nourishes and who are asleep. Second, he watches over them. He pays attention to them all and scans each one of them. He's got to know his flock as a whole, and in detail. Not only must he know where good pastures are, the seasons' laws and the order of things; he must also know each one's particular needs. Once again, a rabbinical commentary on Exodus describes Moses' qualities as a shepherd this way: he would send each sheep in turn to graze — first, the youngest, for them to browse on the tenderest sward; then the older ones; and last the oldest, who were capable of browsing on the roughest grass. The shepherd's power implies individual attention paid to each member of the flock.

These are just themes that Hebraic texts associate with the metaphors of the Shepherd-God and his flock of people. In no way do I claim that that is effectively how political power was wielded in Hebrew society before the fall of Jerusalem. I do not even claim that such a conception of political power is in any way coherent.

They're just themes. Paradoxical, even contradictory, ones. Christianity was to give them considerable importance, both in the Middle Ages and in modern times. Among all the societies in history, ours — I mean, those that came into being at the end of Antiquity on the Western side of the European continent — have perhaps been the most aggressive and the most conquering; they have been capable of the most stupefying violence, against themselves as well as against others. They invented a great many different political forms. They profoundly altered their legal structures several times. It must be kept in mind that they alone evolved a strange technology of power treating the vast majority of men as a flock with a few as shepherds. They thus established between them a series of complex, continuous, and paradoxical relationships.

This is undoubtedly something singular in the course of history. Clearly, the development of "pastoral technology" in the management of men profoundly disrupted the structures of ancient society.

*   *   *

So as to better explain the importance of this disruption, I'd like to briefly return to what I was saying about the Greeks. I can see the objections liable to be made.

One is that the Homeric poems use the shepherd metaphor to refer to the kings. In the *Iliad* and the *Odyssey*, the expression ποιμην λαων crops up several times. It qualifies the leaders, highlighting the grandeur of their power. Moreover, it's a ritual title, common in even late Indo-European literature. In *Beowulf* the king is still regarded as a shepherd. But there is nothing really surprising in the fact that the same title, as in the Assyrian texts, is to be found in archaic epic poems.

The problem arises rather as to Greek thought: There is at least one category of texts where references to shepherd models are made: the Pythagorean ones. The metaphor of the herdsman appears in the *Fragments* of Archytas, quoted by Stobeus. The word νομοζ (the law) is connected with the word νομευζ (shepherd): the shepherd shares out, the law apportions. Then Zeus is called Νομιοζ and Νεμειοζ because he gives his sheep food. And, finally, the magistrate must be Φιλανθρωποζ, i.e., devoid of selfishness. He must be full of zeal and solicitude, like a shepherd.

Grube, the German editor of Archytas' *Fragments*, says that this proves a Hebrew influence unique in Greek literature. Other commentators, such as Delatte, say that the comparison between gods, magistrates, and shepherds was common in Greece. It is therefore not to be dwelt upon.

I shall restrict myself to political literature. The results of the enquiry are clear: the political metaphor of the shepherd occurs neither in Isocrates, nor in Demosthenes, nor in Aristotle. This is rather surprising when one reflects that in his *Areopagiticus*, Isocrates insists on the magistrates' duties; he stresses the need for them to be devoted and to show concern for young people. Yet not a word as to any shepherd.

By contrast, Plato often speaks of the shepherd–magistrate. He mentions the idea in *Critias*, *The Republic* and *Laws*. He thrashes it out in *The Statesman*. In the former, the shepherd theme is rather subordinate. Sometimes, those happy days when mankind was governed directly by the gods and grazed on abundant pastures are evoked (*Critias*). Sometimes, the magistrates' necessary virtue — as contrasted with Thrasymachos' vice, is what is insisted upon (*The Republic*). And sometimes, the problem is to define the subordinate magistrates' role: indeed, they, just as the watchdogs, have to obey "those at the top of the scale" (*Laws*).

But in *The Statesman* pastoral power is the central problem and it is treated at length. Can the city's decision-maker, can the commander, be defined as a sort of shepherd?

Plato's analysis is well known. To solve this question he uses the division method. A distinction is drawn between the man who conveys orders to inanimate things (e.g., the architect), and the man who gives orders to animals; between the man who gives orders to isolated animals (like a yoke of oxen) and he who gives orders to flocks; and he who gives orders to animal flocks, and he who commands human flocks. And there we have the political leader: a shepherd of men.

But this first division remains unsatisfactory. It has to be pushed further. The method opposing *men* to all the other animals isn't a good one. And so the dialogue starts all over again. A whole series of distinctions is established: between wild animals and tame ones; those that live in water, and those that live on land; those with horns, and those without; between cleft- and plain-hoofed animals; between those capable and incapable of mutual reproduction. And the dialogue wanders astray with these never-ending subdivisions.

So, what do the initial development of the dialogue and its subsequent failure show? That the division method can prove nothing at all when it isn't managed correctly. It also shows that the idea of analyzing political power as the relationship between a shepherd and his animals was probably rather a controversial one at the time. Indeed, it's the first assumption to cross the interlocutors' minds when seeking to discover the essence of the politician. Was it a commonplace at the time? Or was Plato rather discussing one of the Pythagorean themes? The absence of the shepherd metaphor in other contemporary political texts seems to tip the scale towards the second hypothesis. But we can probably leave the discussion open.

My personal enquiry bears upon how Plato impugns the theme in the rest of the dialogue. He does so first by means of methodological arguments and then by means of the celebrated myth of the world revolving round its spindle.

The methodological arguments are extremely interesting. Whether the king is a sort of shepherd or not can be told, not by deciding which different species can form a flock, but by analyzing what the shepherd does.

What is characteristic of his task? First, the shepherd is alone at the head of his flock. Second, his job is to supply his cattle with food; to care for them when they are sick; to play them music to get them together, and guide them; to arrange their intercourse with a view to the finest offspring. So we *do* find the typical shepherd-metaphor themes of Oriental texts.

And what's the king's task in regard to all this? Like the shepherd, he is alone at the head of the city. But, for the rest who provides mankind with food? The king? No. The farmer, the baker do. Who looks after men when they are sick? The king? No. The physician. And who guides them with music? The gymnast — not the king. And so, many citizens could quite legitimately claim the title "shepherd of men." Just as the human flock's shepherd has many rivals, so has the politician. Consequently, if we want to find out what the politician really and essentially is, we must sift it out from "the surrounding flood," thereby demonstrating in what ways he *isn't* a shepherd.

Plato therefore resorts to the myth of the world revolving round its axis in two successive and contrary motions.

In a first phase, each animal species belonged to a flock led by a Genius-Shepherd. The human flock was led by the deity itself. It could lavishly avail itself of the fruits of the earth; it needed no abode; and after Death, men came back to life. A crucial sentence adds: "The deity being their shepherd, mankind needed no political constitution."

In a second phase, the world turned in the opposite direction. The gods were no longer men's shepherds; they had to look after themselves. For they had been given fire. What would the politicians's role then be? Would *he* become the shepherd in the gods' stead? Not at all. His job was to weave a strong fabric for the city. Being a politician didn't mean feeding, nursing, and breeding offspring, but binding: binding different virtues; binding contrary temperaments (either impetuous or moderate), using the "shuttle" of popular opinion. The royal art of ruling consisted in gathering lives together "into a community based upon concord and friendship," and so he wove "the finest of fabrics." The entire population, "slaves and free men alike, were mantled in its folds."

The Statesman therefore seems to be classical antiquity's most systematic reflexion on the theme of the pastorate which was later to become so important in the Christian West. That we are discussing it seems to prove that a perhaps initially Oriental theme was important enough in Plato's day to deserve investigation, but we stress the fact that it was impugned.

Not impugned entirely, however. Plato did admit that the physician, the farmer, the gymnast, and the pedagogue acted as shepherds. But he refused to get them involved with the politician's activity. He said so explicitly: how would the politician ever find the time to come and sit by each person, feed him, give him concerts, and care for him when sick? Only a god in a Golden Age could ever act like that; or again, like a physician or pedagogue, be responsible for the lives and development of a few individuals. But, situated between the two — the gods and the swains — the men who hold political power are not to be shepherds. Their task doesn't consist in fostering the life of a group of individuals. It consists in forming and assuring the city's unity. In short, the political problem is that of the relation between the one and the many in the framework of the city and its citizens. The pastoral problem concerns the lives of individuals.

All this seems very remote, perhaps. The reason for my insisting on these ancient texts is that they show us how early this problem — or rather, this series of problems — arose. They span the entirety of Western history. They are still highly important for contemporary society. They deal with the relations between politicical power at work within the state as a legal framework of unity, and a power we can call "pastoral," whose role is to constantly ensure, sustain, and improve the lives of each and every one.

The well-known "welfare state problem" does not only bring the needs or the new governmental techniques of today's world to light. It must be recognized for what it is: one of the extremely numerous reappearances of the tricky adjustment between political power wielded over legal subjects and pastoral power wielded over live individuals.

I have obviously no intention whatsoever of recounting the evolution of pastoral power throughout Christianity. The immense problems this would raise can easily be imagined: from doctrinal problems, such as Christ's denomination as "the good shepherd," right up to institutional ones, such as parochial organization, or the way pastoral responsibilities were shared between priests and bishops.

All I want to do is bring to light two or three aspects I regard as important for the evolution of pastorship, i.e., the technology of power.

First of all, let us examine the theoretical elaboration of the theme in ancient Christian literature: Chrysostom, Cyprian, Ambrose, Jerome, and, for monastic life, Cassian or Benedict. The Hebrew themes are considerably altered in at least four ways:

1. First, with regard to responsibility. We saw that the shepherd was to assume responsibility for the destiny of the whole flock and of each and every sheep. In the Christian conception, the shepherd must render an account — not only of each sheep, but of all their actions, all the good or evil they are liable to do, all that happens to them.

Moreover, between each sheep and its shepherd Christianity conceives a complex exchange and circulation of sins and merits. The sheep's sin is also imputable to the shepherd. He'll have to render an account of it at the Last Judgement. Conversely, by helping his flock to find salvation, the shepherd will also find his own. But by saving his sheep, he lays himself open to getting lost; so if he wants to save himself, he must needs run the risk of losing himself for others. If he does get lost, it is the flock that will incur the greatest danger. But let's leave all these paradoxes aside. My aim was just to underline the force and complexity of the moral ties binding the shepherd to each member of his flock. And what I especially wanted to underline was that such ties not only concerned individuals' lives, but the details of their actions as well.

2. The second important alteration concerns the problem of obedience. In the Hebrew conception, God being a shepherd, the flock following him complies to his will, to his law.

Christianity, on the other hand, conceived the shepherd–sheep relationship as one of individual and complete dependence. This is undoubtedly one of the points at which Christian pastorship radically diverged from Greek thought. If a Greek had to obey, he did so because it was the law, or the will of the city. If he did happen to follow the will of someone in particular (a physician, an orator, a pedagogue), then that person had rationally persuaded him to do so. And it had to be for a strictly determined aim: to be cured, to acquire a skill, to make the best choice.

In Christianity, the tie with the shepherd is an individual one. It is personal submission to him. His will is done, not because it is consistent with the law, and not just as far as it is consistent with it, but, principally, because it is his *will*. In Cassian's *Coenobitical Institutions*, there are many edifying anecdotes in which the monk finds salvation by carrying out the absurdest of his superior's orders. Obedience is a virtue. This means that it is not, as for the Greeks, a provisional means to an end, but rather an end in itself. It is a permanent state; the sheep must permanently submit to their pastors: *subditi*. As Saint Benedict says, monks do not live according to their own free will; their wish is to be under the abbot's command: *ambulantes alieno judicio et imperio*. Greek Christianity named this state of obedience απαθεια. The evolution of the word's meaning is significant. In Greek philosophy, απαθεια denotes the control that the individual, thanks to the exercise of reason, can exert over his passions. In Christian thought, παθος is willpower exerted over oneself, for oneself. Απαθεια delivers us from such wilfulness.

3. Christian pastorship implies a peculiar type of knowledge between the pastor and each of his sheep.

This knowledge is particular. It individualizes. It isn't enough to know the state of the flock. That of each sheep must also be known. The theme existed long before there was Christian pastorship, but it was considerably amplified in three different ways: the shepherd must be informed as to the material needs of each member of the flock and provide for them when necessary. He must know what is going on, what each of them does — his public sins. Last and not least, he must know what goes on in the soul of each one, that is, his secret sins, his progress on the road to sainthood.

In order to ensure this individual knowledge, Christianity appropriated two essential instruments at work in the Hellenistic world: self-examination and the guidance of conscience. It took them over, but not without altering them considerably.

It is well known that self-examination was widespread among the Pythagoreans, the Stoics, and the Epicureans as a means of daily taking stock of the good or evil performed in regard to one's duties. One's progress on the way to perfection, i.e., self-mastery and the domination of one's passions, could thus be measured. The guidance of conscience was also predominant in certain cultured circles, but as advice given — and sometimes paid for — in particularly difficult circumstances: in mourning, or when one was suffering a setback.

Christian pastorship closely associated these two practices. On one hand, conscience-guiding constituted a constant bind: the sheep didn't let itself be led only to come through any rough passage victoriously, it let itself be led every second. Being guided was a state and you were fatally lost if you tried to escape it. The ever-quoted phrase runs like this: he who suffers not guidance withers away like a dead leaf. As for self-examination, its aim was not to close self-awareness in upon itself, but to enable it to open up entirely to its director — to unveil to him the depths of the soul.

There are a great many first-century ascetic and monastic texts concerning the link between guidance and self-examination that show how crucial these techniques were for Christianity and how complex they had already become. What I would like to emphasize is that they delineate the emergence of a very strange phenomenon in Greco-Roman civilization, that is, the organization of a link between total obedience, knowledge of oneself, and confession to someone else.

4. There is another transformation — maybe the most important. All those Christian techniques of examination, confession, guidance, obedience, have an aim: to get individuals to work at their own "mortification" in this world. Mortification is not death, of course, but it is a renunciation of this world and of oneself: a kind of everyday death. A death which is supposed to provide life in another world. This is not the first time we see the shepherd theme associated with death; but here it is other than in the Greek idea of political power. It is not a sacrifice for the city; Christian mortification is a kind of relation from oneself to oneself. It is a part, a constitutive part of the Christian self-identity.

We can say that Christian pastorship has introduced a

game that neither the Greeks nor the Hebrews imagined. A strange game whose elements are life, death, truth, obedience, individuals, self-identity; a game which seems to have nothing to do with the game of the city surviving through the sacrifice of the citizens. Our societies proved to be really demonic since they happened to combine those two games — the city–citizen game and the shepherd–flock game — in what we call the modern states.

As you may notice, what I have been trying to do this evening is not to solve a problem but to suggest a way to approach a problem. This problem is similar to those I have been working on since my first book about insanity and mental illness. As I told you previously, the problem deals with the relations between experiences (like madness, illness, transgression of laws, sexuality, self-identity) knowledge (like psychiatry, medicine, criminology, sexology, psychology), and power (such as the power which is wielded in psychiatric and penal institutions, and in all other institutions which deal with individual control).

Our civilization has developed the most complex system of knowledge, the most sophisticated structures of power: what has this kind of knowledge, this type of power made of us? In what way are those fundamental experiences of madness, suffering, death, crime, desire, individuality connected, even if we are not aware of it, with knowledge and power? I am sure I'll never get the answer; but that does not mean that we don't have to ask the question.

II

I have tried to show how primitive Christianity shaped the idea of a pastoral influence continuously exerting itself on individuals and through the demonstration of their particular truth. And I have tried to show how this idea of pastoral power was foreign to Greek thought despite a certain number of borrowings such as practical self-examination and the guidance of conscience.

I would like at this time, leaping across many centuries, to describe another episode which has been in itself particularly important in the history of this government of individuals by their own verity.

This instance concerns the formation of the state in the modern sense of the word. If I make this historical connection it is obviously not in order to suggest that the aspect of pastoral power disappeared during the ten great centuries of Christian Europe, Catholic and Roman, but it seems to me that this period, contrary to what one might expect, has not been that of the triumphant pastorate. And that is true for several reasons: some are of an economic nature — the pastorate of souls is an especially urban experience, difficult to reconcile with the poor and extensive rural economy at the beginning of the Middle Ages. The other reasons are of a cultural nature: the pastorate is a complicated technique which demands a certain level of culture, not only on the part of the pastor but also among his flock. Other reasons relate to the sociopolitical structure. Feudality developed between individuals a tissue of personal bonds of an altogether different type than the pastorate.

I do not wish to say that the idea of a pastoral government of men disappeared entirely in the medieval church. It has, indeed, remained and one can even say that it has shown great vitality. Two series of facts tend to prove this. First, the reforms which had been made in the Church itself, especially in the monastic orders — the different reforms operating successively inside existing monasteries — had the goal of restoring the rigor of pastoral order among the monks themselves. As for the newly created orders — Dominican and Franciscan — essentially they proposed to perform pastoral work among the faithful. The Church tried ceaselessly during successive crises to regain its pastoral functions. But there is more. In the population itself one sees all during the Middle Ages the development of a long series of struggles whose object was pastoral power. Critics of the Church which fails in its obligations reject its hierarchical structure, look for the more or less spontaneous forms of community in which the flock could find the shepherd it needed. This search for pastoral expression took on numerous aspects, at times extremely violent struggles as was the case for the Vaudois, sometimes peaceful quests as among the Frères de la Vie community. Sometimes it stirred very extensive movements such as the Hussites, sometimes it fermented limited groups like the Amis de Dieu de l'Oberland.

It happened that these movements were close to heresy, as among the Beghards, at times stirring orthodox movements which dwelt within the bosom of the Church (like that of the Italian Oratorians in the fifteenth century).

I raise all of this in a very allusive manner in order to emphasize that if the pastorate was not instituted as an effective, practical government of men during the Middle Ages, it has been a permanent concern and a stake in constant struggles. There was across the entire period of the Middle Ages a yearning to arrange pastoral relations among men and this aspiration affected both the mystical tide and the great millenarian dreams.

*   *   *

Of course, I don't intend to treat here the problem of how states are formed. Nor do I intend to go into the different economic, social, and political processes from which they stem. Neither do I want to analyze the different institutions or mechanisms with which states equipped themselves in order to ensure their survival. I'd just like to give some fragmentary indications as to something midway between the state as a type of political organization and its mechanisms, viz., the type of rationality implemented in the exercise of state power.

I mentioned this in my first lecture. Rather than wonder whether aberrant state power is due to excessive rationalism or irrationalism, I think it would be more appropriate to pin down the specific type of political rationality the state produced.

After all, at least in this respect, political practices resemble scientific ones: it's not "reason in general" that is implemented, but always a very specific type of rationality.

The striking thing is that the rationality of state power was reflective and perfectly aware of its specificity. It was not tucked away in spontaneous, blind practices. It was not brought to light by some retrospective analysis. It was formulated especially in two sets of doctrine: the *reason of state* and the *theory of police*. These two phrases soon acquired narrow and pejorative meanings, I know. But for the 150 or 200 years during which modern states were formed, their meaning was much broader than now.

The doctrine of reason of state attempted to define how the principles and methods of state government differed, say, from the way God governed the world, the father his family, or a superior his community.

The doctrine of the police defines the nature of the objects of the state's rational activity; it defines the nature of the aims it pursues the general form of the instruments involved.

So, what I'd like to speak about today is the system of rationality. But first, there are two preliminaries: (1) Meinecke having published a most important book on reason of state, I'll speak mainly of the policing theory. (2) Germany and Italy underwent the greatest difficulties in getting established as states, and they produced the greatest number of reflexions on reason of state and the police. I'll often refer to the Italian and German texts.

*   *   *

Let's begin with *reason of state*. Here are a few definitions:

BOTERO: "A perfect knowledge of the means through which states form, strengthen themselves, endure, and grow."

PALAZZO: (*Discourse on Government and True Reason of State*, 1606): "A rule or art enabling us to discover how to establish peace and order within the Republic."

CHEMNITZ: (*De Ratione Status*, 1647): "A certain political consideration required for all public matters, councils, and projects, whose only aim is the state's preservation, expansion, and felicity; to which end, the easiest and promptest means are to be employed."

Let me consider certain features these definitions have in common.

1. Reason of state is regarded as an "art," that is, a technique conforming to certain rules. These rules do not simply pertain to customs or traditions, but to knowledge — rational knowledge. Nowadays, the expression *reason of state* evokes "arbitrariness" or "violence." But at the time, what

people had in mind was a rationality specific to the art of governing states.

2. From where does this specific art of government draw its rationale? The answer to this question provokes the scandal of nascent political thought. And yet it's very simple: the art of governing is rational, if reflexion causes it to observe the nature of what is governed — here, the *state*.

Now, to state such a platitude is to break with a simultaneously Christian and judiciary tradition, a tradition which claimed that government was essentially just. It respected a whole system of laws: human laws; the law of nature; divine law.

There is a quite significant text by St. Thomas on these points. He recalls that "art, in its field, must imitate what nature carries out in its own"; it is only reasonable under that condition. The king's government of his kingdom must imitate God's government of nature; or again, the soul's government of the body. The king must found cities just as God created the world; just as the soul gives form to the body. The king must also lead men towards their finality, just as God does for natural beings, or as the soul does, when directing the body. And what is man's finality? What's good for the body? No; he'd need only a physician, not a king. Wealth? No; a steward would suffice. Truth? Not even that; for only a teacher would be needed. Man needs someone capable of opening up the way to heavenly bliss through his conformity, here on earth, to what is *honestum*.

As we can see, the model for the art of government is that of God imposing his laws upon his creatures. St. Thomas's model for rational government is not a political one, whereas what the sixteenth and seventeenth centuries seek under the denomination "reason of state" are principles capable of guiding an actual government. They aren't concerned with nature and its laws in general. They're concerned with what the state is; what its exigencies are.

And so we can understand the religious scandal aroused by such a type of research. It explains why reason of state was assimilated to atheism. In France, in particular, the expression generated in a political context was commonly associated with "atheist."

3. Reason of state is also opposed to another tradition. In *The Prince*, Machiavelli's problem is to decide how a province or territory acquired through inheritance or by conquest can be held against its internal or external rivals. Machiavelli's entire analysis is aimed at defining what keeps up or reinforces the link between prince and state, whereas the problem posed by reason of state is that of the very existence and nature of the state itself. This is why the theoreticians of reason of state tried to stay aloof from Machiavelli; he had a bad reputation and they couldn't recognize their own problem in his. Conversely, those opposed to reason of state tried to impair this new art of governing, denouncing it as Machiavelli's legacy. However, despite these confused quarrels a century after *The Prince* had been written, *reason of state* marks the emergence of an extremely — albeit only partly — different type of rationality from Machiavelli's.

The aim of such an art of governing is precisely not to reinforce the power a prince can wield over his domain. Its aim is to reinforce the state itself. This is one of the most characteristic features of all the definitions that the sixteenth and seventeenth centuries put forward. Rational government is this, so to speak: given the nature of the state, it can hold down its enemies for an indeterminate length of time. It can only do so if it increases its own strength. And its enemies do likewise. The state whose only concern would be to hold out would most certainly come to disaster. This idea is a very important one. It is bound up with a new historical outlook. Indeed, it implies that states are realities which must needs hold out for an indefinite length of historical time — and in a disputed geographical area.

4. Finally, we can see that reason of state, understood as rational government able to increase the state's strength in accordance with itself presupposes the constitution of a certain type of knowledge. Government is only possible if the strength of the state is known; it can thus be sustained. The state's capacity, and the means to enlarge it, must be known. The strength and capacities of the other states must also be known. Indeed, the governed state must hold out against the others. Government therefore entails more than just implementing general principles of reason, wisdom, and prudence. Knowledge is necessary; concrete, precise, and measured

knowledge as to the state's strength. The art of governing, characteristic of reason of state, is intimately bound up with the development of what was then called either political *statistics*, or *arithmetic*; that is, the knowledge of different states' respective forces. Such knowledge was indispensable for correct government.

Briefly speaking, then: reason of state is not an art of government according to divine, natural, or human laws. It doesn't have to respect the general order of the world. It's government in accordance with the state's strength. It's government whose aim is to increase this strength within an extensive and competitive framework.

*   *   *

So what the seventeenth- and eighteenth-century authors understand by "the police" is very different from what we put under the term. It would be worth studying why these authors are mostly Italians and Germans, but whatever! What they understand by "police" isn't an institution or mechanism functioning within the state, but a governmental technology peculiar to the state; domains, techniques, targets where the state intervenes.

To be clear and simple, I will exemplify what I'm saying with a text which is both utopian and a project. It's one of the first utopia-programs for a policed state. Turquet de Mayenne drew it up and presented it in 1611 to the Dutch States General. In his book *Science in the Government of Louis XIV*, J. King draws attention to the importance of this strange work. Its title is *AristoDemocratic Monarchy*; that's enough to show what is important in the author's eyes: not so much choosing between these different types of constitution as their mixture in view to a vital end, viz., the state. Turquet also calls it the City, the Republic, or yet again, the Police.

Here is the organization Turquet proposes. Four grand officials rank beside the king. One is in charge of Justice; another, of the Army; the third, of the Exchecquer, i.e., the king's taxes and revenues; the fourth is in charge of the *police*. It seems that this officer's role was to have been mainly a moral one. According to Turquet, he was to foster among the people "modesty, charity, loyalty, industriousness, friendly cooperation, honesty." We recognize the traditional idea that the subject's virtue ensures the kingdom's good management. But, when we come down to the details, the outlook is somewhat different.

Turquet suggests that in each province, there should be boards keeping law and order. There should be two that see to people; the other two see to things. The first board, the one pertaining to people, was to see to the positive, active, productive aspects of life. In other words, it was concerned with education; determining each one's tastes and aptitudes; the choosing of occupations — useful ones: each person over the age of twenty-five had to be enrolled on a register noting his occupation. Those not usefully employed were regarded as the dregs of society.

The second board was to see to the negative aspects of life: the poor (widows, orphans, the aged) requiring help; the unemployed; those whose activities required financial aid (no interest was to be charged); public health: diseases, epidemics; and accidents such as fire and flood.

One of these boards concerned with things was to specialize in commodities and manufactured goods. It was to indicate what was to be produced, and how; it was also to control markets and trading. The fourth board would see to the "demesne," i.e., the territory, space: private property, legacies, donations, sales were to be controlled; manorial rights were to be reformed; roads, rivers, public buildings, and forests would also be seen to.

In many features, the text is akin to the political utopias which were so numerous at the time. But it is also contemporary with the great theoretical discussions on reason of state and the administrative organization of monarchies. It is highly representative of what the epoch considered a traditionally governed state's tasks to be.

What does this text demonstrate?

1. The "police" appears as an administration heading the state, together with the judiciary, the army, and the exchequer. True. Yet in fact, it embraces everything else. Turquet says so: "It branches out into all of the people's conditions, everything they do or undertake. Its field comprises justice, finance, and the army."

2. The *police* includes everything. But from an extremely particular point of view. Men and things are envisioned as to their relationships: men's coexistence on a territory; their relationships as to property; what they produce; what is exchanged on the market. It also considers how they live, the diseases and accidents which can befall them. What the police sees to is a live, active, productive man. Turquet employs a remarkable expression: "The police's true object is man."

3. Such intervention in men's activities could well be qualified as totalitarian. What are the aims pursued? They fall into two categories. First, the police has to do with everything providing the city with adornment, form, and splendor. Splendor denotes not only the beauty of a state ordered to perfection; but also its strength, its vigor. The police therefore ensures and highlights the state's vigor. Second, the police's other purpose is to foster working and trading relations between men, as well as aid and mutual help. There again, the word Turquet uses is important: the police must ensure "communication" among men, in the broad sense of the word. Otherwise, men wouldn't be able to live; or their lives would be precarious, poverty-stricken, and perpetually threatened.

And here, we can make out what is, I think, an important idea. As a form of rational intervention wielding political power over men, the role of the police is to supply them with a little extra life; and by so doing, supply the state with a little extra strength. This is done by controlling "communication," i.e., the common activities of individuals (work, production, exchange, accommodation).

You'll object: but that's only the utopia of some obscure author. You can hardly deduce any significant consequences from it! But *I* say: Turquet's book is but one example of a huge literature circulating in most European countries of the day. The fact that it is over-simple and yet very detailed brings out all the better the characteristics that could be recognized elsewhere. Above all, I'd say that such ideas were not stillborn. They spread all through the seventeenth and eighteenth centuries, either as applied policies (such as cameralism or mercantilism), or as subjects to be taught (the German *Polizeiwissenschaft*; don't let's forget that this was the title under which the science of administration was taught in Germany).

These are the two perspectives that I'd like, not to study, but at least to suggest. First I'll refer to a French administrative compendium, then to a German textbook.

1. Every historian knows Delamare's *Compendium*. At the beginning of the eighteenth century, this administrator undertook the compilation of the whole kingdom's police regulations. It's an infinite source of highly valuable information. The general conception of the police that such a quantity of rules and regulations could convey to an administrator like Delamare is what I'd like to emphasize.

Delamare says that the police must see to eleven things within the state: (1) religion; (2) morals; (3) health; (4) supplies; (5) roads, highways, town buildings; (6) public safety; (7) the liberal arts (roughly speaking, arts and science); (8) trade; (9) factories; (10) manservants and laborers; (11) the poor.

The same classification features in every treatise concerning the police. As in Turquet's utopia program, apart from the army, justice properly speaking, and direct taxes, the police apparently sees to everything. The same thing can be said differently: Royal power had asserted itself against feudalism thanks to the support of an armed force and by developing a judicial system and establishing a tax system. These were the ways in which royal power was traditionally wielded. Now, "the police" is the term covering the whole new field in which centralized political and administrative power can intervene.

Now, what is the logic behind intervention in cultural rites, small-scale production techniques, intellectual life, and the road network?

Delamare's answer seems a bit hesitant. Now he says, "The police sees to everything pertaining to men's *happiness*"; now he says, "The police sees to everything regulating "*society*" (social relations) carried on between men." Now again, he says that the police sees to *living*. This is the definition I will dwell upon. It's the most original and it clarifies the other two; and Delamare himself dwells upon it. He makes the following remarks as to the police's eleven objects. The police deals with religion, not, of course, from the point of view of dogmatic truth, but from that of the moral quality of life. In seeing to health and supplies, it deals with the preservation of life: concerning trade, factories, workers, the poor and public order, it deals with the conveniences of life. In seeing to the theatre, literature, entertainment, its object is life's pleasures. In short, life is the object of the police: the indispensable, the useful, and the superfluous. That people survive, live, and even do better than just that, is what the police has to ensure.

And so we link up with the other definitions Delamare proposes: "The sole purpose of the police is to lead man to the utmost happiness to be enjoyed in this life." Or again, the police cares for the good of the soul (thanks to religion and morality), the good of the body (food, health, clothing, housing), wealth (industry, trade, labor). Or again, the police sees to the benefits that can be derived only from living in society.

2. Now let us have a look at the German textbooks. They were used to teach the science of administration somewhat later on. It was taught in various universities, especially in Göttingen, and was extremely important for continental Europe. Here is was that the Prussian, Austrian, and Russian civil servants — those who were to carry out Joseph II's and the Great Catherine's reforms — were trained. Certain Frenchmen, especially in Napoleon's entourage, knew the teachings of *Polizeiwissenschaft* very well.

What was to be found in these textbooks?

Huhenthal's *Liber de Politia* featured the following items: the number of citizens; religion and morals; health; food; the safety of persons and of goods (particularly in reference to fires and floods); the administration of justice; citizens' conveniences and pleasures (how to obtain them, how to restrict them). Then comes a series of chapters about rivers, forests, mines, brine pits, housing, and finally, several chapters on how to acquire goods either through farming, industry, or trade.

In his *Précis for the Police*, Willebrand speaks successively of morals, trades and crafts, health, safety, and last of all, of town building and planning. Considering the subjects at least, there isn't a great deal of difference from Delamare's.

But the most important of these texts is Von Justi's *Elements of Police*. The police's specific purpose is still defined as live individuals living in society. Nevertheless, the way Von Justi organises his book is somewhat different. He studies first what he calls the "state's landed property," i.e., its territory. He considers it in two different aspects: how it is inhabited (town vs. country), and then, who inhabit these territories (the number of people, their growth, health, mortality, immigration). Von Justi then analyses the "goods and chattels," i.e., the commodities, manufactured goods, and their circulation which involve problems pertaining to cost, credit, and currency. Finally, the last part is devoted to the conduct of individuals: their morals, their occupational capabilities, their honesty, and how they respect the Law.

In my opinion, Von Justi's work is a much more advanced demonstration of how the police problem was evolved than Delamare's "introduction" to his compendium of statutes. There are four reasons for this.

First, Von Justi defines much more clearly what the central paradox of *police* is. The police, he says, is what enables the state to increase its power and exert its strength to the full. On the other hand, the police has to keep the citizens happy — happiness being understood as survival, life, and improved living. He perfectly defines what I feel to be the aim of the modern art of government, or state rationality: viz., to develop those elements constitutive of individuals' lives in such a way that their development also fosters that of the strength of the state.

Von Justi then draws a distinction between this task, which he calls *Polizei*, as do his contemporaries, and *Politik, Die Politik. Die Politik* is basically a negative task. It consists in the state's fighting against its internal and external enemies. *Polizei*, however, is a positive task: it has to foster both citizens' lives *and* the state's strength.

And here is the important point: Von Justi insists much more than does Delamare on a notion which became increasingly important during the eighteenth century — population. Population was understood as a group of live individuals. Their characteristics were those of all the individuals belonging to the same species, living side by side. (They thus presented mortality and fecundity rates; they were subject to epidemics, overpopulation; they presented a certain type of territorial distribution.) True, Delamare did use the term "life" to characterize the concern of the police, but the emphasis he gave it wasn't very pronounced. Proceeding through the eighteenth century, and especially in Germany, we see that what is defined as the object of the police is population, i.e., a group of beings living in a given area.

And last, one only has to read Von Justi to see that it is not only a utopia, as with Turquet, nor a compendium of systematically filed regulations. Von Justi claims to draw up a *Polizeiwissenschaft*. His book isn't simply a list of prescriptions. It's also a grid through which the state, i.e., territory, resources, population, towns, etc., can be observed. Von Justi combines "statistics" (the description of states) with the art of government. *Polizeiwissenschaft* is at once an art of government and a method for the analysis of a population living on a territory.

Such historical considerations must appear to be very remote; they must seem useless in regard to present-day concerns. I wouldn't go as far as Hermann Hesse, who says that only the "constant reference to history, the past, and antiquity" is fecund. But experience has taught me that the history of various forms of rationality is sometimes more effective in unsettling our certitudes and dogmatism than is abstract criticism. For centuries, religion couldn't bear having its history told. Today, our schools of rationality balk at having their history written, which is no doubt significant.

What I've wanted to show is a direction for research. These are only the rudiments of something I've been working at for the last two years. It's the historical analysis of what we could call, using an obsolete term, the art of government.

This study rests upon several basic assumptions. I'd sum them up like this:

1. Power is not a substance. Neither is it a mysterious property whose origin must be delved into. Power is only a certain type of relation between individuals. Such relations are specific, that is, they have nothing to do with exchange, production, communication, even though they combine with them. The characteristic feature of power is that some men can more or less entirely determine other men's conduct — but never exhaustively or coercively. A man who is chained up and beaten is subject to force being exerted over him. Not power. But if he can be induced to speak, when his ultimate

recourse could have been to hold his tongue, preferring death, then he has been caused to behave in a certain way. His freedom has been subjected to power. He has been submitted to government. If an individual can remain free, however little his freedom may be, power can subject him to government. There is no power without potential refusal or revolt.

2. As for all relations among men, many factors determine power. Yet rationalization is also constantly working away at it. There are specific forms to such rationalization. It differs from the rationalization peculiar to economic processes, or to production and communication techniques; it differs from that of scientific discourse. The government of men by men — whether they form small or large groups, whether it is power exerted by men over women, or by adults over children, or by one class over another, or by a bureaucracy over a population — involves a certain type of rationality. It doesn't involve instrumental violence.

3. Consequently, those who resist or rebel against a form of power cannot merely be content to denounce violence or criticize an institution. Nor is it enough to cast the blame on reason in general. What has to be questioned is the form of rationality at stake. The criticism of power wielded over the mentally sick or mad cannot be restricted to psychiatric institutions; nor can those questioning the power to punish be content with denouncing prisons as total institutions. The question is: how are such relations of power rationalized? Asking it is the only way to avoid other institutions, with the same objectives and the same effects, from taking their stead.

4. For several centuries, the state has been one of the most remarkable, one of the most redoubtable, forms of human government.

Very significantly, political criticism has reproached the state with being simultaneously a factor for individualization and a totalitarian principle. Just to look at nascent state rationality, just to see what its first policing project was, makes it clear that, right from the start, the state is both individualizing and totalitarian. Opposing the individual and his interests to it is just as hazardous as opposing it with the community and its requirements.

Political rationality has grown and imposed itself all throughout the history of Western societies. It first took its stand on the idea of pastoral power, then on that of reason of state. Its inevitable effects are both individualization and totalization. Liberation can only come from attacking, not just one of these two effects, but political rationality's very roots.

5

The Art of Telling the Truth

Foucault interprets Kant's text Was ist
Aufklärung? (What is Enlightenment?) *in this
passage from his first lecture of 1983 at the
Collège de France. In this revised version, Foucault
suggests why this text represents for him a
philosophical riddle or "fetish" which reveals the
critical tradition underlying his theoretical heri-
tage. He examines here the Kantian conception of
the present as a process that embodies thought,
knowledge and philosophy and the role that the
thinking subject plays in it. What Foucault finds
captivating in Kant's essay is his response to a
historical situation which poses the question of
modernity as an ontology of the present. The
notion of the* Aufklärung *thus becomes an exemplary concept in modern thought because of its
ability to interrogate itself concerning the nature
of its present. The following passage appeared in*
Magazine littéraire *207 (May 1984), 35–39. The
translation is by Alan Sheridan.*

It seems to me that this text introduces a new type of question
into the field of philosophical reflection. Of course, it is
certainly neither the first step in the history of philosophy,
nor even the only text by Kant that schematizes a question
concerning history. We find in Kant texts that pose a question
of origin to history: the text on the beginnings of history itself
and the text on the definition of the concept of race. Other
texts pose to history the question of the forms in which it is
carried out: thus, in that same year, 1784, we have *The Idea of a
Universal History from the Cosmopolitical Point of View.* Then
there are others that question the internal finality organizing
historical processes — I'm thinking of the text devoted to the

use of teleological principles. All these questions, which are indeed closely linked, imbue Kant's analyses of history. It seems to me that the text on the *Aufklärung* is a rather different one; in any case, it does not pose any of these questions directly, neither that of origin, nor, despite appearances to the contrary, that of fulfillment, and it poses to itself in a relatively discreet, almost sidelong way, the question of the teleology immanent in the very process of history.

The question that seems to me to appear for the first time in this text by Kant is the question of the present, the question of what is happening now: What is happening today? What is happening now? And what is this "now" within which all of us find ourselves; and who defines the moment at which I am writing? It is not the first time that one finds in philosophical reflection references to the present, at least as a particular historical situation that may be valuable for philosophical reflection. After all, when, at the beginning of the *Discourse on Method*, Descartes recounts his own itinerary and all the philosophical decisions that he has taken both for himself and for philosophy, he refers quite explicitly to something that may be regarded as a historical situation in the order of knowledge, of the sciences in his own time. But in this kind of reference, it is always a question of finding, in this configuration designated as the present, a motive for a philosophical decision; in Descartes, you will not find some such question as: "What precisely, then, is this present to which I belong?" Now it seems to me that the question that Kant is answering — indeed that he is led to answer, because it was asked of him — is a quite different one. It is not simply: what is it in the present situation that can determine this or that decision of a philosophical order? The question bears on what this present actually is, it bears firstly on the determination of a certain element of the present that is to be recognized, to be distinguished, to be deciphered among all the others. What is it in the present that produces meaning now for philosophical reflection?

In the answer that Kant tries to give to this question, he sets out to show how this element becomes the bearer and the sign of a process that concerns thought, knowledge, philosophy; but it is a question of showing how he who speaks as a thinker, as a scientist, as a philosopher, is himself part of this process and (more than that) how he has a certain role to play in this process, in which he is to find himself, therefore, both element and actor.

In short, it seems to me that what we see appearing in Kant's text is the question of the present as the philosophical event to which the philosopher who speaks of it belongs. If one sees philosophy as a form of discursive practice that has its own history, it seems to me that with this text on the *Aufklärung* we see philosophy — and I don't think I'm exaggerating when I say that it is for the first time — problematizing its own discursive contemporaneity: a contemporaneity that it questions as an event, as an event whose meaning, value, philosophical particularity it is its task to bring out and in which it has to find both its own raison d'être and the grounds for what it says. And in doing so we see that when the philosopher asks how he belongs to this present it is a quite different question from that of how one belongs to a particular doctrine or tradition; it is no longer simply the question of how one belongs to a human community in general, but rather that of how one belongs to a certain "us," to an us that concerns a cultural totality characteristic of one's own time.

It is this "us" that is becoming for the philosopher the object of his own reflection. By the same token, the philosopher can no longer avoid the question of the specific way in which he belongs to this "us." All this — philosophy as the problematization of a present, and as the questioning by the philosopher of this present to which he belongs and in relation to which he has to situate himself — might well be said to characterize philosophy as the discourse of modernity on modernity.

To speak very schematically, the question of modernity has already been posed in classical culture in terms of an axis with two poles, that of Antiquity and that of Modernity; it was formulated either in terms of an authority to be accepted or rejected (which authority should we accept? which model should we follow?, etc.), or in the form (which, indeed, is a correlative of the first) of a comparative valuation: are the Ancients superior to the Moderns? Are we living in a period of decline, etc.? We see rising to the surface a new way of posing the question of modernity, not in a longitudinal relation to the Ancients, but in what might be called a "sagital" relation to one's own present. Discourse has to reassess its being in the present on the one hand, to find its proper place in it, and, on the other hand, to decipher its meaning, to specify the mode of action that it is capable of exercising within that present.

What is my present? What is the meaning of this present? And what am I doing when I speak of this present? This, it seems to me, is what this new questioning of modernity means.

But this is nothing more than a trail, which we must now explore more closely. We must try to trace the genealogy, not so much of the notion of modernity, as of modernity as a question. In any case, even if I take Kant's text as the point of emergence of this question, it is evident that this text itself forms part of a broader historical process that must be taken into account. It would no doubt be one of the interesting axes for a study of the eighteenth century in general, and of the *Aufklärung* in particular, to consider the following fact: the *Aufklärung* calls itself *Aufklärung*. It is certainly a very singular cultural process that became aware of itself by naming itself, by situating itself in relation to its past and future, and by designating the operations that it must carry out within its own present.

After all, is not the *Aufklärung* the first period that names itself and which instead of simply characterizing itself, according to an old habit, as a period of decline or prosperity, of splendor or misery, names itself through a certain event that belongs to a general history of thought, of reason, and of knowledge and within which it has itself played a part?

The *Aufklärung* is a period, a period that formulates its own motto, its own precepts, and which says what it has to do, both in relation to the general history of thought and in relation to its present and to the forms of knowledge, ignorance, and illusion in which it is able to recognize its historical situation.

It seems to me that in this question of the *Aufklärung* we see one of the first manifestations of a way of philosophizing that has had a lengthy history over the last two centuries. It is one of the great functions of so-called modern philosophy (which may be said to begin at the very end of the eighteenth century) to question itself about its own present.

One might follow the trajectory of this modality of philosophy through the nineteenth century to the present day. The only thing that I would stress at the moment is that Kant did not forget this question, which he dealt with in 1784 in response to a question that had been asked him from the outside. He was to ask it again and try to answer in relation to another event, one that also never ceased to question itself. That event, of course, was the French Revolution.

In 1798, Kant was in a sense to take up again the text of 1784. In 1784, he was trying to answer the question asked him: "What is this *Aufklärung* of which we are a part?" In 1798 he is answering a question which the present was asking him, but which had been formulated since 1794 by all philosophical discussion in Germany. That question was: "What is the Revolution?"

You know that *The Conflict of the Faculties* is a collection of three dissertations on the relations between the different faculties that make up the University. The second dissertation concerns the conflict between the Faculty of Philosophy and the Faculty of Law. Now the whole field of relations between philosophy and law is concerned with the question: "Is there such a thing as constant progress for mankind?" And it was in order to answer this question that, in paragraph V of this dissertation, Kant reasons in the following way: if one wishes to answer the question "Is there constant progress for mankind?" one must determine whether there exists a possible cause for this progress, but once one has established this possibility, one must show that this cause acts effectively and, to do this, one must locate a certain event that shows that the cause acts in reality. In short, the attribution of a cause will be able to determine only possible effects, or, to be more precise, the possibility of an effect; but the reality of an effect will be able to be established only by the existence of an event.

It is not enough, therefore, to follow the teleological thread that makes progress possible; one must isolate, within history, an event that will have the value of a sign.

A sign of what? A sign of the existence of a cause, of a permanent cause, which, throughout history itself, has guided men on the way of progress. A constant cause that must be shown to have acted in the past, acts now, and will act in the future. Consequently, the event that will be able to allow us to decide whether there is progress will be a sign: *rememorativum, demonstrativum, prognosticum*. It must be a sign that shows that it has always been like that (the rememorative sign), a sign that shows that things are also taking place now (the demonstrative), and a sign that shows that it will always happen like that (the prognostic sign). In this way we can be sure that the cause that makes progress possible has not just acted at a particular moment, but that it guarantees a general tendency of mankind as a whole to move in the direction of progress. That is the question: "Is there around us an event that is rememorative, demonstrative, and prognostic of a permanent progress that affects humankind as a whole?"

You have probably guessed the answer that Kant gives; but I would like to read to you the passage in which he introduces the Revolution as an event that has the value of a sign. "Do not expect this event," he writes at the beginning of paragraph VI, "to consist of noble gestures or great crimes committed by men, as a result of which that which was great among men is made small, or that which was small, made great, nor of gleaming ancient buildings that disappear as if by magic while others rise, in a sense, from the bowels of the earth to take their place. No, it is nothing like that."

In this text, Kant is obviously alluding to the traditional reflections that seek the proofs of the progress or non-progress of humankind in the overthrow of empires, in the great catastrophes by which the best established states disappear, in the reversals of fortune that bring low established powers and allow new ones to appear. Be careful, Kant is telling his readers, it is in much less grandiose, much less perceptible events. One cannot carry out this analysis of our own present in those meaningful values without embarking on a decipherment that will allow us to give to what, apparently, is without meaning and value, the important meaning and value that we are looking for. Now what is this event that is not a "great" event? There is obviously a paradox in saying that the Revolution is not a major event. Is this not the very example of an event that overthrows, that makes what was great small and what was small great, and which swallows up the apparently secure structures of society and states? Now, for Kant, it is not this aspect of the Revolution that is meaningful. What constitutes the event that possesses a rememorative, demonstrative, and prognostic value is not the revolutionary drama itself, not the revolutionary exploits, or the gesticulation that accompanies it. What is meaningful is the way in which the Revolution provided a spectacle, the way in which it was welcomed all around by spectators who did not take part in it, but who observed it, attended it, and, for better or for worse, were carried away by it. It is not the revolutionary upheaval that constitutes the proof of progress; because, firstly, it merely inverts things, and secondly, because if one could carry out the Revolution again, one would not do so. This is an extremely interesting text. "It does not matter," he says, "if the revolution of an intelligent people, such as we have seen in our own time [he's therefore speaking of the French Revolution], it does not matter if it succeeds or fails, it does not matter if it piles up miseries and atrocities, to such an extent that a sensible man who might do it over again in the hope of succeeding would never bring himself to attempt the experience at such a price." It is not, then, the revolutionary process that is important, it does not matter whether it succeeds or fails; this is nothing to do with progress, or at least with the sign of progress we are looking for. The failure or success of the Revolution are not signs of progress or a sign that there is no progress. But even if it were possible for someone to know what the Revolution is, to know how it is carried out, and at the same time to pull it off, then, calculating the necessary cost of this Revolution, this sensible man would not proceed with it. Therefore, as "reversal," as an undertaking that may succeed or fail, as the price that is too heavy to pay, the Revolution cannot in itself be regarded as the sign that there is a cause capable of sustaining the constant progress of humankind through history.

On the other hand, what is meaningful and what is to constitute the sign of progress is that, around the Revolution, there is, says Kant, "a sympathy of aspiration bordering on enthusiasm." What is important in the Revolution is not the Revolution itself, but what takes place in the heads of those who do not make it or, in any case, who are not its principal actors; it is the relationship that they themselves have with that Revolution of which they are not the active agents. The enthusiasm for the Revolution is a sign, according to Kant, of a moral disposition in mankind. This disposition is permanantly manifested in two ways: firstly, in the right possessed by all peoples to give themselves the political constitution that suits them and, secondly, in the principle, in accordance with law and morality, of a political constitution so framed that it avoids, by reason of its very principles, all offensive war. Now it is the disposition that leads mankind to such a constitution that is signified by the Revolution. The Revolution as spectacle, and not as gesture, as a focus for enthusism on the part of those who observe it and not as a principle of overthrow for those who take part in it, is a *"signum rememorativum,"* for it reveals that disposition, which has been present from the beginning; it is a *"signum demonstrativum"* because it demonstrates the present efficacity of this disposition; and it is also a *"signum prognosticum"* for, although the Revolution may have certain questionable results, one cannot forget the disposition that is revealed through it.

We also know very well that these two elements, the political constitution freely chosen by men and a political constitution that avoids war, are also the very process of the *Aufklärung*, in other words the Revolution really is a continuation and culmination of the very process of the *Aufklärung*, and as such the *Aufklärung* and the Revolution are events that can no longer be forgotten. "I maintain," writes Kant, "that I can predict for mankind even without a prophetic spirit, simply from the appearances and premonitory signs of our period, that it will attain that end, that is to say, arrive at such a state that men will be able to give themselves the constitution they wish and the constitution that will prevent an offensive war, and that henceforth this progress will no longer be questioned. Such a phenomenon in the history of mankind is no longer forgotten because it has revealed in human nature a disposition, a faculty for progress such that no politics would be clever enough to free it from the course prior to the events, only nature and liberty combined in mankind, following the internal principles of right were capable of announcing it, though in an indeterminate manner and as a contingent event. But if the aims of this event were not yet attained, even if the Revolution or the reform of the constitution of a people had finally failed, or if, after a certain lapse of time, everything fell back into the old rut, as certain politicians are now predicting, this philosophical prophecy would lose none of its force. For this event is too important, too implicated in the interests of mankind and of too vast an influence over every part of the world not to be recalled to the people's memory on the occasion of favorable circumstances and remembered at a time of crisis when new attempts of the same kind are being made, for in so important a matter for mankind the forthcoming constitution at last attains for a time that solidity that the teaching of repeated experiences cannot fail to give it in all minds."

In any case the Revolution will always run the risk of falling back into the old rut, but as an event whose very content is unimportant, its existence attests to a permanent potentiality that cannot be forgotten: for future history it is the guarantee of the very continuity of progress.

All I wanted to do was to situate for you this text by Kant on the *Aufklärung*; later, I shall try to read it more closely. I also wanted to see how, some fifteen years later, Kant was reflecting on the French Revolution, which had turned out to be so much more dramatic than anticipated. With these two texts, we are in a sense at the origin, at the starting point, of a whole dynasty of philosophical questions. These two questions — "What is the *Aufklärung*? What is the Revolution?" — are the two forms under which Kant posed the question of his own present. They, are also, I believe, the two questions that have not ceased to haunt, if not all modern philosophy since the nineteenth century, at least a large part of that philosophy. After all it seems to me that the *Aufklärung*, both as singular event inaugurating European modernity and as permanent process manifested in the history of reason, in the development and establishment of forms of rationality and technology, the autonomy and authority of knowledge, is for us not just an episode in the history of ideas. It is a philosophical question, inscribed since the eighteenth century in our thoughts. Let us leave in their piety those who want to keep the *Aufklärung* living and intact. Such piety is of course the most touching of treasons. What we need to preserve is not what is left of the *Aufklärung*, in terms of fragments; it is the very question of that event and its meaning (the question of the historicity of thinking about the universal) that must now be kept present in our minds as what must be thought. The question of the *Aufklärung*, or of reason, as a historical problem has in a more or less occult way traversed the whole of philosophical thinking from Kant to our own day. The other face of the present that Kant encountered is the Revolution; the Revolution as at once event, rupture, and overthrow in history, as failure, but at the same time as value, as sign of a disposition that is operating in history and in the progress of humankind. There again the question for philosophy is not to determine what part of the Revolution should be preserved by way of a model. It is to know what is to be done with that will to revolution, that "enthusiasm" for the Revolution, which is quite different from the revolutionary enterprise itself. The two questions — "What is the *Aufklärung*?" and "What is to be done with the will to revolution?" — together define the field of philosophical interrogation that bears on what we are in our present.

Kant seems to me to have founded the two great critical traditions between which modern philosophy is divided. Let us say that in his great critical work Kant laid the foundations for that tradition of philosophy that poses the question of the conditions in which true knowledge is possible and, on that basis, it may be said that a whole stretch of modern philosophy from the nineteenth century has been presented, developed as the analytics of truth.

But there is also in modern and contemporary philosophy another type of question, another kind of critical interrogation: it is the one we see emerging precisely in the question of the *Aufklärung* or in the text on the Revolution. That other critical tradition poses the question: What is our present? What is the present field of possible experiences? This is not an analytics of truth; it will concern what might be called an ontology of the present, an ontology of ourselves, and it seems to me that the philosophical choice confronting us today is this: one may opt for a critical philosophy that will present itself as an analytic philosophy of truth in general, or one may opt for a critical thought that will take the form of an ontology of ourselves, an ontology of the present; it is this form of philosophy that, from Hegel, through Nietzsche and Max Weber, to the Frankfurt School, has founded a form of reflection in which I have tried to work.

6

On Power

In 1978 Foucault agreed to clarify some of the major philosophical issues previously formulated in his works. This interview with Pierre Boncenne delineates the central issue emerging from the totality of Foucault's critical corpus: the nature of power, who exercises it, how it happens and produces a body of knowledge. From anti-psychiatry to the history of sexuality the trajectory of Foucault's thought attests to the pervasiveness of power as a form of social discipline. Segments of this interview appeared for the first time in L'Express on July 6–12 1984, 56–68, shortly after Foucault's death. The translation is by Alan Sheridan.

P.B. In 1961 you published your first book, *Histoire de la folie à l'âge classique*. Why, at the time, were you interested in the problem of madness?

FOUCAULT It would be difficult to give the real reasons and I can only offer you a few memories. To begin with, I would say that I never felt that I had a vocation as a writer: I don't consider that writing is my job and I don't think that holding a pen is — for me, I'm speaking only for myself — a sort of absolute activity that is more important than everything else. It was, therefore, a series of circumstances — studying philosophy, then psychopathology, then training in a psychiatric hospital and being lucky enough to be there neither as a patient nor as a doctor, that is to say, to be able to look at things in a fairly open-minded, fairly neutral way, outside the usual codes — that led me to become aware of this extremely strange reality that we call confinement. What struck me was that this practice of confinement was accepted

by both sides as absolutely self-evident . . . However, I came
to realize that it was far from being self-evident and was the
culmination of a very long history, a culmination that did not
occur until the nineteenth century.

P.B. Wasn't it rather surprising that a philosophy professor should set about researching into the "history of
madness"?

FOUCAULT Indeed it wasn't a subject for a philosopher, in
the sense that it could be presented as a doctoral thesis. And
it took a great deal of unusual understanding on the part of
my professors to convince me that it should be turned into a
thesis. But let's leave these minor, academic questions,
because your question goes much further of course. This type
of subject was certainly not well received in academic circles,
but especially not — and it is this that is surprising and still
causes me problems — in circles that ought to have been
interested in this sort of question. I'm referring, broadly
speaking, to what we might call "left-wing intellectuals" (it
being understood that an "intellectual" and a "left-wing
intellectual" is almost the same thing: the domination of the
left-wing intellectual over the intellectual world was already
overwhelming at that time). Well, in those circles, my
research into the history of madness aroused literally no
interest whatsoever. The only people who showed any
interest in this sort of book were people connected with
literature, like Blanchot or Barthes. But, apart from them, no
intellectual or political review worthy of the name would have
agreed to mention such a book on such a subject — as you can
imagine, *Les Temps Modernes* and *Esprit* were not going to busy
themselves with that . . . [1]

P.B. Why not?

FOUCAULT I think it was bound up with the fact that
theoretical and political discussion was entirely dominated by

1. *Les Temps Modernes*, non-aligned leftist cultural and political journal founded in
October 1945 by Sartre and de Beauvoir. It attempted to reconcile literature with social
reality through a blending of phenomenology with Marxist thought. *Esprit*, leftist
Christian cultural review founded in 1932 by Emmanuel Mounier who believed that
the Catholic Church should become more conscious of its responsibilities toward the
working class and the poor [L.D.K.].

Marxism, understood as a general theory of society, of History, of revolution, etc. To bring into the political field that sort of problem was, therefore, a sort of act of indecency in relation to the acquired hierarchy of speculative values. It was also (but I was quite unaware of this for a lot of reasons) that the Communist parties and the left-wing intellectuals who followed in their wake had no intention of starting.

P.B.   Because behind *Histoire de la folie* lay the problem of Eastern Europe.

FOUCAULT   Of course. I finished writing that book in Poland and I could not fail to think, as I was writing, of what I could see around me. Yet although, by a sort of analogical, non-genealogical relation, I grasped a kinship, a resemblance, I couldn't see exactly how the mechanism of confinement and general disciplinarization of society functioned. In other words, I couldn't see how my research into the history of madness and what I sensed around me could be integrated into an overall analysis stretching from the formation of the capitalist societies in Europe in the seventeenth century to the socialist societies of the twentieth. On the other hand, there were those who did know! And I didn't know what they knew until much later . . . The most Communist of all the French psychiatrists went to Moscow in the 1950s and saw how "mental" patients were treated there. Yet, when he came back, he said nothing! Nothing! Not out of cowardice, but, I believe, out of a sense of horror. He refused to talk about it and died some years later without ever opening his mouth about what he had seen, so traumatized had he been . . . I am convinced, therefore, for political reasons it was not possible to raise the problem of the real practice of confinement, of the real nature of the psychiatric practice that, from the seventeenth century to our own day, had spread throughout Europe.

P.B.   But psychiatrists couldn't simply ignore your *Histoire de la folie*. You have explained how, at first, there was a political blockage. And what happened then? Did they read you or did they never forgive you for writing that book?

FOUCAULT   The reactions were really very odd. At first, there was no reaction on the part of psychiatrists. Then May '68 arrived. Just afterwards, in 1969, certain psychiatrists met at a conference in Toulouse and, led by Marxists, all trumpets blazing, declared that I was an ideologist, a bourgeois ideologist, etc. They literally set up a tribunal of psychiatrists to condemn that book. But, meanwhile, May '68 had taken place and the deep current of "anti-psychiatry" associated with Laing and Cooper was being much talked about and now reached the awareness of the general public. In 1968, the younger psychiatrists or those who, in one way or another, were beginning to familiarize themselves with the ideas of anti-psychiatry began to denounce, quite openly, certain methods used by psychiatry. Suddenly, my book was seen as a work of "anti-psychiatry" and, even today, I have still not been forgiven for it, on those grounds, which is really quite hilarious. I know several psychiatrists who, when referring to the book in conversation with me, call it, by a sort of slip of the tongue that is both flattering and funny, "L'Eloge de la folie" [In Praise of Madness]! I know some who regard it as an apologia for the positive values of madness against psychiatric knowledge . . . Of course, there is absolutely no question of that in *Histoire de la folie* — you only have to read the book to see that.

P.B.   In 1966 you brought out a book, *Les Mots et les choses*, which has been famous ever since. This difficult book . . .

FOUCAULT   Yes, and allow me to make one remark right away: it is the most difficult, the most tiresome book I every wrote, and was seriously intended to be read by about two thousand academics who happen to be interested in a number of problems concerning the history of ideas. Why did it turn out to be so successful? It's a complete mystery. My publisher and I have both thought a great deal about it, since there were three successive reprints of *Les Mots et les choses* before a single review of it appeared in the press . . .

P.B.   Precisely. Didn't the success of this difficult book involve misunderstandings? Take, for example, *Le Petit Larousse*, which sells every year hundreds of thousands of copies. This is what we find: "Michel Foucault . . . author of a philosophy of history based on discontinuity." Now you never agreed with that summary. Why?

FOUCAULT   This idea of "discontinuity" in relation to *Les Mots et les choses* has, indeed, become a dogma. Am I, perhaps, responsible for this? The fact remains, however, that the book says exactly the opposite . . . Forgive me for being dogmatic, but here we go: you only have to know the areas I was concerned with in that book — that's to say, the history of biology, the history of political economy, or the history of general grammar — to see at once, at first sight, what looked like breaks or great ruptures. The effect of which is, for example, that a book of medicine dating from 1750 is, for us, a hilarious object of folklore, of which we understand practically nothing; on the other hand, seventy years later, around 1820, there appeared books of medicine that, even if they contain a lot of things that we regard as erroneous, inadequate, or approximate, are nevertheless part of the same type of knowledge as our own. In *Les Mots et les choses* I set out, therefore, from this self-evident discontinuity and tried to ask myself the question: is this discontinuity really a discontinuity? Or, to be precise, what was the transformation needed to pass from one type of knowledge to another type of knowledge? For me, this is not at all a way of declaring the discontinuity of History; on the contrary, it is a way of posing discontinuity as a problem and above all as a problem to be resolved. My approach, therefore, was quite the opposite of a "philosophy of discontinuity." But, because this book is indeed difficult and because what strikes one most obviously is the heavily stressed — and if you like, sometimes exaggerated, for pedagogical purposes — indication of these discontinuities seen on the surface, many readers saw no further. They failed to see that the whole work of the book consisted precisely in setting out from this apparent discontinuity — on which historians concerned with biology, medicine, or grammar are, I believe, in agreement — and trying, in a way, to dissolve it.

P.B.   After *Les Mots et les choses* (which you complemented with *L'Archéologie de savoir*), you published, in 1975, *Surveiller et punir*. Just as *Les Mots et les choses* was a difficult book, so *Surveiller et punir* was addressed to a much wider public.

FOUCAULT   For *Surveiller et punir*, my idea was to try to write a book that was directly connected with a concrete activity that was taking place on the matter of the prisons. At the time a whole movement had grown up that challenged the prison system and questioned the practices involved in confining offenders. I found myself caught up in this movement, working, for example, with former prisoners, and that is why I wanted to write a history book about prisons. What I wanted to do was not to tell a story, or even to analyze the contemporary situation, because that would have needed much greater experience than I had and a connection with penitential institutions much deeper than I had. No, what I wanted to write was a history book that would make the present situation comprehensible and, possibly, lead to action. If you like, I tried to write a "treatise of intelligibility" about the penitentiary situation, I wanted to make it intelligible and, therefore, criticizable.

P.B.   Making the penitentiary situation intelligible was also to address a wider public, wasn't it?

FOUCAULT   Yes, that was certainly a very important aspect of it. I believe and hope that *Surveiller et punir* is not a difficult book to read — even if I try not to sacrifice precision or historical detail. Anyway, I do know that many people who are not academics in the strict sense of the term or who are not intellectuals in the Parisian sense of the term have read this book. I know that people concerned with the prisons, lawyers, educators, prison visitors, not to mention the prisoners themselves, have read it; and it was precisely such people I was addressing to begin with. For what really interested me in *Surveiller et punir* was being read by a wider public than one made up of students, philosophers, or historians. If a lawyer can read *Surveiller et punir* as a treatise on the history of penal procedure, I'm only too delighted. Or, if you want another example, I'm delighted that historians found no major error in *Surveiller et punir* and that, at the same time, prisoners read it in their cells. To make possible these two types of reading is something important, even if it isn't easy for me to hold the two together.

P.B.   We now come to your latest book, *La volonté de savoir*, which is the first volume in a huge project — a "history of sexuality." How is this research into sexuality related to your previous work?

FOUCAULT   In my studies of madness or the prison, it seemed to me that the question at the center of everything was: what is power? And, to be more specific: how is it exercised, what exactly happens when someone exercises power over another? It seemed to me then that sexuality, in so far as it is, in every society, and in ours in particular, heavily regulated, was a good area to test what the mechanisms of power actually were. Especially as the analyses that were current during the 1960s defined power in terms of prohibition: power, it was said, is what prohibits, what prevents people doing something. It seemed to me that power was something much more complex than that.

P.B.   In order to analyze power, one must not link it *a priori* to repression . . .

FOUCAULT   Exactly . . .

P.B.   That is why, in *Surveiller et punir*, you show with the example of the prisons that it was more useful for power, at a particular moment, to observe than to punish. In *La Volonté de savoir*, with the example of sexuality, you wanted to show, therefore, that it was more useful for power to admit sex than to forbid it, is that so?

FOUCAULT   It is often said that sexuality is something people in our societies dare not talk about. It is true that people dare not say certain things. Nevertheless, I was struck by the following: when one thinks that, since the twelfth century, all Western Catholics have been obliged to admit their sexuality, their sins against the flesh and all their sins in this area, committed in thought or deed, one can hardly say that the discourse on sexuality has been simply prohibited or repressed. The discourse on sexuality was organized in a particular way, in terms of a number of codes, and I would even go so far as to say that, in the West, there has been a very strong incitement to speak of sexuality. Now I was very surprised to see that this more or less self-evident thesis was very ill received. I think that once again we are confronted by a phenomenon of exclusive valorization of a theme: power must be repressive; since power is bad, it can only be negative, etc. In these circumstances, to speak of one's sexuality would necessarily be a liberation. However, it seemed to me, that it was much more complicated than that.

P.B.   In an interview you had with Gilles Deleuze in 1972, you said this: "It's the great unknown at present: who exercises power?[2] And where does he exercise it? Nowadays we know more or less who exploits, where the profit goes, into whose hands it goes and where it is reinvested. But power . . . we know very well that it is not those who govern who hold power. But the notion of 'ruling class' is neither very clear nor very highly developed." Could you explain this analysis of power to me in greater detail?

FOUCAULT   It would be bold of me indeed if I were to tell you that my ideas on this subject are clearer now than at that time. I still believe, then, that the way in which power is exercised and functions in a society like ours is little understood. Of course, there are sociological studies that show us who the bosses of industry are at present, how politicians are formed and where they come from; but there are also more general studies, usually inspired by Marxism, concerning the domination of the bourgeois class in our societies. But, under this general umbrella, things seem to me to be much more complex. In the Western industrialized societies, the questions "Who exercises power? How? On whom?" are certainly the questions that people feel most strongly about. The problem of poverty, which haunted the nineteenth century, is no longer, for our Western societies, of primary importance. On the other hand: Who makes decisions for me? Who is preventing me from doing this and telling me to do that? Who is programming my movements and activities? Who is forcing me to live in a particular place when I work in another? How are these decisions on which my life is completely articulated taken? All these questions seem to me to be fundamental ones today. And I don't believe that this question of "who exercises power?" can be resolved unless that other qustion "how does it happen?" is resolved at the same time. Of course we have to show who those in charge are, we know that we have to turn, let us say, to deputies, ministers, principal private secretaries, etc., etc. But this is not the important issue, for we know perfectly well that even if we reach the point of designating exactly all those people, all those "decision-makers," we will still not really know why and how the decision was made, how it came to be

2.   See "Les intellectuels et le pouvoir," *L'Arc* [issue on Gilles Deleuze] 49 (March 1972), 3–10 [L.D.K.].

accepted by everybody, and how it is that it hurts a particular category of person, etc.

P.B. So we can't study power without what you call the "strategies of power" . . .

FOUCAULT Yes, the strategies, the networks, the mechanisms, all those techniques by which a decision is accepted and by which that decision could not but be taken in the way it was.

P.B. All your analyses tend to show that there is power everywhere, even in the fibers of our bodies, for example, in sexuality. Marxism has been criticized for analyzing everything in terms of economics and even of reducing everything, in the final analysis, to an economic problem. Can you, too, not be criticized for seeing power everywhere and, in the final analysis, of reducing everything to power?

FOUCAULT That's an important question. For me, power is the problem that has to be resolved. Take an example like the prisons. I want to study the way in which people set about using — and late on in history — imprisonment, rather than banishment or torture, as a punitive method. That's the problem. There have been excellent German historians and sociologists of the Frankfurt School who, after studying it, have drawn the following conclusion: in a bourgeois, capitalist, industrial society, in which labor is the essential value, it was considered that people found guilty of crimes could not be condemned to a more useful penalty than to be forced to work. And how were they forced to work? By locking them up in a prison and forcing them to work so many hours a day. This, in brief, is the explanation of the problem posed by those German historians and sociologists. It is an explanation of an economist type. Though I'm not entirely convinced by this reasoning, for the excellent reason . . . that people have never worked in prisons! The profitability of work done in the prisons has always been negligible — it was work for the sake of work. But let's look at the problem more closely. In reality, when we examine how, in the late eighteenth century, it was decided to choose imprisonment as the essential mode of punishment, one sees that it was after all a long elaboration of various techniques that made it possible to locate people, to fix them in precise places, to constrict them to a certain number of gestures and habits — in short, it was a form of "dressage." Thus we see the appearance of garrisons of a type that didn't exist before the end of the seventeenth century; we see the appearance of the great boarding schools, of the Jesuit type, which still did not exist in the seventeenth century; in the eighteenth century, we see the appearance of the great workshops employing hundreds of workers. What developed, then, was a whole technique of human dressage by location, confinement, surveillance, the perpetual supervision of behavior and tasks, in short, a whole technique of "management" of which the prison was merely one manifestation or its transposition into the penal domain. Now what do all these new techniques used to train individuals amount to? I state it very clearly in *Surveiller et punir*: in the case of the workshops, these new techniques did of course respond to the economic necessities of production; in the case of the barracks, they are bound up with problems of both a practical and political kind, with the development of a professional army, which had to perform fairly difficult tasks (knowing how to fire a cannon, for example); and in the case of the schools, with problems of a political and economic character. I say all this in my book. But what I also try to bring out is that, from the eighteenth century onwards, there has been a specific reflection on the way in which these procedures for training and exercising power over individuals could be extended, generalized, and improved. In other words, I constantly show the economic or political origin of these methods; but, while refraining from seeing power everywhere, I also think there is a specificity in these new techniques of training. I believe that the methods used, right down to the way of conditioning individuals' behavior, have a logic, obey a type of rationality, and are all based on one another to form a sort of specific stratum.

P.B.   From a certain point on, then, the "specific techniques of power," as you call them, appear to have functioned of themselves, without any economic justification?

FOUCAULT   There was no really "rational" economic reason to force prisoners to work in prisons. Economically, it served no purpose and yet it was done. There is a whole series of similar ways of exercising power that, while having no economic justification, were nevertheless transposed into the judicial institution.

P.B.   One of your theses is that the strategies of power actually produce knowledge. Contrary to the received idea, there seems to be no incompatibility between power and knowledge.

FOUCAULT   Philosophers or even, more generally, intellectuals justify and mark out their identity by trying to establish an almost uncrossable line between the domain of knowledge, seen as that of truth and freedom, and the domain of the exercise of power. What struck me, in observing the human sciences, was that the development of all these branches of knowledge can in no way be dissociated from the exercise of power. Of course, you will always find psychological or sociological theories that are independent of power. But, generally speaking, the fact that societies can become the object of scientific observation, that human behavior became, from a certain point on, a problem to be analyzed and resolved, all that is bound up, I believe, with mechanisms of power — which, at a given moment, indeed, analyzed that object (society, man, etc.) and presented it as a problem to be resolved. So the birth of the human sciences goes hand in hand with the installation of new mechanisms of power.

P.B.   Your analysis of the relations between knowledge and power takes place in the area of the human sciences. It does not concern the exact sciences, does it?

FOUCAULT   Oh no, not at all! I would not make such a claim for myself. And, anyway, you know, I'm an empiricist: I don't try to advance things without seeing whether they are applicable. Having said that, to reply to your question, I would say this: it has often been stressed that the development of chemistry, for example, could not be understood without the development of industrial needs. That is true and has been demonstrated. But what seems to me to be more interesting to analyze is how science, in Europe, has become institutionalized as a power. It is not enough to say that science is a set of procedures by which propositions may be falsified, errors demonstrated, myths demystified, etc. Science also exercises power: it is, literally, a power that forces you to say certain things, if you are not to be disqualified not only as being wrong, but, more seriously than that, as being a charlatan. Science has become institutionalized as a power through a university system and through its own constricting apparatus of laboratories and experiments.

P.B.   Doesn't science produce "truths" to which we submit?

FOUCAULT   Of course. Indeed, truth is no doubt a form of power. And in saying that, I am only taking up one of the fundamental problems of Western philosophy when it poses these questions: Why, in fact, are we attached to the truth? Why the truth rather than lies? Why the truth rather than myth? Why the truth rather than illusion? And I think that, instead of trying to find out what truth, as opposed to error, is, it might be more interesting to take up the problem posed by Nietzsche: how is it that, in our societies, "the truth" has been given this value, thus placing us absolutely under its thrall?

P.B.   You draw a distinction between the "universal intellectual" of an earlier time, who pronounced on everything under the sun, and a new type of intellectual, the "specific intellectual?" Would you like to say something about this distinction?

FOUCAULT   One of the essential sociological features of the recent evolution of our societies is the development of what might variously be called technology, white-collar workers, the service sector, etc. Within these different forms of activity, I believe that it is quite possible, on the one hand, to get to know how it works and to work within it, that is to say, to do one's job as a psychiatrist, lawyer, engineer, or technician, and, on the other hand, to carry out in that specific area work that may properly be called intellectual, an essentially critical work. When I say "critical," I don't mean a demolition job, one of rejection or refusal, but a work of examination that consists of suspending as far as possible the system of values to which one refers when testing and assessing it. In other words: what am I doing at the moment I'm doing it? At the present time, and this has become more and more evident over the last fifteen years or so, psychiatrists, doctors, lawyers, judges carry out a critical examination, a critical questioning of their own jobs that is an essential element in intellectual life. And I believe that an intellectual, a "professional" intellectual, let's say — a teacher or someone who writes books — will find it easier to find his field of activity, the reality he is looking for, in one of the areas I have just mentioned.

P.B.   Do you regard yourself as a "specific intellectual"?

FOUCAULT   Yes, I do. I work in a specific field and do not produce a theory of the world. Even if, in practice, whenever one works in a particular field, one can do so only by having or arriving at a particular point of view . . .

P.B.   When invited by Bernard Pivot to take part in one of his "Apostrophes" television broadcasts on the publication of *La Volonté du savoir*, you sacrificed, in a sense, the time at your disposal to draw attention to the case of Dr. Stern, then imprisoned by the Soviet authorities.[3]

FOUCAULT   I would not like there to be any ambiguity on this question of the mass media. I regard it as entirely normal that someone who does not have many opportunities of being heard or read should appear on television. I understand perfectly well why writers, even well-known ones, should take part in broadcasts, some of them indeed are excellent, and in that context say something different than they would normally be able to say, because it is true that the relationship to television, to the screen, to the interviewer, or to the viewer brings out things they would not otherwise say. But, personally, I believe that I have had enough opportunities of expressing myself and enough opportunities of being heard not to encumber the mass media with a presentation of my own books. If I want to say something on television, I shall make or propose a film for television. But for someone like me, someone who has plenty of opportunities for self-expression, it seems to me to be indecent to come and talk about my book. So much so that, when I go on television, it is not to substitute for or to duplicate what I have said elsewhere, but to do something that may be useful and to say something that the viewers don't know about. And in saying

---

3.   Bernard Pivot is the moderator of *Apostrophes* the highly popular weekly literary broadcast on French television (*Antenne 2*) [L.D.K.].

this, I repeat, I am not criticizing either book programs or the people who take part in them. If they are young, for example, I can understand perfectly well that they should want to fight for their books and to be heard: I might very well have done the same myself once. But now I prefer to leave room for them.

P.B.   How do you see your success and, more generally, the enthusiasm for the human sciences and for philosophical writings since the 1960s?

FOUCAULT   As far as my success is concerned, we must keep a sense of proportion. Nevertheless, there was this phenomenon of audiences spilling out beyond the lecture hall. It's a phenomenon that began before me with Lévi-Strauss and his book *Tristes tropiques*: suddenly human anthropology was addressing not 200 people, or even 2,000, but 20,000, if not 200,000.[4] That phenomenon, which I was part of, as were also Lévi-Strauss and Barthes, is indeed a disturbing one. What is certain is that we were taken completely by surprise, caught quite unprepared, having really no idea how to address such a public and what to do with it. And indeed that's why we didn't really know how to make use of the mass media. The relationship between us and our reading public was never clearly established. It was as if books were being asked to provide not so much the extra imaginary dimension that used to be expected of them, but rather a more considered, longer-term view of society.

---

4. Claude Lévi-Strauss (1908–). French social anthropologist and founder of structural anthropology. *Tristes tropiques* (1955; English translation 1961) is an autobiographical work that is derived from observation of four primitive South American tribes and reflects psychoanalytic and Marxist concepts [L.D.K.].

7

Power and Sex

The productive power of discourse about sex and its relationship to control and discipline is the subject of this discussion with Bernard-Henri Lévy.[1] In opting for an investigation of what is most hidden in the relations of power, Foucault challenges the essentialized myth of Marxist "class struggle" and thus questions the utopian dream of revolution as a liberating struggle. Originally published as "Foucault: Non au sexe roi" in Le Nouvel observateur, March 12, 1977, this interview was translated by David J. Parent as "Power and Sex," in Telos 32 (1977), 152–61.

B.-H.L.   Your book *La Volonté de savoir* (The Will to Know) marks the beginning of a "history of sexuality" of monumental proportions. What justification is there today for you, Michel Foucault, to undertake so huge an enterprise?

FOUCAULT   So *huge*? No, no, say rather, so *needed*. I do not intend to write the chronicle of sexual behavior over the ages and civilizations. I want to follow a narrower thread: the one that through so many centuries has linked sex and the search for truth in our societies.

B.-H.L.   In precisely what sense?

FOUCAULT   In fact, the problem is this: how is it that in a

1. Bernard-Henri Lévy (1948–   ). One of the leading *nouveaux philosophes* [new French philosophers] who came to prominence in France in the mid 1970s. In *La Barbarie à visage humain* (Paris: Grasset, 1977) [*Barbarism with a Human Face*] Lévy, a former 1968 Maoist, denounces socialism as the most odious form of social control whose myth of a classless society cannot exist without its terrorist truths. Foucault had revealed an initial enthusiasm for the new philosophers' critique of the Marxist conception of centralized power in his review of André Glucksmann's *Les Maîtres Penseurs* [1977] in "La Grande Colère des faits," *Le Nouvel Observateur* 652 (9 May 1977), 84–86 [L.D.K.].

society like ours, sexuality is not simply a means of reproducing the species, the family, and the individual? Not simply a means to obtain pleasure and enjoyment? How has sexuality come to be considered the privileged place where our deepest "truth" is read and expressed? For that is the essential fact: Since Christianity, the Western world has never ceased saying: "To know who you are, know what your sexuality is." Sex has always been the forum where both the future of our species and our "truth" as human subjects are decided.

Confession, the examination of conscience, all the insistence on the important secrets of the flesh, has not been simply a means of prohibiting sex or of repressing it as far as possible from consciousness, but was a means of placing sexuality at the heart of existence and of connecting salvation with the mastery of these obscure movements. In Christian societies, sex has been the central object of examination, surveillance, avowal and transformation into discourse.

B.-H.L.   Hence the paradoxical theme underlying this first volume: far from making sexuality taboo or bringing strong sanctions against it, our societies have never ceased speaking of sex, and making it speak.

FOUCAULT   They could speak very well — and very much — of sexuality, but only to prohibit it.

But I wanted to stress two important facts. First, that the bringing to light, the "clarification" of sexuality occurred not only in discussions but also in the reality of institutions and practices.

Secondly, that numerous, strict prohibitions exist. But they are part of a complex economy along with incitements, manifestations, and evaluations. We always stress the prohibitions. I would like to change the perspective somewhat, grasping in every case the entire complex of apparatuses.

And, as you well know, I have been given the image of a melancholic historian of prohibitions and repressive power, a teller of tales with only two categories: insanity and its incarceration, the anomaly and its exclusion, delinquency and its imprisonment. But my problem has always been on the side of another term: truth. How did the power exerted in insanity produce psychiatry's "true" discourse? The same applies to sexuality: to revive the will to know the source of the power exerted upon sex. My aim is not to write the social history of a prohibition but the political history of the production of "truth."

B.-H.L.   A new revolution in the concept of history? The dawn of another "new history?"

FOUCAULT   A few years ago, historians were very proud to discover that they could write not only the history of battles, of kings and institutions but also of the economy, now they are all amazed because the shrewdest among them have learned that it was also possible to write the history of feelings, behavior and the body. Soon, they will understand that the history of the West cannot be disociated from the way its "truth" is produced and produces its effects.

We are living in a society that, to a great extent, is marching "toward the truth" — I mean, that produces and circulates discourse having truth as its function, passing itself off as such and thus attaining specific powers. The achievement of "true" discourses (which are incessantly changing, however) is one of the fundamental problems of the West. The history as true — is still virgin territory.

What are the positive mechanisms which, producing sexuality in this or that fashion, result in misery?

In any case, what I would like to study, as far as I'm concerned, is the sum total of these mechanisms which, in our society, invite, incite and force one to speak of sex.

B.-H.L.   Still, despite such discourse, you believe that repression, sexual misery also exist . . .

FOUCAULT   Yes, I've heard that objection. You are right: we are all living more or less in a state of sexual misery.

B.-H.L.   Why? Is that a deliberate choice?

FOUCAULT   In subsequent volumes, concrete studies — on women, children, the perverted — I will try to analyze the forms and conditions of this misery. But, for the moment, it is a question of establishing method. The problem is to know whether the misery should be explained negatively by a fundamental interdiction, or positively by a prohibition relative to an economic situation ("Work, don't make love"): or whether it is not the effect of much more complex and much more positive procedures.

B.-H.L.   What could be a "positive" explanation in this case?

FOUCAULT   I will make a presumptuous comparison. What did Marx do when in his analysis of capital he came across the problem of the workers' misery? He refused the customary explanation which regarded this misery as the effect of a naturally rare cause of a concerted theft. And he said substantially: given what capitalist production is, in its fundamental laws, it cannot help but cause misery. Capitalism's raison d'être is not to starve the workers but it cannot develop without starving them. Marx replaced the denunciation of theft by the analysis of production.

Other things being equal, that is approximately what I wanted to say. It is not a matter of denying sexual misery, nor is it however one of explaining it negatively by a repression. The entire problem is to grasp the positive mechanism which, producing sexuality in this or that fashion, results in misery.

Here is one example that I will deal with in a future volume: at the beginning of the 18th century tremendous importance was suddenly ascribed to childhood masturbation, which then was persecuted everywhere like a sudden epidemic, terrible and capable of compromising the whole human race.

Must one conclude from this that childhood masturbation had suddenly become unacceptable for capitalist society in the process of development? This is the position of certain "Reichians," but it does not seem at all satisfactory to me.

On the contrary, what was important at that time was the reorganization of the relations between children and adults, parents, educators; it was an intensification of the intra-family relations; it was childhood as a common area of interest for parents, the educational institutions, the public health authorities; it was childhood as the training-ground for future generations. At the crossroads of body and soul, of health and morality, of education and training, children's sex became both a target and an instrument of power. A specific "sexuality of children" was constituted — precautions, dangerous, constantly in need of supervision.

This resulted in a sexual misery of childhood and adolescence from which our own generations still have not recovered, but the objective was not to forbid, but to use childhood sexuality, suddenly become important and mysterious, as a network of power over children.

B.-H.L.   This idea that sexual misery stems from repression, and that, to be happy, we must have sexual liberation, is held basically by sexologists, doctors, and vice squads . . .

FOUCAULT   Yes, and that is why they present to us a formidable trap. What they are saying, roughly, is this: "You have a sexuality; this sexuality is both frustrated and mute; hypocritical prohibitions are repressing it. So, come to us, tell us, show us all that, confide in us your unhappy secrets . . . "

This type of discourse is, indeed, a formidable tool of control and power. As always, it uses what people say, feel, and hope for. It exploits their temptation to believe that to be happy, it is enough to cross the threshold of discourse and to remove a few prohibitions. But in fact it ends up repressing and dispersing movements of revolt and liberation . . .

B.-H.L.   Hence the misunderstanding of certain commentators: "According to Foucault, the repression or the liberation of sex amounts to the same thing." Or again: groups such as "The MLAC [a radical pro-abortion movement] and Laissez-les vivre [a pro-life movement], employ basically the same discourse . . . "

FOUCAULT   Yes! Matters still have to be cleared up on that point. I was quoted as saying in effect that there is no real difference between the language of condemnation and that against condemnation, between the discourse of prudish moralists and that of sexual liberation. They claimed that I was putting them all in one bag to drown them like a litter of kittens. Diametrically false: that is not what I meant to say. But the important thing is, I didn't say it at all.

FOUCAULT   But a statement is one thing, discourse another. They share common tactics even though they have conflicting strategies.

B.-H.L.   For example?

FOUCAULT   I believe that the movements labeled "sexual liberation" ought to be understood as movements of affirmation "starting with" sexuality. Which means two things: they are movements that start with sexuality, with the apparatus of sexuality in the midst of which we're caught, and which make it function to the limit; but, at the same time, they are in motion relative to it, disengaging themselves and surmounting it.

B.-H.L.   What do these surmountings look like?

FOUCAULT   Take the case of homosexuality. Psychiatrists began a medical analysis of it in the 1870s: a point of departure certainly for a whole series of new interventions and controls.

They began either to incarcerate homosexuals in asylums or to try to cure them. Sometimes they were looked upon as libertines and sometimes as delinquents (hence condemnations — which could be very severe, with burnings at the stake still occurring even in the eighteenth century — were necessarily rare). In the future we will *all* see them as manifesting forms of insanity, sickness of the sexual instinct. But taking such discourses literally, and thereby turning them around, we see responses arising in the form of defiance: "All right, we are the same as you, by nature sick or perverse, whichever you want. And so if we are, let us be so, and if you want to know what we are, we can tell you better than you can." The entire literature of homosexuality, very differently from libertine narratives, appears at the end of the 19th century: recall Wilde and Gide. It is the strategic return of one "same" desire for truth.

B.-H.L.   That indeed is what is happening with all minorities today, women, youth, the blacks in America . . .

FOUCAULT   Yes, of course. For a long time they tried to pin women to their sex. For centuries they were told: "You are nothing but your sex." And this sex, doctors added, is fragile, almost always sick and always inducing illness. "You are man's sickness." And towards the 18th century this ancient movement ran wild, ending in a pathologization of woman: the female body became a medical object *par excellence*. I will try later to write the history of this immense "gynecology" in the broad sense of the term.

But the feminist movements responded defiantly. Are we sex by nature? Well then, let us be so but in its singularity, in its irreducible specificity. Let us draw the consequences and reinvent our own type of existence, political, economic and cultural . . . Always the same movement: to use this sexuality as the starting point in an attempt to colonize them and to cross beyond it toward other affirmations.

B.-H.L. This strategy which you are describing, this strategy of a double *détente*, is it still a strategy of liberation in the classical sense? Or must one not rather say that to liberate sex, one must from now on hate and surmount it?

FOUCAULT A movement is taking shape today which seems to me to be reversing the trend of "always more sex," and "always more truth in sex," which has enthralled us for centuries: it is a matter — I don't say of "rediscovering" — but rather of inventing other forms of pleasures, of relationships, coexistences, attachments, loves, intensities. I have the impression of currently hearing an "anti-sex" grumbling (I am not a prophet, at most a diagnostician), as if an effort were being made, in depth, to shake this great "sexography" which makes us try to decipher sex as the universal secret.

B.-H.L. What are some symptoms for this diagnosis?

FOUCAULT Only an anecdote. A young writer, Hervé Guibert, had written some children's stories: no editor wanted them. He wrote another book, certainly very remarkable and apparently very "sexy." It was the condition for being heard and published. And, presto, he was published (the book is *La Mort Propagande*). Read it: it seems to me the opposite of the sexographic writing that has been the rule in pornography and sometimes in good literature: to move progressively toward naming what is most unmentionable in sex. Hervé Guibert opens with the worst extreme — "You want us to speak of it, well, let's go, and you will hear more than ever before" — and with this infamous material he builds bodies, mirages, castles, fusions, acts of tenderness, races, intoxications; the entire heavy coefficient of sex has been volatilized. But this is only one example of the "anti-sex" challenge, of which many other symptoms can be found. It is perhaps the end of this dreary desert of sexuality, the end of the monarchy of sex.

B.-H.L. Unless we are pledged and chained to sex like an inevitable destiny. And since childhood, as they say . . .

FOUCAULT Exactly, just look at what is happening where children are concerned. Some say that the child's life is sexual. From the milk-bottle to puberty, that is all it is. Behind the desire to learn to read or the taste for comic strips, from first to last, everything is sexuality. Well, are you sure that this type of discourse is effectively liberating? Are you sure that it will not lock children into a sort of sexual insularity? And what if, after all, they didn't give a hoot? If the liberty of not being an adult consisted just in not being a slave of the law, the principle, the *locus communis* of sexuality, would that be so boring after all? If it were possible to have polymorphic relationships with things, people and the body, would that not be childhood? This polymorphism is called perversity by the adults, to reassure themselves, thus coloring it with the monotonous monochrome of their own sex.

B.-H.L. Children are oppressed by the very ones who pretend to liberate them?

FOUCAULT Read the book by Schérer and Hocquenghem.[2] It shows very well that the child has an assortment of pleasure for which the "sex" grid is a veritable prison.

B.-H.L. Is this a paradox?

FOUCAULT This stems from the idea that sexuality is not feared by power, and instead, is far more a means through which power is exercised.

B.-H.L. But consider authoritarian states: can it be said that power is exercised not against but through sexuality?

FOUCAULT Two recent events, apparently contradictory: About ten months ago, China launched a campaign against childhood masturbation, along exactly the same lines that defined this campaign in 18th century Europe (masturbation hampers work, causes deafness, brings about the degeneration of the species). On the other hand, before the year is out, the Soviet Union will, for the first time, host a congress of psychoanalysts (they have to come from abroad since there are none in Russia). Liberalization? A thaw on the part of the

2. Guy Hocquenghem (1946–). Novelist and Gay Activist. René Scherer (1922–). Professor of Philosophy first specializing in German phenomenology and then in the thought of Charles Fourier. Since 1970 he has studied early childhood and has posited the claim that society deprives children of their rights, specifically the desire to express the erotic passion which adults wish to extinguish. *Une érotique puérile* (Paris: Galilée, 1978) denounces the legislation which has segregated adults from children for the past one hundred years [L.D.K.].

subconscious? The springtime of the Soviet libido against the moral bourgeoisificiation of the Chinese?

In Peking's archaic stupidities and the quaint Soviet novelties I see mainly a double recognition of the fact that, formulated *and* prohibited, expressed [*dite*] *and* forbidden [*interdite*], sexuality is a recourse which no modern system of power can do without. We should deeply fear socialism with a sexual physiognomy.

B.-H.L.   In other words, power is no longer necessarily what condemns and encloses?

FOUCAULT   In general terms, I would say that the interdiction, the refusal, the prohibition, far from being essential forms of power, are only its limits, power in its frustrated or extreme forms. The relations of power are, above all, productive.

B.-H.L.   This is a new idea compared with your previous books.

FOUCAULT   If I wanted to pose and drape myself in a slightly fictional style, I would say that this has always been my problem: the effects of power and the production of "truth." I have always felt uncomfortable with this ideological notion which has been used in recent years. It has been used to explain errors or illusions, or to analyze presentations — in short, everything that impedes the formation of true discourse. It has also been used to show the relation between what goes on in people's heads and their place in the conditions of production. In sum, the economics of untruth. My problem is the politics of truth. I have spent a lot of time dealing with it.

B.-H.L.   Why?

FOUCAULT   For several reasons. First, power in the West is what displays itself the most, and thus what hides itself the best: what we have called "political life" since the 19th century is the manner in which power presents its image (a little like the court in the monarchic era). Power is neither there, nor is that how it functions. The relations of power are perhaps among the best hidden things in the social body.

On the other hand, since the 19th century, the critique of society has essentially started with the nature of the economy, which is effectively determining. A valid reduction of "politics," certainly, but a tendency also to neglect the relations of elementary power that could be constitutive of economic relations.

The third reason is the tendency, itself common to institutions, parties, an entire current of revolutionary thought and action, not to see power in any form other than the state aparatus.

All of which leads, when we turn to individuals, to finding power nowhere except in the mind (under the form of representation, acceptance, or interiorization).

B.-H.L.   And faced with this, what did you want to do?

FOUCAULT   Four things: to investigate what might be most hidden in the relations of power; to anchor them in the economic infrastructures; to trace them not only in their governmental forms but also in the infra-governmental or para-governmental ones; to discover them in the material play.

B.-H.L.   What factor did you start with?

FOUCAULT   If you want a bibliographical reference, it was in *Surveiller et Punir*. But I would rather say that it started with a series of events and experiences since 1968 involving psychiatry, delinquency, the schools, etc. These events themselves could never have taken their direction and intensity without the two gigantic shadows of fascism and Stalinism looming in the background. If the workers' misery — this subexistence — caused the political thinking of the 19th century to revolve around the economy, then fascism and Stalinism — these superpowers — induce political anxiety in our current societies.

Hence two problems: power, how does it work? Is it enough for it to issue strong prohibitions in order to really function? And does it always move from above to below and from the center to the periphery?

B.-H.L.   I saw this movement — this sliding — in *La Volonté de Savoir*: this time you made a clean break with the diffuse naturalism that haunts your previous books . . .

FOUCAULT   What you call naturalism refers, I believe, to two things. A certain theory, the idea that under power with its acts of violence and its artifice, we should be able to rediscover the things themselves in their primitive vivacity:

behind the asylum walls, the spontaneity of madness; through the penal system, the generous fever of delinquency; under the sexual interdict, the freshness of desire. And also a certain aesthetic and moral choice: power is bad, ugly, poor, sterile, monotonous and dead; and what power is exercised upon is right, good and rich.

B.-H.L.   Yes. Finally, the theme common to orthodox Marxism and the New Left: "Under the cobblestones lies the beach."

FOUCAULT   If you like. At times, such simplifications are necessary. Such a dualism can be provisionally useful, to change the perspective from time to time and move from *pro* to *contra*.

B.-H.L.   Then comes the time to stop, the moment of reflection and regaining of equilibrium?

FOUCAULT   On the contrary. What should follow is the moment of new mobility and new displacement, for these reversals of *pro* and *contra* are quickly blocked, being unable to do anything except repeat themselves and forming what Jacques Rancière calls the "Leftist *doxa*."[3] As soon as we repeat indefinitely the same refrain of the anti-repressive anthem, things remain in place; anyone can sing the tune, and no one pays attention. This reversal of values and truths, of which I was speaking a while ago, has been important to the extent that it does not stop with simple cheers (long live insanity, delinquency, sex) but allows for new strategies. You see, what often embarrasses me today — in fact, what I regret — is that all this work done in the past fifteen years or so — often under hardship and in solitude — functions for some only as a sign of belonging: to be on the "good side," on the side of madness, children, delinquency, sex.

B.-H.L.   There is no good side?

FOUCAULT   One must pass to the other side — the good side — but by trying to turn off these mechanisms which cause the appearance of two separate sides, by dissolving the

---

3.   Jacques Rancière (1940–). Philosopher and for a certain period collaborator of Louis Althusser with whom he ultimately broke to form the journal *Les Révoltes Logiques*. This publication radically denounces the misdeeds of ideology and valorizes in its place the authenticity of worker's thoughts [L.D.K.].

false unity, the illusory "nature" of this other side with which we have taken sides. This is where the real work begins, that of the present-day historian.

B.-H.L.   Several times already you have defined yourself as an historian. What does that mean? Why "historian" and not "philosopher"?

FOUCAULT   Under as naive a form as a child's fable, I will say that the question of philosophy for a long time has been: "In this world where everything dies, what does not pass away?" It seems to me that since the 19th century, philosophy has never stopped raising the same question: "What is happening right now, and what are we, we who are perhaps nothing more than what is happening at this moment?" Philosophy's question therefore is the question as to what we ourselves are. That is why contemporary philosophy is entirely political and entirely historical. It is the politics immanent in history and the history indispensable for politics.

B.-H.L.   But isn't a return to the most classical, meta-physical kind of philosophy taking place today?

FOUCAULT   I don't believe in any form of return. I would say only this, and only half seriously: The thinking of the first Christian centuries would have had to answer the question: "What is actually going on today? What is this time which we are living in? When and how will this promised return of God take place? What can we do with this intervening time, which is superfluous? And what are we, we who are in this transition?"

We could say that on this incline of history, when the revolution is supposed to hold back and has not yet come, we can ask the same question: "What are we, are we superfluous in this age when what should be happening is not happening? The question of the revolution has dominated all modern thought, like all politics.

B.-H.L.   Are you, on your part, continuing to pose the question and to reflect on it? Does it, in your eyes, remain the question par excellence?

FOUCAULT   If politics has existed since the 19th century, it is because the revolution took place. The current one is not a variant or a sector of that one. Politics always takes a stand on the revolution. When Napoleon said "the modern form of destiny is politics," he was merely drawing the logical conclusions from this truth, for he came after the revolution and before the return of another one.

The return of the revolution — that is surely what our problem is. It is certainly that without it, the question of Stalinism would be purely academic — a mere problem of the organization of societies or of the validity of the Marxist scheme of things. But something quite different is at stake in Stalinism. You know very well what it is: the very desirability of the revolution is the problem today . . .

B.-H.L. Do you want the revolution? Do you want anything more than the simple ethical duty to struggle here and now, at the side of one or another oppressed and miserable group, such as fools or prisoners?

FOUCAULT I have no answer. But I believe that to engage in politics — aside from just party-politics — is to try to know with the greatest possible honesty whether the revolution is desirable. It is in exploring this terrible mole-hill that politics runs the danger of caving in.

B.-H.L. If the revolution were not desirable, would politics remain what you say it is?

FOUCAULT No, I believe not. It would be necessary to invent another one or something else as a substitute for it. We are perhaps experiencing the end of politics. For politics is a field that has been opened by the existence of the revolution, and if the question of the revolution can no longer be posed in these terms, then politics is in danger of disappearing.

B.-H.L. Let us return to your politics in *La Volonté de Savoir*. You say: "Where there is power, there is resistance." Are you not thus bringing back nature, which a while back you wanted to dismiss?

FOUCAULT I think not. This resistance I am speaking of is not a substance. It does not predate the power which it opposes. It is coextensive with it and absolutely its contemporary.

B.-H.L. The inverse image of power? That would come to the same thing. The cobblestones under the beach always appear . . .

FOUCAULT   Absolutely. I am not positing a substance of resistance versus a substance of power. I am just saying: as soon as there is a power relation, there is a possibility of resistance. We can never be ensnared by power: we can always modify its grip in determinate conditions and according to a precise strategy.

B.-H.L.   Power and resistance, tactics and strategy . . . Why this stock of military metaphors? Do you think that power from now on must be visualized in the form of war?

FOUCAULT   I have no idea at the present time. One thing seems certain to me; it is that for the moment we have, for analyzing the relations of power, only two models: a) the one proposed by law (power as law, interdiction, institutions) and b) the military or strategic model in terms of power relations. The first one has been much used and its inadequacy has, I believe, been demonstrated: we know very well that law does not describe power.

The other model is also much discussed, I know. But we stop with words; we use ready-made ideas or metaphors ("the war of all against all," "the struggle for life"), or again formal schemata (strategies are very much in vogue among certain sociologists and economists, especially Americans). I think that this analysis of the power relations would have to be tightened up.

B.-H.L.   But this military conception of the power relations was already used by the Marxists?

FOUCAULT   What strikes me in the Marxist analyses is that they always contain the question of "class struggle" but that they pay little attention to one word in the phrase, namely, "struggle." Here again distinctions must be made. The greatest of the Marxists (starting with Marx himself) insisted sharply on the "military" problems (the army as an instrument of the state, armed insurrection, revolutionary war). But when they speak of the "class struggle" as the mainspring of history, they focus mainly on defining class, its boundaries, its membership, but never concretely on the nature of the struggle. One exception comes to mind: Marx's own non-theoretical, historical texts, which are better and different in this regard.

B.-H.L.   Do you think that your book can fill this gap?

FOUCAULT   I don't make any such claim. In a general way, I think that intellectuals — if this category exists, which is not certain nor perhaps even desirable — are abandoning their old prophetic function.

And by that I don't mean only their claim to predict what will happen, but also the legislative function that they so long aspired for: "See what must be done, see what is good, follow me. In the turmoil that engulfs you all, here is the pivotal point, here is where I am." The Greek wise man, the Jewish prophet, the Roman legislator are still models that haunt those who, today, practice the profession of speaking and writing. I dream of the intellectual who destroys evidence and generalities, the one who, in the inertias and constraints of the present time, locates and marks the weak points, the openings, the lines of force, who is incessantly on the move, doesn't know exactly where he is heading nor what he will think tomorrow for he is too attentive to the present; who, wherever he moves, contributes to posing the question of knowing whether the revolution is worth the trouble, and what kind (I mean, what revolution and what trouble), it being understood that the question can be answered only by those who are willing to risk their lives to bring it about.

As for all the questions of classification and program that are asked of us: "Are you a Marxist?" "What would you do if you had the power?" "Who are your allies and what are your resources?" — these are truly secondary questions compared with the one I have just indicated: it is the question of today.

8

The Dangerous Individual

In this address to the Law and Psychiatry Symposium at York University, Toronto [1978] Foucault observes that the intervention of psychiatry into law begins in the early nineteenth century with the concept of "homocidal mania." The "psychiatrization of crime" was enacted through primitive practices that emphasized the character of the criminal rather than the crime in which he participated. This phenomenon demanded that the judicial system focus on the criminal's potential danger to society instead of on his particular crime. Psychiatry became important in the nineteenth century because it instituted a new medical technology in the treatment of mental disorders as a means to enable the judicial machine to police public hygiene. The "juridico-moral" concept of the dangerous individual threatens us because it gives society the right to censure based on what the individual is. "About the Concept of the Dangerous Individual in 19th Century Legal Psychiatry" was published in the International Journal of Law and Psychiatry 1 (1978), 1–18. It was originally translated by Carol Brown. The new translation that appears here by Alain Baudot and Jane Couchman refers at times to Ms. Brown's version.

I would like to begin by relating a brief exchange which took place the other day in the Paris criminal courts. A man who was accused of five rapes and six attempted rapes, between February and June 1975, was being tried. The accused hardly spoke at all. Questions from the presiding judge:

"Have you tried to reflect upon your case?"

—Silence.

"Why, at twenty-two years of age, do such violent urges overtake you? You must make an effort to analyze yourself. You are the one who has the keys to your own actions. Explain yourself."

—Silence.

"Why would you do it again?"

—Silence.

Then a juror took over and cried out, "For heaven's sake, defend yourself!"

Such a dialogue, or rather, such an interrogatory monologue, is not in the least exceptional. It could doubtlessly be heard in many courts in many countries. But, seen in another light, it can only arouse the amazement of the historian. Here we have a judicial system designed to establish misdemeanors to determine who committed them, and to sanction these acts by imposing the penalties prescribed by the law. In this case we have facts which have been established, an individual who admits to them and one who consequently accepts the punishment he will receive. All should be for the best in the best of all possible judicial worlds. The legislators, the authors of the legal codes in the late 18th and early 19th centuries, could not have dreamed of a clearer situation. And yet it happens that the machinery jams, the gears seize up. Why? Because the accused remains silent. Remains silent about what? About the facts? About circumstances? About the way in which they occurred? About the immediate cause of the events? Not at all. The accused evades a question which is essential in the eyes of a modern tribunal, but which would have had a strange ring to it 150 years ago: "Who are you?"

And the dialogue which I just quoted shows that it is not enough for the accused to say in reply to that question, "I am the author of the crimes before you, period. Judge since you must, condemn if you will." Much more is expected of him. Beyond admission, there must be confession, self-examination, explanation of oneself, revelation of what one is. The penal machine can no longer function simply with a law, a violation and a responsible party. It needs something else, a supplementary material. The magistrates and the jurors, the lawyers too, and the department of the public prosecutor, cannot really play their role unless they are provided with another type of discourse, the one given by the accused about himself, or the one which he makes possible for others, through his confessions, memories, intimate disclosures, etc. If it happens that this discourse is missing, the presiding judge is relentless, the jury is upset. They urge, they push the accused, he does not play the game. He is not unlike those condemned persons who have to be carried to the guillotine or the electric chair because they drag their feet. They really ought to walk a little by themselves, if indeed they want to be executed. They really ought to speak a little about themselves, if they want to be judged. The following argument used recently by a French lawyer in the case of the kidnapping and murder of a child clearly indicates that the judicial stage cannot do without this added element, that no judgment, no condemnation is possible without it being provided, in one way or another.

For a number of reasons, this case created a great stir, not only because of the seriousness of the crime, but also because the question of the retention or the abolition of the death penalty was at stake in the case. In his plea, which was directed against the death penalty more than in favor of the accused, the lawyer stressed the point that very little was known about him, and that the nature of the man had only barely been glimpsed at in the interrogations and in the psychiatric examinations. And he made this amazing remark (I quote approximately): "Can one condemn to death a person one does not know?"

This is probably no more than one illustration of a well-known fact, which could be called the law of the third element, or the Garofalo principle, since Garofalo was the one who formulated it with complete clarity: "Criminal law knew only two terms, the offense and the penalty. The new criminology recognizes three, the crime, the criminal and the means of repression." In large part, the evolution, if not of the penal systems, at least of the day to day penal practice in many countries, is determined by the gradual emergence in the course of the 19th century of this additional character. At first a pale phantom, used to adjust the penalty determined by the judge for the crime, this character becomes gradually more substantial, more solid and more real, until finally it is the crime which seems nothing but a shadow hovering about the criminal, a shadow which must be drawn aside in order to reveal the only thing which is now of importance, the criminal.

Legal justice today has at least as much to do with criminals as with crimes. Or more precisely, while, for a long time, the criminal had been no more than the person to whom a crime could be attributed and who could therefore be punished, today, the crime tends to be no more than the event which signals the existence of a dangerous element — that is, more or less dangerous — in the social body.

From the very beginning of this development, resorting to the criminal over and above the crime was justified by a double concern: to introduce more rationality into penal practice, and to adjust the general provisions of laws and legal codes more closely to social reality. Probably, it was not realized, at least at first, that to add the notion of psychological symptomatology of a danger to the notion of legal imputability of a crime was not only to enter an extremely obscure labyrinth, but also to come slowly out of a legal system which had gradually developed since its birth during the medieval inquisition. It could be said that hardly had the great eighteenth-century legal reformers completed the systematic codification of the results of the preceding evolution, hardly had they developed all its possibilities, when a new crisis began to appear in the rules and regulations of legal punishment. "What must be punished, and how?" That was the question to which, it was believed, a rational answer had finally been found; and now a further question arose to confuse the issue: "Whom do you think you are punishing?"

In this development, psychiatry and psychiatrists, as well as the notion of "danger," played a permanent role. I would like to draw attention to two stages in what one might call the psychiatrization of criminal danger.

The intervention of psychiatry in the field of law occurred in the beginning of the nineteenth century, in connection with a series of cases whose pattern was about the same, and which took place between 1800 and 1835.

Case reported by Metzger: a retired officer who lives a solitary life becomes attached to his landlady's child. One day, "with absolutely no motive, in the absence of any passion, such as anger, pride, or vengeance," he attacks the child and hits him twice with a hammer, though not fatally.

Selestat case: in Alsace, during the extremely hard winter of 1817, when famine threatens, a peasant woman takes advantage of her husband's being absent at work to kill their little daughter, cuts off her leg and cooks it in the soup.

In Paris in 1827, Henriette Cornier, a servant, goes to the neighbor of her employers and insists that the neighbor leave her daughter with her for a time. The neighbor hesitates, agrees, then, when she returns for the child, Henriette Cornier has just killed her and has cut off her head which she has thrown out the window.

In Vienna, Catherine Ziegler kills her illegitimate child. On the stand, she explains that her act was the result of an irresistible force. She is acquitted on grounds of insanity. She is released from prison. But she declares that it would be better if she were kept there, for she will do it again. Ten months later, she gives birth to a child which she kills immediately, and she declares at the trial that she became pregnant for the sole purpose of killing her child. She is condemned to death and executed.

In Scotland, a certain John Howison enters a house where he kills an old woman whom he hardly knows, leaves without stealing anything and does not go into hiding. Arrested, he denies the fact against all evidence; but the defense argues that it is the crime of a madman since it is a crime without material motive. Howison is executed, and his comment to an official at the execution that he felt like killing him, was considered in retrospect as supplementary evidence of madness.

In New England, out in the open fields, Abraham Prescott kills his foster mother with whom he had always gotten along very well. He goes home and breaks into tears in front of his foster father, who questions him. Prescott willingly confesses his crime. He explains later that he was overcome by a sudden and acute toothache and that he remembers nothing. The inquiry will establish that he had already attacked his foster parents during the night, an act which had been believed to be the result of a fit of sleepwalking. Prescott is condemned to death but the jury also recommends a commutation. He is nevertheless executed.

(The psychiatrists of the period, Metziger, Hoffbauer, Esquirol and Georget, William Ellis, and Andrew Combe refer tirelessly to these cases and to others of the same type.)

Out of all the crimes committed, why did these particular ones seem important; why were they at issue in the discussions between doctors and jurists? First, of all, it must be noted that they present a picture very different from what had hitherto constituted the jurisprudence of criminal insanity. In general terms, until the end of the eighteenth century, the question of insanity was raised under penal law only in cases where it was also raised in the civil code or in canon law, that is when it appeared either in the form of *dementia* and of imbecility, or in the form of *furor*. In both cases, whether it was a matter of a permanent state or a passing outburst, insanity manifested itself through numerous signs which were easy enough to recognize, to the extent that it was debated whether a doctor was really necessary to authenticate it. The important thing is that criminal psychiatry did not develop from a subtle redefining of the traditional question of *dementia* (e.g., by discussing its gradual evolution, its global or partial character, its relationship to congenital disabilities of individuals) nor through a closer analysis of the symptomatology of *furor* (its remissions, its recurrences, its rhythm). All these problems, along with the discussions which had gone on for years, were replaced by a new problem, that of crimes which are neither preceded, nor accompanied, nor followed by any of the traditional, recognized, visible symptoms of insanity. It is stressed in each case that there was no previous history, no earlier disturbance in thought or behavior, no delirium; neither was there any agitation, nor visible disorder as in furor; indeed, the crime would arise out of a state which one might call the zero degree of insanity.

The second common feature is too obvious to be dealt with at any length. The crimes in question are not minor offenses but serious crimes, almost all murders, sometimes accompanied by strange cruelties (cannibalism in the case of the woman from Selestat). It is important to note that the psychiatrization of delinquency occurred in a sense "from above." This is also a departure from the fundamental tendency of previous jurisprudence. The more serious the crime, the less usual it was to raise the question of insanity (for a long period, it was not taken into consideration in cases involving sacrilege or lèse-majesté). That there is a considerable area of overlap between insanity and illegality was readily admitted in the case of minor offenses — little acts of violence, vagrancy — and these were dealt with, at least in some countries such as France, by the ambiguous measure of internment. But it was not through the ill-defined zone of day to day disorders that psychiatry was able to penetrate penal justice in full force. Rather it was by tackling the great criminal event of the most violent and rarest sort.

Another common feature of these great murders is that they take place in a domestic setting. They are family crimes, household crimes, and at most neighborhood crimes — parents who kill their progeny, children who kill their parents or guardians, servants who kill their employers' or their neighbors' child, etc. As we can see, these are crimes which bring together partners from different generations. The child-adult or adolescent-adult couple is almost always present. In those days, such relationships of age, of place, of kinship were held to be at the same time the most sacred and the most natural, and also the most innocent. Of all relationships, they were the ones which ought to have been the least charged with material motive or passion. Rather than crimes against society and its rules, they are crimes against nature, against those laws which are perceived to be inscribed directly on the human heart and which link families and generations. At the beginning of the nineteenth century, the form of crime about which it appeared that the question of insanity could properly be raised was thus the crime against nature. The individual in whom insanity and criminality met in such a way as to cause specialists to raise the question of their relationship, was not the man of the little everyday disorder, the pale silhouette moving about on the edges of law and normality, but rather the great monster. Criminal psychiatry first proclaimed itself a pathology of the monstrous.

Finally, all of these crimes were committed without reason, I mean without profit, without passion, without motive, even based on disordered illusions. In all the cases which I have mentioned, the psychiatrists do justify their intervention by insisting that there existed between the two actors in the drama no relationship which would help to make the crime intelligible. In the case of Henriette Cornier, who had decapitated her neighbor's daughter, it was carefully established that she had not been the father's mistress, and that she had not acted out of vengeance. In the case of the woman from Selestat, who had boiled up her daughter's thigh, an important element of the discussion had been, "Was there or was there not famine at the time? Was the accused poor or not, starving or not?" The public prosecutor had said: "If she had been rich, she could have been considered deranged, but she was poverty-stricken; she was hungry; to cook the leg with the cabbage was interested behavior; she was therefore not insane."

At the time when the new psychiatry was being established, and when the principles of penal reform were being applied nearly everywhere in Europe and in North America, the great and monstrous murder, without reason, without preliminaries, the sudden eruption of the unnatural in nature, was the singular and paradoxical form taken by criminal insanity or pathological crime. I say paradoxical since there was an attempt to grasp a type of derangement which manifested itself only in the moment and in the guise of the crime, a derangement which would have no symptom other than the crime itself, and which could disappear once the crime had been committed. And conversely, it entailed identifying crimes whose reason, whose author, whose "legally responsible agent" so to speak, is that part of the subject which is beyond his responsibility; that is, the insanity which hides in him and which he cannot even control because he is frequently not even aware of it. Nineteenth-century psychiatry invented an entirely fictitious entity, a crime which is insanity, a crime which is nothing but insanity, an insanity which is nothing but crime. For more than half a century this entity was called homicidal monomania. I do not intend to go over the theoretical background of the notion, nor to follow up the innumerable discussions which it prompted between men of the law and doctors, lawyers and magistrates. I simply want to underline this strange fact, that psychiatrists have tried very stubbornly to take their place in the legal machinery. They justified their right to intervene, not by searching out the thousand little visible signs of madness which may accompany the most ordinary crimes, but by insisting — a preposterous stance — that there were kinds of insanity which manifested themselves only in outrageous crimes, and in no other way. And I would also like to underline the fact that, in spite of all their reservations about accepting this notion of monomania, when the magistrates of the time finally accepted the psychiatric analysis of crime, they did so on the basis of this same notion, so foreign and so unacceptable to them.

Why was the great fiction of homicidal mania the key notion in the protohistory of criminal psychiatry? The first set of questions to be asked is probably the following: at the beginning of the nineteenth century, when the task of psychiatry was to define its specificity in the field of medicine and to assure that its scientific character was recognized among other medical practices, at the point, that is, when psychiatry was establishing itself as a medical specialization (previously it had been an aspect rather than a field of medicine), why then did it want to meddle in an area where so far it had intervened very discretely? Why did doctors want so badly to describe as insane, and thus to claim, people whose status as mere criminals had up to that point been unquestioned? Why can they be found in so many countries, denouncing the medical ignorance of judges and jurors, requesting pardons or the commutation of punishment for certain convicts, demanding the right to be heard as experts by the tribunals, publishing hundreds of reports and studies to show that this criminal or that one was a madman? Why this crusade in favor of the "pathologification" of crime, and under the banner, no less, of homicidal mania? This is all the more paradoxical in that, shortly before, at the end of the eighteenth century, the very first students of insanity (especially Pinel) protested against the practice followed in many detention centers of mixing delinquents and the mentally ill. Why would one want to renew a kinship which one had taken such trouble to break down?

It is not enough to invoke some sort of imperialism on the part of psychiatrists seeking a new domain for themselves or even the internal dynamics of medical knowledge attempting to rationalize the confused area where madness and crime mix. Crime then became an important issue for psychiatrists, because what was involved was less a field of knowledge to be conquered than a modality of power to be secured and justified. If psychiatry became so important in the nineteenth century, it was not simply because it applied a new medical rationality to mental or behavioral disorders, it was also because it functioned as a sort of public hygiene.

In the eighteenth century, the development of demography, of urban structures, of the problem of industrial labor, had raised in biological and medical terms the question of human "populations," with their conditions of existence, of habitation, of nutrition, with their birth and mortality rate, with their pathological phenomena (epidemics, endemic diseases, infant mortality). The social "body" ceased to be a simple juridico-political metaphor (like the one in the *Leviathan*) and became a biological reality and a field for medical intervention. The doctor must therefore be the technician of this social body, and medicine a public hygiene. At the turn of the nineteenth century, psychiatry became an autonomous discipline and assumed such prestige precisely because it had been able to develop within the framework of a medical discipline conceived of as a reaction to the dangers inherent in the social body. The alienists of the period may well have had endless discussions about the organic or psychic origin of mental illnesses; they may well have proposed physical or psychic therapies. Nonetheless, through all their differences, they were all conscious that they were treating a social "danger," either because insanity seemed to them to be linked to living conditions (overpopulation, overcrowding, urban life, alcoholism, debauchery), or because it was perceived as a source of danger for oneself, for others, for one's contemporaries, and also for one's descendants through heredity. Nineteenth-century psychiatry was a medical science as much for the societal body as for the individual soul.

One can see why it was important for psychiatry to prove the existence of something as extravagant as homicidal mania. One can see why for half a century there were continuous attempts to make that notion work, in spite of its meager scientific justification. Indeed, if it exists, homicidal mania shows:

First, that in some of its pure, extreme, intense manifestations, insanity is entirely crime, nothing but crime — that is, at least at the ultimate boundaries of insanity, there is crime;

Second, that insanity can produce not just behavioral disorders, but absolute crime, the crime which transgresses all the laws of nature and of society; and

Third, that even though this insanity may be extraordinarily intense, it remains invisible until it explodes; that for this reason no one can forecast it, unless he has considerable experience and a trained eye. In short, only a specialist can spot monomania. The contradiction is more apparent than real when the alienists eventually define monomania as an illness which manifests itself only in crime while at the same time they reserve the right to know how to determine its premonitory signs, its predisposing conditions.

So, homicidal mania is the danger of insanity in its most harmful form; a maximum of consequences, a minimum of warning. The most effects and fewest signs. Homicidal mania thus necessitates the intervention of a medical eye which must take into account not only the obvious manifestations of madness but also the barely perceptible traces, appearing randomly where they are the least expected, and foretelling the worst explosions. Such an interest in the great crimes "without reason" does not, I think, indicate on the part of psychiatry a desire to take over criminality, but a desire to justify its functions: the control of the dangers hidden in human behavior. What is at stake in this great issue of homicidal mania is the function of psychiatry. It must not be forgotten that in most Western countries psychiatry was then striving to establish its right to impose upon the mentally ill a therapeutic confinement. After all, it had to be shown that madness, by its nature, and even in its most discrete manifestations, was haunted by the absolute danger, death. The functioning of modern psychiatry is linked to this kinship between madness and death, which was not scientifically established, but rather symbolically represented in the figure of homicidal mania.

However, there is another question to be asked, this time from the point of view of the judges and the judicial apparatus. Why indeed did they accept, if not the notion of monomania, at least the problems that it entailed? It will probably be said that the great majority of magistrates refused to recognize this notion which made it possible to transform a criminal into a madman whose only illness was to commit crimes. With a great deal of tenacity and, one might add, with a certain degree of good sense. They did everything they could to dismiss this notion which the doctors proposed to them and which lawyers used spontaneously to defend their clients. And yet, through this controversy about monstrous crimes, about crimes "without reason," the idea of a possible kinship between madness and delinquency became acclimatized even within the judicial institution. Why was this accomplished, and relatively easily at that? In other words, why did the penal institution, which had been able to do without medical intervention for so many centuries, which had been able to judge and condemn without the problem of madness being raised except in a few obvious cases, why did this penal institution so willingly have recourse to medical knowledge from the 1820s on? For there is no mistaking the fact that English, German, Italian, and French judges of the time quite often refused to accept the conclusions of the doctors. They rejected many of the notions which the doctors proposed to them. After all, the doctors did not take them by force. They themselves solicited — following the laws, the rules, the jurisprudence which vary from country to country — the duly formulated advice of psychiatrists, and they solicited it especially in connection with those famous crimes "without reason." Why? Was it because the new codes written and applied at the beginning of the nineteenth century took into account psychiatric expertise or gave a new emphasis to the problem of pathological irresponsibility? Not at all. Surprisingly enough these new laws hardly modified the previous situation. Most of the codes based on the Napoleonic model incorporated the old principle that the state of mental disorder is incompatible with legal responsibility and thus is immune from the usual legal consequences. Most of the codes also incorporate the traditional notions of *dementia* and *furor* used in the older legal systems. Neither the great theoreticians like Beccaria and Bentham, nor those who actually wrote up the new penal laws, tried to elaborate upon these traditional notions, nor to establish new relationships between punishment and criminal medicine, except to affirm in a very general way that penal justice must cure this illness of societies, i.e., crime. It was not "from above," by way of legal codes or theoretical principles, that psychiatric medicine penetrated the penal system. Rather, it was "from below," through the mechanics of punishment and through the interpretation given to them. Among all the new techniques for controlling and transforming individuals, punishment had become a system of procedures designed to reform lawbreakers. The terrifying example of torture or exile by banishment could no longer suffice in a society where exercise of power implied a reasoned technology applied to individuals. The forms of punishment to which all the late eighteenth-century reformers, and all the early nineteenth-century legislators rallied — that is, imprisonment, forced labor, constant surveillance, partial or total isolation, moral reform — all this implies that punishment bears on the criminal himself rather than on the crime, that is on what makes him a criminal, on his reasons, his motives, his inner will, his tendencies, his instincts. In the older systems, the horror of the punishment had to reflect the enormity of the crime; henceforth, the attempt was made to adapt the modalities of punishment to the nature of the criminal.

In these circumstances, one sees why the great unmotivated crimes posed a difficult problem for the judges. In the past, to impose a punishment for a crime one had only to find the author of the crime, and it was enough that he had no excuse and that he had not been in a state of *furor* or *dementia*. But how can one punish someone whose reasons are unknown, and who keeps silent before his judges, except to admit the facts and to agree that he had been perfectly conscious of what he was doing? What is to be done when a woman like Henriette Cornier appears in court, a woman who has killed a child whom she hardly knew, the daughter of people whom she could neither have hated nor loved, who decapitates the girl but is unable to give the slightest explanation, who does not try for a moment to hide her crime, and who had nonetheless prepared for her act, had chosen the moment, had procured a knife, had eagerly sought an opportunity to be alone for a moment with her victim? Thus, in a person who had given no sign of madness, there arises an act which is at once voluntary, conscious, and reasoned — that is, all that is necessary for a condemnation according to the terms of the law — and yet nothing, no reason, no motive, no evil tendencies, which would have made it possible to determine what should be punished in the guilty woman. It is clear that there should be a condemnation, but it is hard to understand why there should be a punishment, except of course for the external but insufficient reason of setting an example. Now that the reason for the crime had become the reason for the punishment, how could one punish if the crime was without reason? In order to punish, one needs to know the nature of the guilty person, his obduracy, the degree of his evilness, what his interests or his leanings are. But if one has nothing more than the crime on one hand and the author on the other, pure and simple judicial responsibility formally authorizes punishment, yet does not allow one to make sense of it.

One can see why these great unmotivated crimes, which the psychiatrists had good reason to emphasize, were also, but for very different reasons, such important problems for the judicial apparatus. The public prosecutors obstinately referred to the law: no *dementia*, no *furor*, no recognized evidence of derangement; on the contrary, perfectly organized acts; therefore, the law must be applied. But no matter how hard they tried, they could not avoid the question of motivation, for they knew very well that from now on, in practice, the judges would link punishment, at least in part, to the determination of motives. Perhaps Henriette Cornier had been the mistress of the girl's father, and sought revenge; perhaps, having had to abandon her own children, she was jealous of the happy family living near her. All the indictments prove that in order for the punitive mechanism to work, the reality of an offense and a person to whom it can be attributed are not sufficient; the motive must also be established, that is, a psychologically intelligible link between the act and the author. The Selestat case, in which a cannibalistic woman was executed because she *could* have been hungry, seems to me to be very significant.

The doctors who were normally called in only to certify cases of *dementia* or of *furor* began now to be called upon as "specialists in motivation"; they had to evaluate not only the subject's reason but also the rationality of the act, the whole system of relationships which link the act to the interests, the plans, the character, the inclinations, and the habits of the subject. And even though the judges were often reluctant to accept the diagnosis of monomania so relished by the doctors, they were obliged to entertain willingly the set of problems raised by the notion: that is, in slightly more modern terms, the integration of the act into the global behavior of the subject. The more clearly visible this integration, the more clearly punishable the subject. The less obvious the integration, the more it seems as if the act has erupted in the subject, like a sudden and irrepressible mechanism, and the less punishable the responsible party appears. And justice will then agree that it cannot proceed with the case since the subject is insane, and will commit him to psychiatric confinement.

Several conclusions can be drawn from this:

First, the intervention of psychiatric medicine in the penal system starting in the 19th century is neither the consequence nor the simple development of the traditional theory of the irresponsibility of those suffering from *dementia* or *furor*.

Second, it is due to the regulating of two phenomena arising necessarily, one from the functioning of medicine as a public hygiene, the other from the functioning of legal punishment as a technique for transforming the individual.

Third, these two new demands are both bound up with the transformation of the mechanism of power through which the control of the social body has been attempted in industrial societies since the eighteenth century. But in spite of their common origin, the reasons for the intervention of medicine in the criminal field and the reasons for the recourse of penal justice to psychiatry are essentially different.

Fourth, the monstrous crime, both anti-natural and irrational, is the meeting point of the medical demonstration that insanity is ultimately always dangerous, and of the court's inability to determine the punishment of a crime without having determined the motives for the crime. The bizarre symptomatology of homicidal mania was designed at the point of convergence of these two mechanisms.

Fifth, in this way, the theme of the dangerous man is inscribed in the institutions of psychiatry as well as of justice. Increasingly in the nineteenth and twentieth century, penal practice and then penal theory will tend to make of the dangerous individual the principal target of punitive intervention. Increasingly, nineteenth-century psychiatry will also tend to seek out pathological stigmata which may mark dangerous individuals: moral insanity, instinctive insanity, and degeneration. This theme of the dangerous individual will give rise on the one hand to the anthropology of criminal man as in the Italian school, and on the other to the theory of social defense first represented by the Belgian school.

Sixth, another important consequence is that there will be a considerable transformation of the old notion of penal responsibility. This notion, at least in certain respects, was still close to civil law. It was necessary, for instance, in order to impute a violation to someone, that he be free, conscious, unafflicted by *dementia*, untouched by any crisis of *furor*. Now responsibility would no longer be limited only to this form of consciousness but to the intelligibility of the act with reference to the conduct, the character, the antecedents of the individual. The more psychologically determined an act is found to be, the more its author can be considered legally responsible. The more the act is, so to speak, gratuitous and undetermined, the more it will tend to be excused. A paradox, then: the legal freedom of a subject is proven by the fact that his act is seen to be necessary, determined; his lack of responsibility proven by the fact that his act is seen to be unnecessary. With this untenable paradox of monomania and of the monstrous act, psychiatry and penal justice entered a phase of uncertainty from which we have yet to emerge; the play between penal responsibility and psychological determinism has become the cross of legal and medical thought.

I would now like to turn to another moment which was particularly fertile for the relationship between psychiatry and penal law: the last years of the nineteenth century and the first few of the twentieth from the first congress on Criminal Anthropology (1885) to Prinz's publication of his *Social Defence* (1910).

Between the period which I was recalling previously and the one I would like to speak about now, what happened? First of all, within the discipline of psychiatry in the strict sense of the term, the notion of monomania was abandoned, not without some hesitations and reversions, shortly before 1870. Abandoned for two reasons: first because the essentially negative idea of a partial insanity, bearing on only one point and unleashed only at certain moments, was gradually replaced by the idea that a mental illness is not necessarily an affliction of thought or of consciousness, but that it may attack the emotions, the instincts, spontaneous behavior, leaving the forms of thought virtually intact. (What was called moral insanity, instinctive insanity, aberration of the instincts, and finally perversion, corresponds to this elaboration, whose favored example since about the 1840s has been the deviations in sexual conduct.) But there was another reason for abandoning monomania; that is, the idea of mental illness, whose evolution is complex and polymorphous, and which may present one particular symptom or another at one stage or another of their development, not only at the level of the individual but also at the level of several generations; in short, the idea of degeneration.

Because of the fact that these great evolutive ramifications can be defined, it is no longer necessary to make a distinction between the great monstrous and mysterious crimes which could be ascribed to the incomprehensible violence of *insanity* and minor delinquency, which is too frequent, too familiar to necessitate a recourse to the pathological. From then on, whether one had to deal with incomprehensible massacres or minor offenses (having to do with property or sexuality), in every case one might suspect a more or less serious perturbation of instincts or the stages in an uninterruped process. Thus there appear in the field of legal psychiatry new categories, such as necrophilia around 1840, kleptomania around 1860, exhibitionism in 1876, and also legal psychiatry's annexation of behavior like pederasty and sadism. There now exists, at least in principle, a psychiatric and criminological continuum which permits one to pose questions in medical terms at any level of the penal scale. The psychiatric question is no longer confined to some great crimes; even if it must receive a negative answer, it is to be posed across the whole range of infractions.

Now this has important consequences for the legal theory of responsibility. In the conception of monomania, suspicions of pathology were aroused precisely when there was no reason for an act; insanity was seen as the cause of that which made no sense, and legal non-responsibility was established in view of this inconsistency. But from this new analysis of instinct and emotions, it will be possible to provide a causal analysis for all kinds of conduct, whether delinquent or not, and whatever their degree of criminality. Hence the infinite labyrinth in which the legal and psychiatric problem of crime found itself. If an act is determined by a causal nexus, can it be considered to be free? Does it not imply responsibility? And is it necessary, in order to be able to condemn someone, that it be impossible to reconstruct the causal intelligibility of his act?

Now, as background for this new way of posing the problem, I must mention several transformations which were, at least in part, the conditions of its being possible. First the intensive development of the police network, which led to a new mapping and closer surveillance of urban space and also to a much more systematic and efficient prosecution of minor delinquency. It must be added that social conflicts, class struggles and political confrontations, armed revolts — from the machine-smashers of the beginning of the century to the anarchists of the last few years of the century, including the violent strikes, the revolutions of 1848 and the Commune of 1870 — prompted those in power to treat political misdemeanors in the same way as ordinary crimes in order to discredit them. Little by little an image was built up of an enemy of society who can equally well be a revolutionary or a murderer, since after all revolutionaries do sometimes kill. Corresponding to this, throughout the whole second half of the century there developed a "literature of criminality," and I use the word in its largest sense, including miscellaneous news items (and, even more, popular newspapers) as well as detective novels and all the romanticized writings which developed around crime — the transformation of the criminal into a hero, perhaps, but, equally, the affirmation that ever-present criminality is a constant menace to the social body as a whole. The collective fear of crime, the obsession with this danger which seems to be an inseparable part of society itself, are thus perpetually inscribed in each individual consciousness.

Referring to the 9,000 murders then recorded annually in Europe, not counting Russia, Garofalo said in the Preface to the first edition of his *Criminology* (1887): "Who is the enemy who has devastated this land? It is a mysterious enemy, unknown to history; his name is: the criminal."

To this must be added another element: the continuing failure of the penitentiary system, which is very frequently reported. It was the dream of the eighteenth-century reformers, then of the philanthropists of the following period, that incarceration, provided that it be rationally directed, might serve as a true penal therapy. The result was meant to be the reform of the prisoners. It soon became clear that prison had exactly the opposite result, that it was on the whole a school for delinquency and that the more refined methods of the police system and the legal apparatus, far from insuring better protection against crime, brought about a strengthening of the criminal milieu, through the medium of prison itself.

For all sorts of reasons, a situation existed such that there was a very strong social and political demand for a reaction to, and for repression of, crime. This demand had to do with a criminality which in its totality had to be thought of in judicial and medical terms, and yet, the key notion of the penal institution since the Middle Ages, that is, legal responsibility, seems utterly inadequate for the conceptualization of this broad and dense domain of medico-legal criminality.

This inadequacy became apparent, both at the conceptual and at the institutional level, in the conflict between the so-called school of Criminal Anthropology and the Internation Association of Penal Law around the 1890s. In attempting to cope with the traditional principles of criminal legislation, the Italian School (the Criminal Anthropologists) called for nothing less than a putting aside of legality — a true "depenalization" of crime, by setting up an apparatus of an entirely different type from the one provided for by the Codes.

For the Criminal Anthropologists this meant totally abandoning the judicial notion of responsibility, and posing as the fundamental question not the degree of freedom of the individual, but the level of danger he represents for society. Moreover, it meant noting that the accused whom the law recognized as not responsible because he was ill, insane, a victim of irresistible impulsed, was precisely the most seriously and immediately dangerous. The Criminal Anthropologists emphasized that what is called "penalty" does not have to be a punishment, but rather a mechanism for the defense of society, and therefore noted that the relevant difference is not between legally responsible subjects to be found guilty, and legally irresponsible subjects to be released, but between absolutely and definitively dangerous subjects and those who can cease to be dangerous provided they receive certain treatment. They concluded that there should be three main types of social reaction to crime or rather to the danger represented by the criminal: definitive elimination (by death or by incarceration in an institution) temporary elimination (with treatment), and more or less relative and partial elimination (sterilization and castration).

One can see the series of shifts required by the anthropological school: from the crime to the criminal; from the act as it was actually committed to the danger potentially inherent in the individual; from the modulated punishment of the guilty party to the absolute protection of others. All these shifts implied quite clearly an escape from a universe of penal law revolving around the act, its imputability to a *de jure* subject, the legal responsibility of the latter and a punishment proportionate to the gravity of this act as defined by law. Neither the "criminality" of an individual, nor the index of his dangerousness, nor his potential or future behavior, nor the protection of society at large from these possible perils, none of these are, nor can they be, juridical notions in the classical sense of the term. They can be made to function in a rational way only within a technical knowledge-system, a knowledge-system capable of characterizing a criminal individual in himself and in a sense beneath his acts; a knowledge-system able to measure the index of danger present in an individual; a knowledge-system which might establish the protection necessary in the face of such a danger. Hence the idea that crime ought to be the responsibility not of judges but of experts in psychiatry, criminology, psychology, etc. Actually, that extreme conclusion was not often formulated in such an explicit and radical way, no doubt through practical prudence. But it followed implicitly from all the theses of Criminal Anthropology. And at the second meeting of this Association (1889), Pugliese expressed it straightforwardly. We must, he said, turn around the old adage: the judge is the expert of experts; it is rather up to the expert to be the judge of judges. "The commission of medical experts to whom the judgment ought to be referred should not limit itself to expressing its wishes; on the contrary it should render a real decision."

It can be said that a point of break-down was being reached. Criminology, which had developed out of the old notion of monomania, maintaining a frequently story relationship with penal law, was in danger of being excluded from it as excessively radical. This would have led to a situation similar to the original one; a technical knowledge-system incompatible with law, besieging it from without and unable to make itself heard. As the notion of monomania could be used to overlay with madness a crime with no apparent reasons, so, to some extent, the notion of degeneration made it possible to link the most insignificant of criminals to a peril of pathological dimensions for society, and, eventually, for the whole human species. The whole field of infractions could be held together in terms of danger and thus of protection to be provided. The law had only to hold its tongue. Or to plug its ears and refuse to listen.

It is usual to say that the fundamental propositions of criminal anthropology were fairly rapidly disqualified for a number of reasons: because they were linked to a form of scientism, to a certain positivist naïveté which the very development of the sciences in the twentieth century has taken upon itself to cure; because they were related to historical and social evolutionism which was itself quickly discredited; because they found support in a neuropsychiatric theory of degeneration which both neurology and psychoanalysis have quickly dismantled; and because they were unable to become operational within the format of penal legislation and within legal practice. The age of criminal anthropology, with its radical naïvetés, seems to have disappeared with the 19th century; and a much more subtle psycho-sociology of delinquency, much more acceptable to penal law, seems to have taken up the fight.

It seems to me that, at least in its general outlines, criminal anthropology has not disappeared as completely as some people say, and that a number of its most fundamental theses, often those most foreign to traditional law, have gradually taken root in penal thought and practice. But this could not have happened solely by virtue of the truth of this psychiatric theory of crime, or rather solely through its persuasive force. In fact there had been a significant mutation within the law. When I say "within the law," I probably say too much, for, with a few exceptions (such as the Norwegian code, but after all it was written for a new state) and aside from some projects left in limbo (such as the Swiss plan for a penal code), penal legislation remained pretty well unchanged. The laws relating to suspension of sentence, recidivism, or relegation were the principal modifications somewhat hesitantly made in French legislation. This is not where I see the significant mutations, but rather in connection with an element at the same time theoretical and essential, namely the notion of responsibility. And it was possible to modify this notion not so much because of the pressure of some internal shock but mainly because a considerable evolution had taken place in the area of civil law during the same period. My hypothesis would be that it was civil law, not criminology, which made it possible for penal thought to change on two or three major points. It was civil law which made it possible to graft onto criminal law the essential elements of the criminological theses of the period. It may well be that without the reformulation which occurred first in civil law, the jurists would have turned a deaf ear to the fundamental propositions of criminal anthropology, or at least would never have possessed the proper tool for integrating them into the legal system. In a way which may at first seem strange, it was civil law which made possible the articulation of the legal code and of science in penal law.

This transformation in civil law revolves around the notion of accident and legal responsibility. In a very general way, it is worth emphasizing the significance which the problem of accidents had, not only for law but also for economics and politics, especially in the second half of the nineteenth century. One could object that since the sixteenth century, insurance plans had shown how important the idea of risk had already become. But on the one hand, insurance dealt only with more-or-less individual risks and on the other, it entirely excluded the legal responsibility of the interested party. In the nineteenth century, the development of wage-earning, of industrial techniques, of mechanization, of transportation, of urban structures, brought with it two important things. First, risks were incurred by third parties (the employer exposed his employees to work-related accidents; transport companies exposed not only their passengers to accidents but also people who just happened to be there). Then, the fact that these accidents could often be linked to a sort of error — but a minor error (inattention, lack of precaution, negligence) committed moreover by someone who could not carry the civil responsibility for it nor pay the ensuing damages. The problem was to establish in law the concept of no-fault responsibility. It was the effort of Western civil legislators and especially German jurists, influenced as they were by the demands of Bismarckian society — a society characterized not only by discipline but also by security-consciousness. In this search for a no-fault responsibility, the civil legislators emphasized a certain number of important principles:

First, this responsibility must be established not according to the series of errors committed but according to the chain of causes and effects. Responsibility is on the side of cause, rather than on the side of fault. This is what German jurists meant by *Causahaftung*.

Second, these causes are of two orders which are not mutually exclusive: the chain of precise and individual facts, each of which has been induced by the preceding one; and the creation of risks inherent in a type of action, of equipment, of enterprise.

Third, granted, these risks are to be reduced in the most systematic and rigorous way possible. But they will certainly never be made to disappear; none of the characteristic undertakings of modern society will be without risk. As Saleilles said, "a causal relationship linked to a purely material fact which in itself appears as an adventurous fact, not in itself irregular, nor contrary to the customs of modern life, but contemptuous of that extreme caution which paralyzes action, in harmony with the activity which is imperative today and therefore defying hatreds and accepting risks, that is the law of life today, that is the common rule, and law is made to reflect this contemporary conception of the soul, in the course of its successive evolution."

Fourth, since this no-fault liability is linked to a risk which can never entirely be eliminated, indemnity is not meant to sanction it as a sort of punishment, but to repair its effects and also to tend, in an asymptotic way, towards an eventual reduction of its risks. By eliminating the element of fault within the system of liability, the civil legislators introduced into law the notion of causal probability and risk, and they brought forward the idea of a sanction whose function would be to defend, to protect, to exert pressure on inevitable risks.

In a rather strange way, this depenalization of civil liability would constitute a model for penal law, on the basis of the fundamental propositions formulated by criminal anthropology. After all, what is a "born criminal" or a degenerate, or a criminal personality, if not someone who, according to a causal chain which is difficult to restore, carries a particularly high index of criminal probability, and is in himself a criminal risk? Well, just as one can determine civil liability without establishing fault, but solely by estimating the risk created and against which it is necessary to build up a defense (although it can never be eliminated), in the same way, one can render an individual responsible under law without having to determine whether he was acting freely and therefore whether there was fault, but rather by linking the act committed to the risk of criminality which his very personality constitutes. He is responsible since by his very existence he is a creator of risk, even if he is not at fault, since he has not of his own free will chosen evil rather than good. The purpose of the sanction will therefore not be to punish a legal subject who has voluntarily broken the law; its role will be to reduce as much as possible — either by elimination, or by exclusion or by various restrictions, or by therapeutic measures — the risk of criminality represented by the individual in question.

The general idea of the *Social Defence* as it was put forward by Prinz at the beginning of the twentieth century was developed by transferring to criminal justice formulations proper to the new civil law. The history of the conferences on Criminal Anthropology and conferences on penal law at the turn of the century, the chronical of the conflicts between positivist scholars and traditional jurists, and the sudden *détente* which occurred at the time of Liszt, of Saleilles, of Prinz, the rapid eclipse of the Italian School after that, but also the reduction of the jurists' resistance to the psychological approach to the criminal, the establishment of a relative consensus around a criminology which would be accessible to the law, and of a system of sanctions which would take into account criminological knowledge — all of these seem indeed to indicate that at that moment the required "shunting switch" had just been found. This "switch" is the key notion of *risk* which the law assimilates through the idea of a no-fault liability, and which anthropology, or psychology, or psychiatry can assimilate through the idea of imputability without freedom. The term, henceforth central, of "dangerous being," was probably introduced by Prinz at the September 1905 session of the International Union of Penal Law.

I will not list here the innumerable legal codes, rules, and memoranda which carried into effect, in one way or another, this notion of the *dangerous state* of an individual in penal institutions throughout the world. Let me simply underline a couple of things.

First, since the great crimes without reason of the early 19th century, the debate did not in fact revolve so much around freedom, even though the question was always there. The real problem, the one which was in effect throughout, was the problem of the dangerous individual. Are there individuals who are intrinsically dangerous? By what signs can they be recognized, and how can one react to their presence? In the course of the past century, penal law did not evolve from an ethic of freedom to a science of psychic determinism; rather, it enlarged, organized, and codified the suspicion and the locating of dangerous individuals, from the rare and monstrous figure of the monomaniac to the common everyday figure of the degenerate, of the pervert, of the constitutionally unbalanced, of the immature, etc.

It must also be noted that this transformation took place not only from medicine towards law, as though the pressure of rational knowledge on older prescriptive systems; but that it also operated through a perpetual mechanism of summoning and of interacting between medical or psychological knowledge and the judicial institution. It was not the latter which yielded. A set of objects and of concepts was born at their boundaries and from their interchanges.

This is the point which I would like to stress, for it seems that most of the notions thus formed are operational for legal medicine or for psychiatric expertise in criminal matters. But has not something more been introduced into the law than the uncertainties of a problematic knowledge — to wit, the rudiments of another type of law? For the modern system of sanctions — most strikingly since Beccaria — gives society a claim to individuals only because of what they do. Only an act, defined by law as an infraction, can result in a sanction, modifiable of course according to the circumstances or the intentions. But by bringing increasingly to the fore not only the criminal as author of the act, but also the dangerous individual as potential source of acts, does one not give society rights over the individual based on what he is? No longer, of course, based on what he is by statute (as was the case in the societies under the Ancien Régime), but based on what he is by nature, according to his constitution, character traits, or his pathological variables. A form of justice which tends to be applied to what one is, this is what is so outrageous when one thinks of the penal law of which the eighteenth-century reformers had dreamed, and which was intended to sanction, in a completely egalitarian way, offenses explicitly defined beforehand by the law.

It could be objected that in spite of this general principle, even in the nineteenth century the right to punish was applied and varied on the basis not only of what men do, but also of what they are, or of what it is supposed that they are. Hardly had the great modern codes been established when attempts were made to mitigate them by legislation such as the laws dealing with extenuating circumstances, with recidivism, and with conditional release. It was a matter of taking into account the author behind the acts that had been committed. And a complete and comparative study of the legal decisions would no doubt easily show that on the penal stage the offenders were at least as present as their offenses. A form of justice which would be applied only to what one does is probably purely utopian and not necessarily desirable. But since the eighteenth century at least, it has constituted the guiding principle, the juridico-moral principle which governs the modern system of sanctions. There was therefore no question, there can still be no question, of suddenly putting it aside. Only insidiously, slowly, and as it were from below and fragmentally, has a system of sanctions based on what one *is* been taking shape. It has taken nearly one hundred years for the notion of "dangerous individual," which was potentially present in the monomania of the first alienists, to be accepted in judicial thought. After one hundred years, although this notion may have become a central theme in psychiatric expertise (in France psychiatrists appointed as experts speak about the dangerousness of an individudal much more than about his responsibility), the law and the codes seem reluctant to give it a place. The revision of the penal code presently underway in France has just barely succeeded in replacing the older notion of *dementia* (which made the author of an act not responsible), with the notions of discernment and control which are in effect only another version of the same thing, hardly modernized at all. Perhaps this indicates a foreboding of the dreadful dangers inherent in authorizing the law to intervene against individuals because of what they are; a horrifying society could emerge from that.

Nonetheless, on the functional level, judges more and more need to believe that they are judging a man as he is and according to what he is. The scene which I described at the beginning bears witness to this. When a man comes before his judges with nothing but his crimes, when he has nothing else to say but "this is what I have done," when he has nothing to say about himself, when he does not do the tribunal the favor of confiding to them something like the secret of his own being, then the judicial machine ceases to function.

9

Practicing Criticism

Conducted by Didier Eribon for the French
newspaper Libération this interview, granted
shortly after the 1981 election of Socialist President
François Mitterrand, uncovers the Foucauldian
imperative to place thought before the "sacrilization
of the social." To practice criticism demands not
only a liberation of thought, but also an intellectual
activity that makes conflicts visible through the
action of theory. If transformation is to be
achieved, it can only be realized in a permanent
state of criticism. This interview was published
under the title "Is it really important to think?" on
May 30–31, 1981. The translation is by Alan
Sheridan.

D.E.   On election night we asked you for your first
reactions. You didn't want to make any comment. But now
you feel more at ease to speak . . .

FOUCAULT   Indeed, I consider that voting in itself is a
form of action. It is then up to the government to act in its
turn. Now the time has certainly come to react to what is
beginning to be done. Anyway, I believe people are grown up
enough to make up their own minds when they vote and then
to celebrate if they feel so inclined. Indeed it seems to me that
they managed very well.

D.E.   What, then, are your reactions today?

FOUCAULT   I'm struck by three things. Over the last
twenty years at least, a series of questions have been raised
within society itself. And for a long time these questions have
not had a place in "serious" institutional politics.

The socialists seem to have been the only ones to grasp
the reality of those problems and to react to them — which

probably has something to do with their victory.

Secondly, in relation to these problems (I am thinking above all of the administration of justice or the question of the immigrants), the first steps or the first declarations have been absolutely at one with what one might call a "left-wing logic" — the logic for which Mitterrand was elected.

Thirdly, which is more remarkable, the measures taken do not conform to majority opinion. Neither on the death penalty, nor on the question of the immigrants have the declared choices of the government followed majority public opinion.

This gives the lie to all that has been said about the pointlessness of these questions that had been debated over the past ten or fifteen years; all that has been said about the non-existence of a left-wing logic in the way a government is run; all that has been said about how, in the first measures to be taken by the new government, it had given into popular feeling. On nuclear weapons, the immigrants, and the law, the government has anchored its decision in problems that really have been seen in reference to a logic that went against majority opinion. And I'm sure the majority approves this way of proceeding, if not the measures themselves. In saying this, I'm not saying that things have been done and now we can sit back. Those first steps are not a charter, but nevertheless they are more than symbolic gestures.

Compare them with what Giscard did immediately after his election: a handshake to the prisoners. It was a purely symbolic gesture addressed to an electorate that was not his. Today we have the first set of effective measures that may run counter to the feelings of a part of the electorate, but which mark the style of government.

D.E. Indeed it does seem that a quite new way of governing is being established.

FOUCAULT Yes, that's an important point and one that may have appeared for the first time with Mitterrand's electoral victory. It seems to me that this election has been felt by many people as a sort of victory, a modification in the relationship between those who govern and the governed. Not that the governed have taken the place of those who govern. After all, what has happened is a shift within the political class. We are entering into a government by party, with all the dangers that this involves, and we should never forget that.

But the question that is raised by this change is whether it is possible to establish between those who govern and the governed a relationship that is not one of obedience, but one in which work will play an important role.

D.E.   You mean it will be possible to work with this government?

FOUCAULT   We must escape from the dilemma of being either for or against. After all, it is possible to face up to a government and remain standing. To work with a government implies neither subjection nor total acceptance. One may work with it and yet be restive. I even believe that the two things go together.

D.E.   After Michel Foucault the critic, are we now going to see Michel Foucault the reformist? After all, the reproach was often made that the criticism made by intellectuals leads to nothing.

FOUCAULT   First I'll answer the point about "that leads to nothing." There are hundreds and thousands of people who have worked for the emergence of a number of problems that are now on the agenda. To say that this work produced nothing is quite wrong. Do you think that twenty years ago people were considering the problems of the relationship between mental illness and psychological normality, the problem of prison, the problem of medical power, the problem of the relationship between the sexes, and so on, as they are doing today?

Furthermore, there are no reforms as such. Reforms are not produced in the air, independently of those who carry them out. One cannot not take account of those who will have the job of carrying out this transformation.

And, then, above all, I believe that an opposition can be made between critique and transformation, "ideal" critique and "real" transformation.

A critique is not a matter of saying that things are not right as they are. It is a matter of pointing out on what kinds of assumptions, what kinds of familiar, unchallenged, unconsidered modes of thought the practices that we accept rest.

We must free ourselves from the sacrilization of the social

as the only reality and stop regarding as superfluous something so essential in human life and in human relations as thought. Thought exists independently of systems and structures of discourse. It is something that is often hidden, but which always animates everyday behavior. There is always a little thought even in the most stupid institutions; there is always thought even in silent habits.

Criticism is a matter of flushing out that thought and trying to change it: to show that things are not as self-evident as one believed, to see that what is accepted as self-evident will no longer be accepted as such. Practicing criticism is a matter of making facile gestures difficult.

In these circumstances, criticism (and radical criticism) is absolutely indispensable for any transformation. A transformation that remains within the same mode of thought, a transformation that is only a way of adjusting the same thought more closely to the reality of things can merely be a superficial transformation.

On the other hand, as soon as one can no longer think things as one formerly thought them, transformation becomes both very urgent, very difficult, and quite possible.

It is not therefore a question of there being a time for criticism and a time for transformation, nor people who do the criticism and others who do the transforming, those who are enclosed in an inaccessible radicalism and those who are forced to make the necessary concessions to reality. In fact I think the work of deep transformation can only be carried out in a free atmosphere, one constantly agitated by a permanent criticism.

D.E.   But do you think the intellectual must have a programmatic role in this transformation?

FOUCAULT   A reform is never only the result of a process in which there is conflict, confrontation, struggle, resistance . . .

To say to oneself at the outset: what reform will I be able to carry out? That is not, I believe, an aim for the intellectual to pursue. His role, since he works specifically in the realm of thought, is to see how far the liberation of thought can make those transformations urgent enough for people to want to carry them out and difficult enough to carry out for them to be profoundly rooted in reality.

It is a question of making conflicts more visible, of making them more essential than mere confrontations of interests or mere institutional immobility. Out of these conflicts, these confrontations, a new power relation must emerge, whose first, temporary expression will be a reform. If at the base there has not been the work of thought upon itself and if, in fact, modes of thought, that is to say modes of action, have not been altered, whatever the project for reform, we know that it will be swamped, digested by modes of behavior and institutions that will always be the same.

D.E. After taking part in a number of movements, you have somewhat withdrawn lately. Are you now going to participate in such movements once again?

FOUCAULT Whenever I have tried to carry out a piece of theoretical work, it has been on the basis of my own experience, always in relation to processes I saw taking place around me. It is because I thought I could recognize in the things I saw, in the institutions with which I dealt, in my relations with others, cracks, silent shocks, malfunctionings . . . that I undertook a particular piece of work, a few fragments of autobiography.

I'm not an activist who has retired from the fray and who would now like to return to service. My mode of work hasn't changed much; but what I do expect from it is that it will continue to change me more.

D.E. People say you are fairly pessimistic. Hearing you, I would say instead you were rather optimistic.

FOUCAULT There's an optimism that consists in saying that things couldn't be better. My optimism would consist rather in saying that so many things can be changed, fragile as they are, bound up more with circumstances than necessities, more arbitrary than self-evident, more a matter of complex, but temporary, historical circumstances than with inevitable anthropological constants . . . You know, to say that we are much more recent than we think isn't a way of taking the whole weight of history on our shoulders. It's rather to place at the disposal of the work that we can do on ourselves the greatest possible share of what is presented to us as inaccessible.

The Politics of
Contemporary Life

10

Social Security

In this interview Michel Foucault discusses the "perverse effects" of the social security system in France. He describes this phenomenon as producing both an attack on autonomy and institutional dependency through either integration or marginalization. Foucault speaks here about the issue of the right to "health" and the regulatory criteria used to establish the norm from which this "rational" economy of protection is carried out. In this context Foucault examines the meaning of the word "subjected" in the discourse of social security. The problem raised by this system is the value of life and the ways in which one confronts an infinite demand. This interview was conducted by Robert Bono; it was published under the title "A Finite Security System Confronting an Infinite Demand" as an appendix to the collective work (with the CFDT) Sécurité sociale: l'enjeu (Paris: Syros, 1983). The translation is by Alan Sheridan.

R.B.   Traditionally, social security guarantees individuals against a number of risks resulting from illness, family organization, and old age. Obviously, this is a function that it must continue to exercise.

But between 1946 and our own day, things have changed. New needs have appeared. We see a growing aspiration on the part of individuals and groups for autonomy — there is the aspiration of children in relation to their parents, women in relation to men, the sick in relation to the medical profession, the handicapped in relation to institutions of all kinds. The has also emerged the need to check various forms of marginalization caused very largely by unemployment, but also, in certain cases, by the inadequacies of our social security machinery.

It seems to us that these two needs at least ought to be taken into account by the forthcoming meetings of the management committees within the social security service, so that this service will be given newly defined roles capable of leading to a revision of its benefit system. Does it seem to you that these needs really do exist in our society? Would you suggest others? And how, in your opinion, can social security help us respond to them?

FOUCAULT   I think we have to stress three things at the outset.

Firstly, our system of social guarantees, as it was implemented in 1946, is now coming up against economic obstacles that are only too familiar.

Secondly, this system, worked out in the period between the two wars — that is to say, at a time when one of the aims was to reduce if not to overcome a number of social conflicts, and when a conceptual model was used that was still impregnated by a certain rationality produced at the time of the First World War — this system is now reaching its limits, as it comes up against the political, economic, and social rationality of modern societies.

Lastly, social security, whatever its positive effects, has also had "perverse effects": an increasing rigidity of certain mechanisms and a growth in dependence. One notes the following fact, which is inherent in the functional mechanisms of the machinery: on the one hand, more security is being given to people and, on the other, they are being made increasingly dependent. But what one ought to be able to expect from security is that it gives each individual autonomy in relation to the dangers and situations likely to lower his status or subject him.

R.B.   If indeed people seem disposed to abdicate a little of their freedom and autonomy providing their security is extended and strengthened, how are we to reconcile this "infernal couple": security-dependence?

FOUCAULT   This is a problem in which the terms are negotiable. What we must try to appreciate is people's capacity for assuming such a negotiation and the level of compromise of which they are capable. People look at things differently now. In the 1930s and just after the War, the problem of security was of such acuteness and of such immediacy that the question of dependence hardly came into it. From the 1950s onwards, however, and still more from the 1960s onwards, the notion of security has begun to be associated with the question of independence. This development has been an extremely important cultural, political, and social phenomenon. One cannot now not take it into account.

There is a certain anti-security view current today that opposes in a rather simplistic way and regards as dangerous claims derived from the "Security and Liberty" law. We should be fairly prudent about that.

But there certainly does exist a positive demand: that for a security that opens the way to richer, more numerous, more diverse, and more flexible relations with oneself and with one's environment, while guaranteeing to each individual a real autonomy. This is a new fact that ought to be taken into account in discussions on social protection.

That is how, in a very schematic way, I would situate this question of the demand for autonomy.

R.B. The negotiation you mentioned can only be carried out on a watershed: on the one hand, we are aware that certain rigidities in our social security machinery, combined with its centralist character, threaten the autonomy of groups and individuals by keeping them in an administrative straightjacket which (if the Swedish experience is to be believed) becomes ultimately unbearable; but, on the other hand, the form of liberalism described by Jules Guesde, when he spoke of "free foxes in free henhouses" is hardly more attractive — one has only to look at the United States to be convinced of this . . . [1]

FOUCAULT It's precisely the difficulty of striking a compromise on this watershed that makes as subtle an analysis as possible of the present situation necessary. By "present situation" I don't mean the totality of economic and social

1.   Jules Guesde, real name Mathieu Basile (1845–1922). French Socialist. Known for his defense of the Paris Commune (1871) and rejection of all compromise with capitalist government which caused a split amongst socialists [L.D.K.].

mechanisms, which others can describe better than I: I'm speaking rather of the kind of interface between, on the one hand, people's feelings, their moral choices, their relationship with themselves, and, on the other hand, the institutions that surround them. It is here that malfunctionings, malaise, and, perhaps, crises are born.

Considering what might be called the "negative effects" of the system, it seems to me that we should distinguish between two tendencies: an effect of dependency *by integration* and an effect of dependency *by marginalization or exclusion*. We have to combat both.

I believe that there is a need to resist the phenomenon of integration. A whole machinery of social coverage in fact, fully benefits the individual only if that individual is *integrated*, whether in terms of family, work place, or geographical area.

R.B.   That isn't so much the case now: certain arrangements have been reconsidered, from this point of view, especially in the case of family allowances, so that they now concern the whole population, without reference to professional and familial criteria. In the areas of health and pensions, we are also seeing the beginnings of a readjustment. The principle of integration, though still with us, has lost its preeminence.

On the other hand, where the movements of marginalization are concerned, the problem has not been tackled at all.

FOUCAULT   It is true that some pressures towards integration may have been relaxed. I mentioned them at the same time as the phenomenon of marginalization because I wonder whether we ought not to try to grasp the two together. We can probably do something to correct the effects of dependence through integration, just as we could probably correct a number of things concerning marginalization. But is making a few partial corrections, smoothing out a few corners enough? Would that satisfy our needs? Ought we not rather to be trying to think out a whole system of social coverage that takes into account this demand for autonomy, so that these effects of dependence will disappear almost entirely?

R.B.   Doesn't this question of integration also arise in relations between the individual and the state?

FOUCAULT   We are witnessing, in this respect, an important phenomenon: up until what we call "the crisis" [the economic recession] and, more specifically, up until the obstacles that we are now encountering, it seems to me that the individual hardly gave a thought to the question of his relationship with the state in so far as that relation, taking into account the way the great centralizing institutions function, was made up of an "input" (his contributions) and an "output" (the allowances he received). The effects of dependence were perceived rather at the level of the people around him.

Nowadays we have to confront a problem of limits. What is in question is not equal access by all to security, but the infinite access of each individual to a number of possible allowances. We say to people: "You can't go on consuming indefinitely." And when the authorities declare "You no longer have a right to that," or "You will no longer be covered for such operations," or "You have to pay a proportion of the hospital costs," and even "It wouldn't be any use extending your life by three months, so we're going to let you die," then the individual wonders about the nature of his relationship with the state and begins to feel his dependence on an institution whose decision-making powers he had hitherto only dimly perceived.

R.B. Isn't this problematic of dependence perpetuating the ambivalence that lay, even before any machinery of social security had been set up, at the creation of the first health institutions? Wasn't the aim of the first hospitals both to alleviate penury and to keep the poor and sick out of society's view, while making them incapable of disturbing public order?

Can we not, in the twentieth century, free ourselves of a logic that links charity and confinement and work out less alienating systems, which people might — let's use the word — "appropriate"?

FOUCAULT It's true that, in a sense, history in the long term does reveal the permanence of certain problems.

Having said that, I am very mistrustful of two intellectual attitudes whose persistence during the last decade one may deplore. The first consists of presupposing the repetition and extension of the same mechanisms through the history of our societies. Sometimes it seems as if a sort of cancer will envelope the whole social body. It's an unacceptable theory. The way in which certain categories of the population were confined in the seventeenth century, to take this example, is very different from the hospitalization practiced in the nineteenth century, and still more so from the machinery of security we have at the present time.

Another attitude, which is just as frequent, consists in maintaining the fiction of the "good old days," when the social body was alive and warm, families united and individuals autonomous. Those happy times were supposed to have come to an end with the advent of capitalism, the bourgeoisie, and industrial society. This is, of course, a historical absurdity.

The continuist reading of history and the nostalgic reference to a golden age of social life still haunt many minds, and a number of political and sociological analyses are marked by them. They must be rooted out.

R.B.   Having said that, perhaps we should return to the question of marginality . . . It seems that our society is divided into a "protected" sector and a sector exposed to precariousness. Although social security alone cannot remedy this situation, nevertheless a system of social protection can help to reduce marginalization and segregation by taking adequate measures on behalf of the handicapped, immigrants, and all categories subjected to a precarious status. That, at any rate, is how I see it. Do you?

FOUCAULT   It can probably be said that certain phenomena of marginalization are bound up with factors of separation between an "assured" population and an "exposed" population. Indeed this sort of cleavage was specifically predicted by a number of economists in the 1970s, who believed that the post-industrial societies would confirm it — the exposed sector necessarily having to grow considerably in relation to what it then was. However, such a "programming" of society has not often been implemented and it cannot be accepted as the sole explanation of the processes of marginalization.

In some marginalizations there are what I will call another aspect of the phenomenon of dependence. Our systems of social security impose a particular way of life to which individuals are subjected, and any person or group that, for one reason or another, will not or cannot embrace that way of life is marginalized by the very operation of the institutions.

R.B. There's a difference between marginality that has been chosen and marginality that is imposed . . .

FOUCAULT That's true, and we should delineate these two concepts in a more detailed analysis. Nevertheless, taking the situation as a whole, there are good grounds for elucidating the relations that exist between the functioning of social security and lifestyles. Over the past ten years or so, people have begun to observe these lifestyles, but it's a study that would require much further research, and yet avoid a strict "sociologism," divorced from certain ethical problems.

R.B. Our aim is to give people both security and autonomy. Perhaps we could get closer to it in two ways: first, by abandoning the absurd legal red tape that we're so fond of in France and which piles up mountains of paperwork about everybody (and thus puts the marginals in an even more unfavorable position) and try out an a posteriori legislation in such a way as to facilitate the access of all to allowances and to social facilities; and, secondly, by implementing a real decentralization, using a personnel and premises properly geared to receiving people.

What do you think of this and would you subscribe to it?

FOUCAULT Yes, of course. The aim of optimal social security combined with maximum independence is clear enough. As to attaining it . . .

I believe that such an aim requires two types of means. Firstly, we need a certain empiricism. We have to transform the field of social institutions into a vast experimental field, in such a way as to decide which taps need turning, which bolts need to be loosened here or there, to get the desired change; we certainly need to undertake a process of decentralization, for example, to bring the decision-making centers and those who depend on them closer and to bring together the decision-making processes, thus avoiding the kind of grand totalizing integration that leaves people in complete ignorance of what is involved in this or that regulation. What we have to do then is to increase the experiments wherever possible in this particularly interesting and important area of social life, bearing in mind that a whole institutional complex, at present very fragile, will probably have to undergo a restructuring from top to bottom.

Secondly — and this is a crucial point — there would be considerable work to be done in renewing the conceptual categories that dominate the way we approach all these problems of social guarantees and security. We are still bound up with an outlook that was formed between 1920 and 1940, mainly under the influence of Beveridge, a man who was born over a hundred years ago.[2]

For the moment, then, we completely lack the intellectual tools necessary to envisage in new terms the form in which we might attain what we are looking for.

R.B.   Perhaps to illustrate the obsolete outlook you were talking about, wouldn't there be some point in a linguistic study of the meaning of the word "subjected" in the language of social security?

FOUCAULT   Absolutely! And we have to ask the question how things could be so arranged that the individual would no longer be a "subject" in the sense of subjected . . .

As for the intellectual inadequacies I have just referred to, one may well wonder where such new forms of analysis, such a new outlook, might come from.

What I do know, to put things in a rather schematic way, is that in the late eighteenth century in England and in the nineteenth century in certain other European countries, parliament was such a place where new projects (tax laws and customs duties, in Great Britain, for example) could be worked out. It was there that huge campaigns, involving discussion and reflection, began. In the second half of the nineteenth century, a great many problems and projects were born in what was then a new form of association, in the unions, the political parties, and various other associations. In the first half of the twentieth century, a great deal of very important work — of a theoretical kind — was carried out in the political, economic, and social spheres by people like Keynes or Beveridge, as well as by a number of intellectuals, academics, and administrators.

2.   William Henry Beveridge (1879–1963). British economist known for his report on comprehensive unemployment insurance (1942) [L.D.K.].

But, we have to agree, the crisis that we are going through and which will soon be ten years old has given rise to nothing interesting or new in those quarters. It would seem that a sort of sterilization has taken place there: no significant invention seems to have emerged.

R.B.   Can the unions be the seed-beds for such ideas?

FOUCAULT   If it is true that the present malaise puts in question whatever may be on the side of state institutional authority, it is a fact that the answers will not come from those who administer that authority: answers ought rather to come from those who are trying to counter-balance the prerogative of the state and who constitute counter-powers. What comes from union action may possibly, indeed, open up a space for invention.

R.B.   Does this need to change mental attitudes to social security provide an opportunity for "civil society" — of which the unions are a part — in opposition to "state society"?

FOUCAULT   Although this opposition between civil society and state may quite rightly have been greatly used in the late eighteenth century and in the nineteenth century, I'm not at all sure that it is still operational. The Polish example in this respect is interesting: when one assimilates the powerful social movement that has just traversed that country to a revolt of civil society against the state, one misunderstands the complexity and multiplicity of the confrontations. It is not only against the state-party that the Solidarity movement has had to fight.

The relations between the political power, the systems of dependence that they engender, and individuals are too complex to be reduced to such a schema. In fact, the notion of an opposition between civil society and state was formulated in a given context and with a particular intention: liberal economists proposed it in the late eighteenth century with a view to limiting the state's sphere of action, civil society being conceived as the locus of an autonomous economic process. It was a quasi-polemical concept, opposed to the administrative power of the states at the time, in order to bring victory to a certain liberalism.

But there is something else that bothers me about this

notion: it's that the reference to this antagonistic couple is never exempt from a sort of Manichaeism that afflicts the notion of "state" with a pejorative connotation while idealizing "society" as a good, living, warm whole.

What I am attentive to is the fact that every human relation is to some degree a power relation. We move in a world of perpetual strategic relations. Every power relation is not bad in itself, but it is a fact that always involves danger.

Let us take the example of penal justice, which is more familiar to me than that of social security: a whole movement is at work at present in Europe and the United states in favor of an "informal justice" or certain forms of arbitration carried out by the group itself. To believe society capable, by mere internal regulation, of solving the problems that it is presented with is to have a very optimistic notion of society. In short, to get back to what we were saying, I remain fairly circumspect as regards a certain way of opposing civil society and state, and to any project for transferring to the first a power of initiative and decision that the second is seen as having annexed in order to exercise it in an authoritarian fashion: whatever scenario one takes, a power relation would be established, and the question would still remain of how to limit its effects, this relation being in itself neither good nor bad, but dangerous, so that one would have to reflect, at every level, on the way it should channel its efficacity in the best possible way.

R.B.   What we are very aware of is that social security, in its present form, is perceived as a distant institution, having a state character — even if this isn't so — because it is a huge centralized machine. Our problem, then, is the following: in order to open up participation to its users, they must be brought closer to the centers of decision. How are we to do this?

FOUCAULT   This problem is an empirical one, rather than one of an opposition between civil society and state: it's what I choose to call "decisional distance." In other words, it is a question of measuring the optimal distance between a decision made and the individual it concerns, in such a way that the individual has a say in what is done and in such a way that this decision is intelligible to him, while at the same time being geared to his situation, without having to go through an inextricable maze of regulations.

R.B.   These questions raise another, directly connected with the economic situation. It is, in fact, in a situation of crisis that we have to formulate hypotheses capable of responding to these questions about "decisional distance," to the demand for autonomy, and to the importance of the struggle against marginalization. Now, the CFTD, in a fairly demanding way, conceives health not only as a state of physical and mental well-being, but, beyond matters within the purview of the state, as the ability to overcome the conflicts, tensions, and acts of aggression that affect the individual in his personal and social life.[3] Such a view calls for the setting up of a whole machinery of education and prevention over and above a machinery concerned with care; it concerns society as a whole. In such circumstances, can one oppose it with the argument of what it would cost?

Furthermore, what is your position with regard to the notion of a "right to help," which is part of our claims?

FOUCAULT   Here we come to the heart of an extremely interesting problem.

When the system of social security that we know today was set up on a large scale, there was a sort of more or less explicit and largely silent consensus as to what could be called "health needs." In short, it was the need to remedy "accidents," that is to say, incapacities caused by illness and handicaps, congential or acquired.

Two processes have stemmed from this. Firstly, a technical acceleration of medicine, which has increased its theoretical power, but even more quickly its capacity for examination and analysis. Secondly, a growth in the demand for health that has demonstrated the fact that the need for health (as experienced) has no internal principle of limitation.

Consequently, it is not possible to lay down objectively a theoretical, practical threshold, valid for all, on the basis of which it might be said that health needs are entirely and definitively satisfied.

3. CFTD. *Confederation Française des Travailleurs Democratique.* This former Catholic trade union federation took on a more aggressive stance for labor demands in relation to the Communist-controlled CGT in the post-1968 period [L.D.K.].

The question of rights appears to be a particularly thorny one in this context. I would like to make a few simple remarks about it. It is clear that there is hardly any sense in speaking of a "right to health." Health — good health — cannot derive from a right; good and bad health, however crude or subtle the criteria used, are facts: physical states and mental states. And even if one corrects that statement at once, with the observation that the frontier between health and illness is partly defined by the ability of doctors to recognize an illness, by the subject's lifestyle or activity, and by what is or is not recognized as illness in a particular culture, this relativity does not mean that there is no such thing as a right to be on this or that side of the dividing line.

On the other hand, one may have a right to conditions of work that do not significantly increase the risks of illness or of various handicaps. One may also have a right to compensation, to medical care, and to damages, when one's health suffers in one way or another that comes within the responsibility of a particular authority.

But that is not the problem we are facing today. It is, I believe, the following: must a society try to satisfy by collective means individuals' need for health? And can those individuals legitimately claim satisfaction of those needs?

It seems — if those needs are likely to increase indefinitely — that a positive answer to this question could take no acceptable or even conceivable form. On the other hand, one may speak of "means of health"; and by that we shall mean not only hospital equipment and pharmaceuticals, but everything that a society has at its disposal, as far as is technically feasible, to remedy or alleviate ill-health. These means define a moving line — which results from the technical capacities of medicine, the economic capacities of a community, and what a society wishes to devote as resources and means to health. And one may define the right of access to these means of health. Such a right may be seen in different ways. There is the problem of the equality of all before this access — a problem that is easy enough to answer in principle, though it is not always easy to guarantee this equality in practical terms. There is the problem of indefinite access to these means of health; here we should be under no illusion. The problem probably has no theoretical solution.

The important thing is to know by what constantly flexible, constantly provisional arbitration the limits of this access will be defined. We must bear in mind that these limits cannot be established once and for all by a medical definition of health or by some absolutely expressed notion of "health needs."

R.B. This poses a number of problems, including the rather trivial problem of inequality: the life expectancy of a manual laborer is much lower than that of a priest or a teacher. How is one to arrange things so that the arbitrations from which a "health norm" would result take account of this situation?

Furthermore, expenditures on health now represent 8.6% of the gross national product. This has not been programmed: the cost of health — and this is the problem — is induced by a multiplicity of individual decisions and by a process of renewing these decisions. Are we not by this fact, while claiming equality of access to health, actually in a situation of "rationed" health?

FOUCAULT   I think our preoccupation is the same: the question is how — and it's a formidable problem, with political, economic, and cultural implications — and on what criteria and according to what combinatory mode we are to establish the norm on the basis of which one might, at any given moment, define a right to health.

The question of cost, which crops up constantly, as we know, brings a new dimension to this problem.

I don't see, and nobody can explain to me how, technically, it would be possible to satisfy all health needs however much they may expand. And even though I have no idea where the line ought to be drawn, it would in any case be impossible to allow expenditure on health to increase at the rate seen in recent years.

A machinery set up to give people a certain security in the area of health has, then, reached a point in its development at which we will have to decide what illness, what type of pain, will no longer receive coverage — a point at which, in certain cases, life itself will be at risk. This poses a political and moral problem not unrelated, all things consider-ed, to the question of the right enjoyed by a state to ask an individual to go and get himself killed in war. That question, though it has lost none of its intensity, has been perfectly integrated into people's consciousness through long historical developments, in such a way that soldiers have actually agreed to get themselves killed — and therefore to place their lives beyond protection. The question that now arises is how people are going to accept being exposed to certain risks without being protected by the all-providing state.

R.B.   Does this mean that we are going to question the automatic use of incubators, consider euthanasia, and go back on the very thing against which social security has struggled, namely a certain way of eliminating the most biologically weak individuals? Are we to allow the victory of the slogan "We must choose — let us choose the strongest"? Who will choose between the constant development of therapeutics, the development of post-natal medicine, and improvements in working conditions (every year, in French enterprises, twenty women out of a hundred have nervous breakdowns . . .)?

FOUCAULT   Such choices are being made all the time, even though it is not being admitted. They are made in the logic of a certain rationality and are then justified in various ways.

The question I'm asking is whether a "health strategy" — this problematic of choice — must remain silent . . . There is a paradox here: this strategy is acceptable, in the present state of things, providing it remains silent. If it is given voice, even in the form of a more or less acceptable rationality, it becomes morally unbearable. Take the example of dialysis machines: how many patients are being treated in this way, how many others cannot benefit from them? Supposing the choices by which one ends up with this inequality of treatment were revealed: the exposure of such guidelines would cause a scandal! In this area a certain rationality becomes a scandal.

I have no solution to offer. But I think it is pointless to avert one's gaze: we must try to get to the bottom of things and confront them.

R.B.   Would there not also be some point in carrying out an analysis of costs sufficiently detailed to bring out the possibility of certain economies before making more painful, or even "scandalous" choices? I'm particularly thinking of iatrogenic affections, which represent at present, if certain figures are to be believed, 8% of health problems: isn't this one of the "perverse effects" that may be specifically imputed to some defect in rationality?

FOUCAULT   Re-examining the rationality that governs our choices in health matters is certainly a task that ought to be attacked resolutely.

Thus we see that a number of disturbances like dyslexia, because they are regarded as benign, are given very little cover by social security, whereas their social cost may be enormous (has anyone calculated everything that a case of dyslexia may involve in terms of educational investment, quite apart from the cost of care?). It's the type of situation to be reconsidered as soon as one reexamines what might be called "normality" in health matters. There's an enormous amount of work to be carried out, in terms of inquiries, experiments, measures, intellectual and moral rethinking, on this matter.

Obviously, we've a difficult turning-point to negotiate.

R.B.   The definition of a norm in health matters, the search for a consensus around a certain level of expenditure and around certain ways of allocating that expenditure — isn't all this an extraordinary opportunity for people to assume responsibility for what affects them fundamentally, namely, their life and well being, as well as being a somewhat daunting task?

How are we to open up discussion at every level of public opinion?

FOUCAULT   It is true that when attempts are made to stimulate rethinking in this area, there is a general outcry.[4] What is significant is that the protests are aimed at statements about things that are immediately a source of scandal — life and death. By bringing out these problems of health, one is entering an order of values that gives rise to an absolute, infinite demand. The problem raised is, therefore, that of the relationship between an infinite demand and a finite system.

This is not the first time that mankind has faced this problem. After all, were not the religions created to resolve it? But today we must find a solution in technical terms.

R.B.   Doesn't the project of engaging the responsibility of each individual or his own choices provide one element of a

4.   Reference to Jacques Attali's *L'ordre Cannibale* [L.D.K.].

solution? When a smoker is asked to pay a surtax, for example, doesn't this amount to imposing on him responsibility for the costs of the risk that he is taking? Can we not, similarly, point out to people the significance and consequences of their individual decisions instead of laying down frontiers beyond which life would no longer have the same value?

FOUCAULT   I quite agree. When I speak of decisions and norms, I'm not thinking that some committee of the great and good could declare each year: "In view of the circumstances and state of our finances, this risk will be covered and that one won't be." I imagine, in a more overall way, something like a "cloud of decisions" that would broadly define the norm decided upon. It remains to be seen how that normative axis would be as representative as possible of a certain state of people's awareness — that's to say, of the nature of their demand and of the extent of their consent. I believe the decisions made ought to be the effect of a kind of ethical consensus so that the individual may recognize himself in the decisions made and in the values that inspired them. Only then would such decisions be acceptable, even if there might be protests here and there.

Having said this, it is true that people who smoke and drink ought to realize that they are taking a risk. It is also true that too much salt is dangerous when one suffers from arteriosclerosis, just as it is dangerous to eat sweet things when one is diabetic . . . I stress this to show how complicated the problems are and to suggest that decisions, a "decisional cloud," should never take the form of strict regulations. Any rational, uniform model leads too rapidly to paradoxes!

It is quite obvious, indeed, that the cost of diabetes and arteriosclerosis is tiny compared with the expenditure caused by tobacco-smoking and alcoholism . . .

R.B.   . . . which amount to veritable scourges, and the cost of which is also a social cost: I'm thinking of certain kinds of crime, abused children, beaten wives . . .

FOUCAULT   Let's remember, too, that alcoholism was literally implanted in the French working-class milieu in the nineteenth century, through the opening of the bistros by decree. Let's also remember that neither the problem of home distillers, nor the problem in wine-growing areas has ever been resolved . . . One can speak of a veritable policy of organized alcoholism in France. Perhaps we are in a period when it is becoming possible to take the bull by the horns and move towards less coverage for the risks attached to alcoholism.

In any case, I am not advocating, it goes without saying, any kind of wild liberalism that would lead to individual coverage for those with means and an absence of cover for the rest . . .

I am simply stressing that the fact of "health" is a cultural fact in the broadest sense of the term, which is to say at once political, economic, and social. Which is to say that it's bound up with a certain state of individual and collective consciousness. Each period has its own notion of "normality." Perhaps we shall have to turn to a system that will define, in the field of the *abnormal*, of the pathological, illnesses *normally* covered by society.

R.B.   Don't you think that in order to clarify the debate it would in fact be better to discriminate, prior to any definition of a norm of health, between what belongs to the medical sphere and what belongs to social relations? Haven't we witnessed, over the last thirty years, a sort of "medicalization" of what might be called social problems? We have, for example, given a response of a medical type to the question of absenteeism in enterprises, when we ought rather to have improved working conditions. This kind of "displacement" puts a strain on the health budget . . .

FOUCAULT   Innumerable things, in fact, have been "medicalized," not to say "over-medicalized," which really belong to something other than medicine. It so happens that, when faced with certain problems, we believed that the medical solution was the most effective and most economic. The same goes for certain educational problems, sexual problems, problems concerned with imprisonment . . . Certainly we ought to revise a lot of practices of this type.

R.B.   We haven't talked about the problem of old age. Hasn't our society a tendency to banish its old people to "homes," as if to forget them?

FOUCAULT   I must admit that I have reservations about all that is being said about the present status of old people, about their isolation and their neglect in our societies.

Of course, old people's homes in Nanterre and Ivry do have a rather sordid image. But the fact that they have caused a scandal is indicative of a new sensibility, itself bound up with a new situation. Before the war, families pushed their old people into a corner of the house and complained what a burden they were for them, making them pay for their presence in the home by innumerable acts of humiliation and hatred. Today, old people receive pensions on which they can live, and one finds in all the cities of France "clubs for senior citizens" that are attended by people who meet one another, travel, consume, and form a section of the population whose importance is becoming considerable. Even if a number of individuals remain marginalized, the condition of old people has improved a great deal in the last few decades. This is why we are so sensitive — and a very good thing, too — to what is still happening in some institutions.

R.B.   How, in fact, can the social security system contribute to an ethics of the human person?

FOUCAULT   Without going over everything that has been said in this interview that might contribute towards answering this question, I will say that social security has at least contributed by posing a number of problems, notably by posing the question of what life is worth and the way in which one can confront death.

The idea of bringing together individuals and the decision-making centers ought to involve, at least as a consequence, a recognized right for everybody to kill himself when he wishes in decent conditions . . . If I won a few billion francs in the national lottery, I'd set up an institute where people who wanted to die could come and spend a weekend, a week or a month, enjoying themselves as far as possible, perhaps with the help of drugs, and then disappear, as if by obliteration . . .

R.B.   A right to suicide?

FOUCAULT   Yes.

R.B.   What is to be said about the way in which we die

today? What are we to think of this aseptic death, often in a hospital, without one's family around one?

FOUCAULT   Death becomes a non-event. Generally speaking, people die under a blanket of drugs, if not in some accident, so that they lose consciousness entirely in a few hours, a few days, or a few weeks: they are obliterated. We live in a world in which the medical and pharmaceutical accompaniment of death deprives it of much of its pain and drama.

I don't go along entirely with everything that is said about the "asepticization" of death, as opposed to something like an integrating, dramatic ritual. The noisy wailing around the coffin was not always exempt from a certain cynicism: the anticipated pleasure of the legacy may well have been mingled with it. I prefer the gentle sadness of disappearance to this sort of ceremonial.

The way in which one dies nowadays seems to me significant of a sensibility, a system of values that is current today. It seems to me that there is something chimerical about wanting to revive, in a great wave of nostalgia, practices that no longer have any meaning.

Let's try rather to give meaning and beauty to death-obliteration.

11

Confinement, Psychiatry, Prison

A dialogue with Michel Foucault, David Cooper,
Jean-Pierre Faye, Marie-Odile Faye and Marine
Zecca.[1]
Foucault engages here in an acrimonious
attack on the psychiatric establishment. Starting
from the hypothesis that psychiatrists are always
functionaries of the social order, Foucault claims
that the imperative to "medically" police both
private and social hygiene is not an aberration
particular only to Soviet life. From the outset,
psychiatry regarded itself as responsible for identifying and supervising those who were considered
as dangerous from both penal and medical
perspectives. More recently, as Foucault suggests,
a discourse on sexuality has emerged that has
become one of general psychiatrization functioning as a means to police public health. To
transcend this cancerous bureaucracy the intellectual must extricate himself from the ideological
basis of dissidence and engage in a radical
analysis of the networks of power as they pass
through the body.
Originally published as "Enfermement, psy-
chiatrie, prison," this dialogue appeared in a
special issue of Change 32–33 (1977), 76–110

1. David Cooper (1931–). Medical doctor and psychiatrist. Founder with R.D. Laing of the British school of anti-psychiatry. He is highly critical of the institution of psychoanalysis which, he claims, inflicts violence on individuals.

Jean-Pierre Faye (1925–). Writer, philosopher, and editor of the journal Change. With the support of François Mitterrand's socialist government he founded the Collège International de Philosophie. Best known in the Anglo-Saxon world for his Langages totalitaires (1974).

Marie-Odile Faye. Editorial Assistant for Change.

Marine Zecca. Collaborator of David Cooper [L.D.K.].

on "La Folie encerclée". This translation is by Alan
Sheridan.

J.-P.F. This interference between two domains — those
you have just described: British anti-psychiatry and the
confinement of dissidents [of "those who think otherwise"] —
these two facts are so fundamental, and so close to the central
problem of your thought, that it seems to me impossible not
to think about them *with* you.

This, then, is the question: the self-evident connection
between, on the one hand, the *critique* made by the British
anti-psychiatrists and, on the other, the *fact* of "special"
psychiatric repression.

Fainberg has explained to us how this terrible phenomenon began very quitely: in fact, it was a result of trying to
find a replacement for Stalinism.[2] It began above all as a form
of "liberalization," after a speech given by Khrushchev,
following the Twentieth Congress. This is not very different
from the way the asylum came about, as you describe it: after
the brutal repression of the "madman," chained up in a cell,
came Pinel and the freeing of the chained inmates of Bicêtre
. . . The *Nouveau Larousse Illustré*, published in the late
nineteenth century, described this as "a veritable revolution in
the treatment of the insane . . . But you point out that "Pinel's
reform[3] is much more a visible culmination than a modification of this repression of madness *as forbidden speech.*"

*After demanding that the camps be opened, Khrushchev made
that 1958 speech, which indeed harks back to the opposite, or other-
thinking, thought on madness. But there was a precursor to this, in
the time of Nicholas I:[4] this was Chadaev, Pushkin's friend, whom
the tsar — "the enemy of Revolutions", "the policeman of Europe"*

2. Victor Fainberg. Soviet Jew who was committed to a psychiatric hospital in
Leningrad for protesting the 1968 invasion of Czechoslavakia [L.D.K.].

3. Philippe Pinel (1745–1828). Founder of modern psychology, he based his
treatment on the systematic study of clinically ill patients. He believed in isolation
and supervision as a "moral treatment" for those suffering from mental illness
[L.D.K.].

4. "The Tsar Nicholas . . . was honored for his domestic virtues and for the skill
of his government . . . This prince . . . subjected dissidents to all manner of
vexations" (M.N. Bouillet, *Dictionnaire universel d'Histoire*, Paris, 1872).

— would have condemned, if he had read his pamphlets, to being treated at home by a psychiatrist . . .

FOUCAULT   But I'd say that perhaps he wasn't a precursor. It's true that we seem to be seeing two very different functions — the medical function of psychiatry, on the one hand, and the strictly represive function of the police, on the other — coming together at a given moment, in the system we're talking about. But in fact the two functions were only *one*, from the outset. You must have read Castel's book on the *birth* of the psychiatric order: he shows very well how psychiatry, as it developed in the early nineteenth century was not at all localized within the asylum, with a medical function, and then became generalized and extended to the entire social body, right up to the confusion we see today — somewhat discreet in France, but much more evident in the Soviet Union. But from the outset, psychiatry has had as its project to be a function of social order.

After the revolution, during which the great structures of confinement had been shaken and abolished, what could be done to reconstitute controls that did not take the form of confinement, but which nevertheless would be effective? Psychiatry immediately perceived itself as a permanent function of social order and made use of the asylums for two purposes: first, to treat the most obvious, the most embarrassing cases and, at the same time, to provide a sort of guarantee, an image of scientificity, by making the place of confinement look like a hospital. The renaming of the place of confinement as a hospital was a way of declaring that the practice of psychiatry was indeed medical — since it, too, like medicine, had a hospital. But the main point of Castel's book is to show that the hospital was not at all the most important thing about this business . . .

J.-P.F.   It was a cover operation.

FOUCAULT   That's right — an operation of justification, in relation to a psychiatric project that appears very clearly in the periodicals of the time and in the speeches of psychiatrists: everywhere society is meeting a mass of problems, in the street, at work, in the family, etc. — and we psychiatrists are *the* functionaries of social order. It is up to us to make good these disorders. We have a function in public hygiene. That is the true vocation of psychiatry. And that is its true context, its destiny.

So much so that psychiatry has never abandoned this dream, nor this context. Indeed what is happening in the Soviet Union is not the monstrous coupling of a medical function and a police function, which really have nothing to do with one another. It is simply the intensification, the ossification of a kinship structure that has never ceased to function.

J.-P.F.   In a way, it's an uncovering.

FOUCAULT   Yes, and a *condensation*. In this respect, the Soviet Union has taken up this inheritance.

One could write its history. For this function has always intervened where "public hygiene" — in the sense of public order — is perceived as most threatened, that is to say, by crime. As early as 1830, psychiatry began to stick its nose in. When Italian criminology developed, of course, psychiatry was there, supporting the discourse of Lombrosian criminology. And around the 1890s, when there were congresses of criminology all over the place, one was held at St. Petersburg in 1892 (around 1891–93), in which a certain Monsieur Léveillé — he was French — told the Russians: we Europeans are having a lot of trouble dealing with certain individuals, who are criminals, of course, but who are, above all, mental patients — criminals because they are mental patients and mental patients in so far as they are criminals — and we don't really know what to do with them, because we have no structures to receive them. But you Russians, who have at your disposal great virgin territories in Siberia, you might very well — with the sort of people we have to banish to Cayenne or New Caledonia — you might very well organize big work camps in Siberia for all those people, on the border between medicine and penality. You will use them to do *that* and thus exploit all the potential wealth of those lands . . . Good old Léveillé had defined the Gulag.

J.-P.F.   Was there any response, at the time?

FOUCAULT   No response and no thanks. He wasn't decorated — even posthumously.

J.-P.F.   But did he come back pleased with what he had seen?

FOUCAULT   Delighted. Deportation to Siberia already existed, but if we are to judge from this text, I believe it must have functioned quite simply as exile, for political prisoners. The idea that there could be set up there a politico-medical — politico-penal-medical, or *medico-politico-penal* — confinement, with an *economic* function, which would allow the exploitation of the wealth of a still virgin country, that, I think, was a new idea. Anyway, it was new to his mind, when he formulated it.

J.-P.F.   It wasn't Dostoyevsky's experience.

FOUCAULT   When we reread the texts on deportation in the nineteenth century, we find that it did not in fact function *like that*.

D.C.   During the press conference given by Fainberg and Pliuch, I was very struck by Claude Bourdet's question to Viktor Fainberg: why do they use psychiatry in the Soviet Union? When they have that whole police and penitentiary apparatus, which is perfect in itself, and which could take charge of anybody, why use psychiatry?

FOUCAULT   There's no answer. Except, perhaps, that the question is inappropriate. Because *it* always functioned like that.

J.-P.F.   It was already there . . .

FOUCAULT   It was already there. Once again it is not a question of a *distortion* of the use of psychiatry: that was its fundamental project.

D.C.   The movement in the 1930s towards depsychiatrization in the Soviet Union was reversed under Stalin. The legal prohibition of psychological tests — *and of lobotomy*, around 1936 — was then followed by a resumption of it, though not as widespread as in the West . . .

J.-P.F.   Who was behind the prohibition of lobotomy in the USSR?

D.C.   . . . The new Western technique being to implant twenty electrodes into the cerebellum — into a tiny area no more than a centimeter — in order to achieve long-distance supervision far more advanced than Delagado's apparatus at Yale — this practice and this degree of sophistication was still lacking in the Soviet Union. But there is this going back, now.

J.-P.F.   The use of lobotomy in the 1950s in the United

States — in France, too, but probably more in the USA for *political* purposes, if we are attentive to Breggin's work and to the texts that appeared in *Les Temps modernes* [April 1973] — that converges dangerously with the post-Stalinist facts of psychiatric repression.

FOUCAULT   The question raised by David is indeed crucial: the brake put on psychiatry . . .

J.-P.F.   . . . Soviet psychiatry.

FOUCAULT   Yes, on Soviet psychiatry before 1940 — and the sudden acceleration after 1945. What does it mean? We would have to bring in the whole problem of reflexology, which for a long time — after 1945, in any case, and perhaps even up till now — was the only theoretical background accepted by Soviet psychiatry. All others were regarded as ideological, idealist, irrationalist, etc. Reflexology was used to the full in the period between 1945 and 1965. I remember meeting Marthe Robert and Michel de M'uzan after the Kafka centenary, which took place in Prague: they came back horrified, having learnt of the reflexological Pavlovian treatment to which homosexuals were being subjected. And, indeed, the method used was extremely simple: they were shown a woman's photograph — and given a pleasure inducing injection. A man's photograph — and an injection that made them feel sick, etc. This was shown to visitors, as if it was a highly remarkable discovery . . . Then, when the officials noted the visitors' unenthusiastic attitude and had to listen to their questions, they presented their material rather differently . . . We may even wonder whether visitors weren't shown it, ostensibly to convince them, but, in fact, to expose a scandal perceived as much by the doctors themselves. I really don't know, the phenomenon was highly ambiguous . . .

   If I am talking about this reflexology it's because, in France, it was certainly one of the reasons why anti-psychiatry failed to develop. In France, the psychiatrists, for reasons of political choice, would have been in a position to question the psychiatric apparatus; let's say, broadly speaking, that the left-wing psychiatrists felt they could do nothing because of a political situation in which they really had no wish for this question to be raised, because of what was happening in the Soviet Union — whether or not they had any very clear idea of what was happening. Then they had imposed on them, as an ideology, against the various contemporary "irrationalisms" — existentialism, psychoanalysis, etc. — this reflexological ideology. Thirdly, they were given as a concrete task, not a radical questioning of psychiatric practice and of the mental institution, but the defense of the psychiatric profession. So there were these three reasons for their refusal to budge.

J.-P.F.   The interesting consequence of reflexology, in the case of birth clinics — of clinics specializing in "painless birth" — had as its counterpart, in psychiatry, an absolute refusal to do anything about it, or to have anything to do with it! The same political body functioned in this double way.

But the incredible paradox is that at the time when police activity was at its most repressive, in the 1930s, at the height of the Stalinist purges, there was probably still a revolutionary inheritance in Soviet medicine, which had the effect of forbidding, suspending, or diverting the appearance of lobotomy as a psychiatric technique. It was probably not Stalin in his infinite wisdom who took this position . . . It must have been decided at the level of the medical authorities.

D.C.   But isn't it illegal now?

M.-O.F.   It's by no means sure . . .

J.-P.F.   Do we know who was behind this decision, or what his political tendency was?

FOUCAULT   What I'm going to say is probably very vague, compared with the precise explanations that we ought to be able to provide, but, generally speaking, the 1930s and 1940s in the Soviet Union were dominated by a double theme. Firstly: nature is good in itself and whatever distorts it is the result of historical, economic, and social alienation. Secondly: it's man's task to transform nature and he can transform it. The infinite bounty of nature, the gradual transformability of nature: this was the ideological background of all discourse — including Lysenko's for example.

J.-P.F.   Michurinism . . .

FOUCAULT   I believe that the prohibition of lobotomy was the result of much more precise aims than that. But I can see very well in what kind of climate it could be forbidden. For it is an amputation of nature. And it is a renunciation of the transformation of nature itself by man . . .

M.Z.   This is similar to Henri Laborit's explanation.[5]

FOUCAULT   That was the ideological background. It is likely that, as for Lysenko, there was a precise reason why it was triggered off: it wasn't simply this ideology that produced the *Lysenko effect*. Similarly, there must be something else behind the prohibition of lobotomy. I remember the time when cybernetics and the various information techniques began to be known in the West, just after the war: the official reviews of the French Communist Party set about denouncing this pseudo-science, this typically capitalistic technology, etc. Technologies that had not been mastered in the USSR were *ipso facto* disqualified.

J.-P.F.   Of course, the cybernetic ideology is now highly fashionable in those circles.

D.C.   At the Milan Congress, the contribution made by Peter Breggin, of Washington, was highly important: in the German psychiatric hospitals, in the 1930s, SS officers appeared to have been trained — by psychiatrists — in "scientific" euthanasia.[6] Many of those psychiatrists emigrated to the United States — some of them are now eminent figures in the American Psychiatric Association . . . With this American background . . . Breggin was sued for defamation, but he defended himself well.

M.Z.   All the states in the USA that had for a time abolished surgical operations on the brain have now authorized them. On two conditions: that the patient cannot be treated by any other technique than psycho-surgery; that it is a "good surgeon" that is doing the operation; and that several individuals, outside the medical profession, attest to the fact that the patient is a "real patient" . . . it's absolutely absurd.

FOUCAULT   A "real patient" and a "good doctor" . . . And

5. Henri Laborit (1914–). Researcher on the vegetal nervous system and pharmo-psychology [L.D.K.].

6. Peter Breggin (1936–). Specialist in forensic psychiatry. Research on psychosurgery for political purposes and the control of violence [L.D.K.].

supposing one had a "good patient" and a "real surgeon?" Wouldn't that work? That's usually how things are . . .

D.C. But the psychiatric definitions of the "great patients" are very interesting . . . Working class first. Jew rather than non-Jew. Black rather than non-black.

M.Z. And women . . .

D.C. Rather than men. Obviously, a black woman would be the perfect patient.

M.Z. On whom surgical operations of the brain would have a positive result,

J.-P.F. I don't know whether by going back we're moving further away from the subject or getting closer to the source, but Royer-Collard's report on Sade, on Sade's confinement, is a sort of primary document.[7] The first *written* document perhaps to provide the medical account of an avowed politically motivated psychiatric confinement. And it occurred at the threshold of the century of the asylum.

FOUCAULT Yes, and it shows very clearly what the problem was. By abolishing for political and above all juridical, judicial reasons (so as not to leave it to the executive) the right to confine people without a properly supervised procedure, the Revolution had opened the institutions of confinement. This then created a whole series of problems that were to be discussed throughout the Revolution: what are we going to do with those people? There was now no question of confinement, and a man no longer had the right to confine his children or wife, nor did a wife have the right to confine her husband (statistically the two were more or less equivalent) — so what is to be done? After all, we cannot deprive people of a right so fundamental, so necessary to the correct functioning of society as the right to confine a member of one's family who is being a nuisance.

In France, the right of confinement, which was never expressly formulated, was *practiced* in fact for over a century and a half. And it was ultimately that right which then

7.   Royer-Collard (1763–1845). French Jansenist philosopher who opposes sensualism which he regards as an essentially sceptical philosophy capable of undermining social order [L.D.K.].

resurfaced, in an elaborate, sophisticated form, in the law of 1838 — and its successors.

M.-O.F. Was the shift from the Bastille to Charenton progress?

FOUCAULT Oh, yes. Before, a letter of denunciation could be sent to the police superintendent, who carried out a counter-investigation, and answered yes or no: the person in question was confined or not.

M.-O.F. Did those who were not nobles also have this "right" to confinement, similar to the *lettres de cachet?*[8]

FOUCAULT That's a very important question. I, too, thought for a long time that the *lettres de cachet* were a privileged institution, in the hands of the king himself, and which could be used only against his immediate enemies . . . but as I went through the archives at the Arsenal, I came to see that it was a very widespread practice indeed. The *lettres de cachet* were in no way confined to royal use and to the upper aristocracy. But, from the late seventeenth century onwards, two correlative and more or less simultaneous institutions developed. On the one hand, the police had divided up the cities into closely supervised sectors, with a superintendent for each district; inspectors and informers swarmed the streets, arresting prostitutes, homosexuals, etc. On the other hand, and side by side with it, were the *lettres de cachet*, which were in widespread use and by which anybody could ask the district superintendent to arrest and confine somebody . . .

M.-O.F. But where?

FOUCAULT At Bicêtre, where there were between three and six thousand individuals. At La Salpêtrière, where women were confined, etc.

Piles of those letters have been found, which were written *by public writers*, at street corners. Perhaps the cobbler's or fishmonger's wife wanted to get rid of her husband, or her son, her uncle, her father-in-law, etc. — then she would dictate her complaints to the public writer. They are astonishing documents — because the public writer

8. *lettre de cachet*: originally a royal letter that could denounce, arrest, and confine someone [L.D.K.].

explained to his client that it would be better to use this or that compulsory formula. So it usually began with something like: "My lord, I have the honor of prostrating myself at your feet in order to . . . " Then came, with the request, a list of the reasons "justifying" it in the plaintiff's own vocabulary, with all his demands, his hatreds, his anger, his grudges. In the middle of this solemn language, redolent of the administration of Louis XIV's time, we find such phrases as "she's a filthy whore . . . " In fact people, including the "lowest" classes of society, had been given an instrument of denunciation and confinement that ended up, after a century's use, as a veritable *right*, which people sorely missed during the Revolution. And during the whole Revolutionary period this problem was posed constantly: a means must be found for families to be able to confine lawfully those individuals who are a nuisance to them . . . Hence the setting up of family courts, which existed and functioned for a time in the nineteenth century. And then, finally, the law of 1838, which was merely a substitute for all that — with, over and above the family's request, an administrative supervision by the prefect, countersigned by a doctor.

What's more, there was no difficulty in obtaining this counter-signature, since the psychiatrists regarded themselves not so much as doctors — in the sense we understand it today — as civil servants concerned with public hygiene: that is, their job was to supervise whatever was in a state of disorder, whatever presented a *danger*. In the end, it is this notion of "danger," which was introduced at that time, theorized in psychiatry and criminology in the nineteenth century, that you find again in Soviet legislation. This legislation may say: you're claiming that a patient is being put in prison (or a prisoner put in hospital), but that's not at all the case! Someone is being confined because he has been "dangerous." They even reached the point of describing *as an offense* in the penal code the fact of being perceived *as dangerous* . . .

We haven't got to that point here yet . . . But in the British, American, Italian, German, and French practice of psychiatry *and* of penal law, we see that the notion of "danger" is still the guiding thread. And all these things — police, psychiatry — are institutions intended to react *to danger*.

D.C.   The formula still is: "dangerous *for others* or *for himself*" . . .

FOUCAULT   In other words, he is dangerous "for himself," when it can't be proved that he is dangerous "for others . . . "

M.-O.F.   What is emerging there, then, is a "social police" . . . But what about the "political police"? It's a problem that was posed by the Commune: we saw this quite clearly when studying Da Costa's memorandum on the police of the Second Empire and, above all, on its *political police*.[9]

J.-P.F.   Da Costa criticizes his friend Rigault, the Commune's delegate to the Sûreté générale, of which for a time he was *chef de cabinet*, of having as a "dream" . . . "the continuation of the police methods of the Empire."[10] Of the Second Empire, but also the First — Fouché's, the regime that locked Sade up at Charenton and produced Royer-Collard's report.

FOUCAULT   The political police? It has always existed, at least since the sixteenth century. But there have been various stages in its formation. In France, there was a sizeable policing, on the borders between the political and social if you like, of the Protestants, after the revocation of the Edict of Nantes. The pursuit of Protestants, their circulation in the country, their meetings, their services, all that had to be supervised: this meant considerable "progress" . . . Then there was the post-Revolutionary period, of course.

J.-P.F.   The Napoleonic period.

FOUCAULT   Yes. Then, after 1848, there was Napoleon III's police — and the Commune.

J.-P.F.   The contradictions of the Commune . . . For Da Costa's Report "to the Police Delegate," that is to say, to Ferré, Rigault's second successor, sees its task as *"abandoning the system of terror, the regime of fear*, which is unworthy of us" and, more specifically, as removing the fears that the

9.   *Change* 15: Police fiction (1973): Memorandum from Da Costa, chef de cabinet of the Délégué à la Sûreté Générale (of the Ministry of the Interior) of the Commune: Report written two days after his condemnation to death, June 29, 1871.

10.   Ibid., p. 17.

memories of the September Days[11] inspire in certain prisoners."[12] It is rare to find the servants of a revolutionary regime
expressing, in so many terms, such a wish to *abandon* the
police methods inherited from the monarchist and bourgeois
state. At the same time, Da Costa specifically saw his task, as
he writes himself, "the pursuit of persons accused of having
been part of *Bonaparte's former political police*."[13] But what he
proposes to Ferré — in May '71 — "to get out of this terrible
situation," is "*to abolish absolutely the present organization of the
police*," and "to reorganize it on democratic, moral, and
fraternal bases . . . " For him, the concrete objective was to
annul the repressive law on hostages, which had not been
applied. (At the same time, Marx was congratulating the
Commune on it!) Here the notion of "danger" is entirely
turned inside out. But as far as psychiatry goes . . .

D.C.   "Danger" functions in a very simple way for
psychiatrists. There are these *forms*, these formulas: danger for
others, danger for oneself . . . One can cross out one of the
terms and leave the other. It is even simpler to leave both . . .
The forms of short detention may be renewed, if "necessary."
To renew them for a whole year, it is necessary to write a
paragraph — that's all.

J.-P.F.   The paragraphs are already written.

FOUCAULT   In France at the moment, the first question
posed to a psychiatric specialist in the courts is: Is this
individual dangerous? To the question of article 64 — is he
responsible for his acts? — psychiatrists do not answer very
often, because they cannot answer it. They *consider* that they
cannot answer it, because they say that it is meaningless. But
they *admit* — and this is highly significant — that they can

11.   September 1792: the massacres of the first "Paris Commune." Da Costa also
occupied the posts of Danton and Hébert — substitute for the Procurator of the
Commune.

12.   *Change* 9, May 1971: 176–80.

13.   This is precisely the view of the Permanent Congress of Santiago, which
opened on February 25, 1976 with a reading from Julio Cortazar, of the verdict of the
Second Russell Tribunal with contributions from Mario Pedrosa, Miguel Rojas-Mix,
Ariel Dorfman, Manuel Scorza, and Saul Yurkievich, from Mando Aravantinou on
behalf of the Khnari Collective of Athens, and with a message from Vratislav
Effenberger and the Prague Surrealist Group, read by Vincent Bounoure. It was to
continue in the exhibition of the Museum of Chilean Resistance.

answer the question: Is the individual dangerous?

And yet, all the same, when you look closely at the penal code, whether it is of an Anglo-Saxon or a Napoleonic type, *danger* has never constituted an offense. To be dangerous *is not an offense*. To be dangerous *is not an illness*. It is not a symptom. And yet we have come, as if it is self-evident, and for over a century now, to *use* the notion of danger, by a perpetual movement backwards and forwards between the penal and the medical. The penal says: listen, I don't really know what to do with this man, I'd like your opinion about him — is he dangerous? And if the psychiatrist is told: come now, you must reply to *this* question, will reply: obviously, "danger" is not a psychiatric notion — but it is the question *asked me by the judge*. And there you are! If one considers the whole thing, taken together, one sees that it all functions on the notion of danger.

J.-P.F.   The ball is hit from one side of the court to the other.

FOUCAULT   And the Soviet system functions in exactly the same way.

J.-P.F.   The concept of "torpid schizophrenia" . . . a syndrome that has no symptoms. Schizophrenia is an illness that may not have any symptoms: a sort of "noumenon," a "thing-in-itself." Very "dangerous" . . .

D.C.   A few days ago, the American psychiatrists protested against this form of diagnosis in the Soviet Union. Because there are forms of schizophrenia diagnosed in the USSR that (for them) are "really" pseudo-schizophrenic neuroses or neurotic pseudo-schizophrenias . . . it's all becoming a question of linguistics!

J.-P.F.   If the concept of schizophrenia can be used in this way, outside any symptom, in a "non-Western" space — this does indeed pose the question as to how it was constructed at the outset, in the West.

D.C.   There *is*, in fact, a danger in "madness." But it is the danger of the unexpected, of the spontaneous. Because the madman doesn't actually strike others . . . He does so *"in our words"* . . . In this sense, all madmen are political dissidents. But each delusion — or supposed delusion — may be found in political declarations.

There is something else — "paranoia," which is a form of hyper-normality . . . a fascist form of existence.

J.-P.F.   Usually, perfectly *accepted*.

D.C.   But what one doesn't accept very easily is the proposition that all madmen are political dissidents. Yet it's true. We must *extend this concept of dissidence* — I prefer to say: dis-*sension*, difference of feeling, of thinking . . . Dis-*sidence* means: to sit in another camp. Now, in the Soviet Union, there are dissidents who don't want "to sit in another camp." Or, in East Germany, Wolf Biermann *wants* the socialist camp — but he wants *to think differently*. This is the *dissent* of the *dissenter*, in the English sense. It is something different. At the Venice Biennale, some Italian socialists proposed as a theme dissidence in Eastern Europe. Why not dissidence in general? That would provide plenty of material for a very good congress . . . It's not only psychiatric dissidence that is in question, in the capitalist world. But dissidence throughout the Third World, where we find the *criticism of weapons*. The socialist countries have dissidents, too — but they are precisely dissidences on which, on its side, capitalism is *based*: through the over-exploitation of the Third World. Those thousands and millions of dissidents. How can you constitute an ideological basis for dissidence *in general*, throughout the world? Through an analysis of *power*. That's what you have done, Michel, in several areas: in *Surveiller et punir* and in the first volume of *La Volonté de savoir*. Perhaps by using the analysis of the Budapest School in terms of "radical needs," which opens up a lot of perspectives. And which must be rather *unacceptable* over there . . .

To form an ideological basis of dissidence throughout the world: that's *our* question. Perhaps to develop international action — on a basis that is still to be *found*.

J.-P.F.   The events in Argentina this winter have shown that a whole area of repression in Latin America also involves *psychiatry*. And in an odd way. What exactly is being targeted? Left-wing psychiatrists, belonging to tendencies close to anti-psychiatry or to psychoanalysis, have become the targets. (For example, Bauleo and his friends.) And where did the blow come from? And what was the "model" that served as a measure for this repression? A "good psychiatry" for Latin America, which is "thinkable" somewhere out there?

FOUCAULT I don't know Argentina very well. I know Brazil a little. The situation out there is highly complex. For it is absolutely true that, on the one hand, doctors in Brazil take part in interrogation involving torture. They give advice . . . And it is certain that there are psychiatrists *who take part in that*. I think I can state that there is at least one psychoanalyst, in Rio, who is a torture-advisor. Anyway, that is what I have been told as a fact. And he isn't some minor psychoanalyst either, but someone who is conversant with the most sophisticated forms of present-day psychoanalysis . . .

On the one hand, it is absolutely certain that there are psychoanalysts and psychiatrists out there who are *victims* of political repression and who have taken the initiative in action in the opposite direction, in the opposition. At the head of a very important demonstration against repression, in the years 1968–69, there was a Rio psychoanalyst.

D.C. But one of the fascist generals and "gorillas" in the pre-Geisel period was the honorary president of the World Association of Psycho-surgery. It was probably at the time of Medici.[14]

FOUCAULT Medici was in fact a policeman.

I think what you are proposing there, David, is a crucial problem: what ideological basis can be given to dissidence *in general*? But as soon as one tries to give it an ideology, don't you think that one is already preventing it from being truly dissidence?

I think it must be given tools . . .

D.C. But not *an* ideology: an ideological *base*, which is rather different. And maybe include, for example, an analysis of power, like yours — a phenomenon that for me is still difficult to grasp. It seems to me that you are struggling, in your work, to understand it. But it is something totally multiform: something at the base — and which is not "an ideology."

FOUCAULT This work to be done would be rather an

14. Ernesto Geisel (1907–). Brazilian army officer, business executive, and politician. President of Brazil, 1974–79 [L.D.K.].

ideological tool, a tool of analysis, of perception, of de-coding — a possibility of defining practice, etc. That, indeed, is the thing to be worked at.

D.C.   How, with whom?

M.Z.   I think it can also be done in teams. In Italy, where there may be a lack of this basic theoretical work, a lot has been done in practice over the last ten years.

D.C.   The most important work is probably that of Mario Tomasini in Parma. He is a worker in the PCI [Italian Communist Party] and became an assessor for Health, in the Parma region. The occupation of the hospital there led to "the expulsion of the psychiatrists" and to "the self-management of affective problems" in the community . . .

M.Z.   The juvenile prison, the orphanage, three institutions for those suffering from physical and motor handicaps, and half the psychiatric hospital were "emptied," the other institutions were closed and the people brought back into the community, finding work, an apartment — there was a whole movement to find individual or collective apartments . . . That really is a very important piece of work and one that, in the last analysis, has turned the economic crisis to good account: as a situation that enables them to set up self-managed factories, to take over land that was not cultivated and to form collectives of young people who will cultivate the land. Their work is very important. But I have the feeling that something is missing, something that is stopping them going any further. I feel, too, that Mario has somewhat lost his way in this astonishing experiment: he cannot *theorize* it and — which amounts to the same thing — *he cannot take it across the frontiers of the province of Parma.*

D.C.   In the PCI there are two tendencies — around Berlinguer's evident schism.[15] There is that of Amendola, on the one hand. On the other, there is a group like that of Tomasini, which believes in a radical self-management of all aspects of life, including affective problems and problems of madness. There is here a whole tendency that is somewhat hidden in the Italian situation today, but one that is

---

15.   Enrico Berlinguer (1922–84). Former Secretary-General of the Italian Communist party who advocated a moderate brand of communism [L.D.K.].

fundamental. There is also a mistrust of it on the part of left-wing psychiatrists in Italy.

FOUCAULT   Jervis's attitude is typical. The last sentence in his book is amazing. It amounts to saying: psychiatry, but of course!, it may be useful in so far as it allows someone to reconstitute the wholeness of his personality, to bring together again the disintegrated syntheses, etc. This definition is pretty close to those of Royer-Collard . . .

M.Z.   There's a notion, in Italy, that is almost more important than "dangerousness" — and that is the notion of "pain" . . .

D.C.   Ah yes, the ideology of pain, of "relieving pain," which *translates* the whole language of psychiatry into a language of pain.

M.Z.   It's a way of justifying the whole psychiatric apparatus . . . which, with a little more centralization and planning, will be able to put an end to the experiments being made today, which have favored decentralization.

In a lecture at the Collège de France, you talked about your trip to Brazil, and of a "health plan" that is being worked out there — which isn't specifically a plan for mental health, but for health in general, which, nevertheless, through its institutions, will constitute a new relationship with the body, with illness, and, ultimately, a social order based on illness, *on the fear of illness*. And this is quite close to the Italian situation, or rather what is threatening it.

FOUCAULT   What is certain is that there is today a place where one can take up militant action that has a meaning, and which is not simply *the injection of an ideology* that happens to be present in our heads, but which puts ourselves in question, and that is the question of illness.

Let me take the example of northeast Brazil. The morbidity rate there reaches 100%, parasitosis — however "anti-doctor" one may be — really does exist; and parasitosis can be eliminated. The problem is to know how one may actually obtain therapeutic results, which it would be pitiful to deny, without the setting up of a type of medical power, and a type of relationship to the body, and a type of authoritarianism — a *system of obedience*, in the end, because that is what it is about, characteristic of our relationship to the doctor and to medicine today.

There's a tremendous amount at stake here. And one cannot but feel pretty helpless in the face of it. With the Brazilian friends I see, we talk about it endlessly. They've done some excellent work, but it remains very local, it's immediately stifled — they're forced to leave the region in which they work, for political reasons, and six months later, something else is going on.

What is certain is that the networks of power now pass through health and the body. They used to pass "through the soul." Now through the body . . .

J.-P.F. It's the inquisition of the body.

M.Z. Techniques are so highly developed, so sophisticated, and so effective that, although psychiatry once practiced the segregation of individuals without really being able to "treat" them, now it has total power to "normalize" them and to "cure" them. Through surgery, drugs, behavior-therapy . . .

J.-P.F. With a view to "relieving pain" — and the danger?

D.C. The ideology of "pain" is the ideology of "personal salvation." These are the most "advanced techniques: EST (Erhard Sensitivity Training), "Transcendental Meditation", "Rebirth Therapy": all this constitutes a "third force" in therapeutics — after psychoanalysis and behavior theory. Then there's transactional analysis, the "primal scream," etc. Imported into Mexico for the poor people over there, like cheap techniques. At Pueblo, they're now practicing "anti-psychiatry" . . . T-shirts are being sold carrying the slogan: "I'm a human being, not an object . . . " So we have anti-psychiatry advertising.

FOUCAULT We're in a labyrinth of paradoxes . . .

Recently there appeared in a newspaper of which we are particularly fond, and in line with the anti-medicine struggle, an investigation into the scandals of official medicine, of medicine as run by the senior consultants in the area of cardiovascular illnesses in particular. Against this medicine of the mandarins, somebody was proposing something that consisted of a small electrical apparatus stuck into the navel and the behind, and which was supposed, by provoking discharges, to shake out your coagulated bloodcells and get it all back moving in the right way.

What must be rejected, absolutely, is that sort of empirical medicine from the eighteenth century, which is still hanging around . . .

J.-P.F. "Shocks" . . .

FOUCAULT The article ended with the name of the book where you can find out how to use this wonderful instrument and the name of the individual who had made it. And — as you've probably guessed — it was a doctor.

M.-O.F. We're at the stage of criticism . . . Is there a stage at which we might propose something?

FOUCAULT My position is that it is not up to us to propose. As soon as one "proposes" — one proposes a vocabulary, an ideology, which can only have effects of domination. What we have to present are instruments and tools that people might find useful. By forming groups specifically to make these analyses, to wage these struggles, by using these instruments or others: this is how, in the end, possibilities open up.

But if the intellectual starts playing once again the role that he has played for a hundred and fifty years — that of prophet, in relation to what "must be," to what "must take place" — these effects of domination will return and we shall have other ideologies, functioning in the same way.

It is simply in the struggle itself and through it that positive conditions emerge.

J.-P.F. In other words, it's a "positive philosophy" . . .

FOUCAULT Yes, otherwise a positive philosophy emerges.

J.-P.F. But to what type of injection of socialized pain does this ideology of "relieving pain" referred to by David just now specifically lead in practice? There's a type of pain that is normalized in such a way that it is regarded as "non-dangerous," as *healthy*. But it may be more intolerable for the patient. There are, on the other hand, forms of pain labeled as bad.

D.C. The ideology of pain and of "relieving pain" means relieving the pain of everybody around *that object* — everybody else . . .

J.-P.F.   But this object — which one?

D.C.   The madman, our madness.

J.-P.F.   It's to relieve others' pain. Never mind him. As soon as he's out of danger . . .

D.C.   The madman . . . but I've followed your advice, Michel, and *abolished* the word "madness" in the last pages of my book.

What matters to me is the analysis of depsychiatrization in the Third World: non-medical administration and pre-psychiatrization — the *avoidance* of psychiatry — in certain Third World countries. In Mexico, Cuba, Tanzania, Nigeria.

FOUCAULT   And in Italy, in Belgium — and here.

J.-P.F.   In Trieste, the closing of the psychiatric hospital has reached its final stage.

M.Z.   But two fundamental questions remain: how does one respond to the *crisis* in the community, hasn't one simply broken up the hospital into tiny external centers that play the same role — that of confinement? Have those responsible for that "breaking up" managed to find, in the general hospitals, *beds,* so that someone may be hospitalized for two or three days, if really necessary? A whole question of legislation is involved here as well, which *Psychiatria democratica* is trying to resolve. The important question is whether it isn't ultimately a policy of "sectorization." They've avoided this at Parma, but we'll have to see what happens at Trieste.

J.-P.F.   There's a precursor to this — the inverse of Sade's case. At Tübingen, as we know, there's the famous Hölderlin house, the Hölderlin Tower, where the poet lived, for almost forty years, calling himself Scardanelli. What is not so well known is how he ended up there: *who* put him there. In fact it was the director of the hospital nearby, which was simply the former theology faculty, of the pre-Lutheran period, where Malancthon (a big plaque reminds one of this) studied. It's a large, very beautiful, fifteenth-century building and is now the philosophy faculty. There, in the hospital, *a few beds* were kept at the time for "psychical" or "mental" cases. Hölderlin was hospitalized there for a time, after being brought to Würtemberg in a state described as "dangerous," "demential," and which, in fact, occurred in a whole *political* context. For after the arrest of his friend and protector Isaac Sinclair, for complicity with the German revolutionary movements sympathetic to the French Revolution, he felt that he was in danger himself — politically, this time. Put by force into a carriage that was supposed to take him back to Württemberg, to his "native country," he had a strong feeling that he was going to be arrested on arrival. (The Duke of Württemberg was an energetic supporter of the Counter-Revolution.) It was at that moment that he had the "delusional" attack that brought about his confinement in the Tübingen hospital — in that space situated by its history somewhere between theology and philosophy, and containing at the time a semi-psychiatric "department" . . . But the astonishing and brilliant decision of the hospital director was to remove him immediately from this confinement and to find him a non-place: the house of the master joiner Zimmer. There begins the story of Hölderlin in his tower, in the "Hölderlin Turm." He would go for walks along the Neckar, without ever going back to the seminary in which he had been a student with Hegel and Schelling and which was only *a few hundred yards away*. It was in that world that he wrote the second group of the "Poems of Madness" — not the hymns, written in a fragmented, incomplete language, but the quatrains, written in rhyming, regular meter, the "quiet" quatrains.

The *Hölderlin Turm*, a few yards away from the hospital and its "mental" beds, was a micro-operation of de-psychiatrization. A Hölderlinian micro-Trieste, a small "Basaglia experiment" in the romantic age. It was Tübingen's Trieste . . .

D.C.   Things got much worse after that. With Kretschmer and his "somatic types" . . . If one is too tall and thin, one is probably schizophrenic. If one is too fat, one is manic depressive. If one is very muscular — epileptic . . .

J.-P.F.   One is guilty in advance. But at the time of the joiner Zimmer nobody had yet invented "torpid schizophrenia."

In Trieste, in the hospital itself, what's going to happen? The Congress will be taking place there . . .

Are *you* going?

FOUCAULT   To the "Network" Congress? No, I won't be there.

I've another problem now — one concerned with the same area — that I'd like to talk to you about.

My question is this. In France today there's a Commission for the reform of penal law. It has already been at work for several months (with the possibility of a change of government?), and has not so far taken any decisions of importance. To my great surprise, they telephoned me. They told me that they were studying the legislation on sexuality. They were in some difficulty and would like to know what I thought about it . . . I asked them what questions they would like to ask me. They sent me some questions, which I received *this morning*.

Well, everything concerning legislation about films, books, etc., none of that is any problem to me. I think one can say in principle that, in no circumstances, should sexuality be subject to any kind of legislation whatever. O.K. But there are two areas that for me present a problem. One is rape and the other is children.

What should be said about rape?

D.C.   That's the most difficult question.

FOUCAULT   One can always produce the theoretical discourse that amounts to saying: in any case, sexuality can in no circumstances be the object of punishment. And when one punishes rape one should be punishing physical violence and nothing but that. And to say that it is nothing more than an act of aggression: that there is no difference, in principle, between sticking one's fist into someone's face or one's penis into their sex . . . But, to start with, I'm not at all sure that women would agree with this . . .

M.Z.   No, not really. Not at all, in fact.

FOUCAULT   So you accept that there is a "properly sexual" offense.

M.Z.   Oh, yes.

M.-O.F.   For all the little girls who have been attacked, in parks, in the underground, in all those experiences of everyday life, at eight, ten, or twelve: extremely traumatizing . . .

J.-P.F.   But that's "psychical" rape, not violence, isn't it?

FOUCAULT   You're talking about exhibitionism, aren't you?

M.-O.F.   Yes, but if at that point there is nobody else around, anybody who might intervene, one thing leads to another — and that happens every day, in wastelands, etc. And that's something rather different from getting a smack from an adult.

FOUCAULT   I discussed all this yesterday with a magistrate. He said: there's no reason to make rape a crime. Rape could be outside the criminal law. It could quite simply come under civil law, with damages.

What do you think? I say: you, women . . . because, in this area, men, perhaps unfortunately, have less experience.

M.Z.   I can't place myself on the legislative level. Or on that of "punishment" — that's what bothers me.

J.-P.F.   From the point of view of women's liberation, one is on the "anti-rape" side. And from the point of view of anti-repression, it's the opposite. Is that right?

D.C.   One ought to invent "another crime." A single "crime" (rather as in China, where the whole of criminal law seems to have been reduced to fifteen points . . .) A crime that would be *failure to respect* the right of another *to say no.* A crime without punishment, but one involving political education . . . This, apart from cases of rape involving physical damage.

M.-O.F.   In the new climate, in which sexuality must be freely consented to, not subject to the criminal law, it is obvious that rape is its "opposite."

J.-P.F.   It has itself a repressive side . . . But how are we to think of repressing rape?

FOUCAULT   The answer from both of you, Marie-Odile and you, too, Marine, was very clear when I said: it may be regarded as an act of violence, possibly more serious, but of the same type, as that of punching someone in the face. Your answer was immediately: No — it's quite different. It's not just a punch in the face, but more serious.

M.Z.   Of course!

FOUCAULT   Then there are problems, because what we're saying amounts to this: sexuality as such, in the body, has a preponderant place, the sexual organ isn't like a hand, hair, or a nose. It therefore has to be protected, surrounded, invested in any case with legislation that isn't that pertaining to the rest of the body.

M.Z.   I was thinking more specifically about children. But, where children are concerned, I don't think it's any longer simply a sexual act. I believe it's really an act of physical violence.

D.C.   Rape is non-orgasmic. It's a sort of rapid masturbation in someone else's body. It isn't sexual. It's a wound.

M.Z.   That's what I meant. It's no longer sexuality, we're in a different area. That of physical violence.

FOUCAULT   In that case, then we come back to what I was saying. It isn't a matter of sexuality, it's the physical violence that would be punished, without bringing in the fact that sexuality was involved. I apologize for insisting on this. Your first reaction, on the other hand, was to say: it's quite different, it's not the same as a punch in the face.

M.Z.   It depends . . . on the point of view, it's very difficult to analyze. I was saying to myself: I sense a distance in relation to that, and I regard it as an act of physical violence, because I was thinking of a child. But I *also* think that it's really a trauma.

M.-O.F.   There's a lot of talk at the moment about one's right to pleasure. Well, by such an act, one can deprive a human being of just that . . .

J.-P.F.   In that case it's a wound that can affect one's very sexuality.

M.-O.F.   In Chile, in the shanty-towns, the *poblaciones*, in the appalling housing conditions there (which have been made much worse since the Junta), there are frequent cases of rapes of little girls, of eight or nine, by their fathers, brothers, etc. One can find there children who have become completely disabled, like in India as a result of child marriages.

J.-P.F.   If one is thinking in terms of damages, the peculiarity here is that it is a matter of the future.

FOUCAULT   On this theme, couldn't we say — for example, when a woman's frigidity (or possibly a man's impotence) is said to have been caused by the trauma of rape, or even of an insistent experience of exhibitionism — can't we admit that what we are doing is giving rape the same role as that played by the Oedipus Complex in facile psychoanalysis?

J.-P.F. During the discussion at "Shakespeare & Co." Kate Millett explained publicly that in Paris she had been seriously raped, by "physical rape" . . . [16] She provided all the details: in a café the psychical rapist sat down at the table next to hers and, when she went to another café, he followed her and sat down once again next to her . . .

I've been told of a more disturbing example. A little girl of eight, raped by a young farmworker of twenty-eight, in a barn. She thought the man wanted to kill her, he tore off her clothes. She went home — her father is a doctor, a cardiologist, though at the same time he is interested in Reich: hence the contradiction. He saw the little girl come home — she didn't say a word. She remained completely silent, for several days — she had a high fever. She therefore said nothing by definition. However, after a few days, she showed that she had been hurt, physically. Her father treated the wound and stitched it up. As a doctor and a Reichian, was he to bring a charge? He did no more than talk to the day laborer, before he left. No legal action was brought. They talked — and said no more about it. But the story continues with the description of an enormous psychical difficulty at the sexual level, later. One that was verifiable only some ten years later.

It's very difficult to think of anything here at the legal level. It's difficult enough at the psychical level — whereas it seems simple enough at the physical level.

FOUCAULT In other words, are we to have specific laws against physical attack involving sex? That's the problem.

J.-P.F. There's a lesion that is both physical, as in the case of a punch on the nose, and at the same time anticipates a "psychical lesion" — in inverted commas. It may not be irreversible, but it seems very difficult to assess. At the level of civil responsibility, it's difficult to "assess damages." At the

16. Katharine Murray Millett (1934–). American feminist and author of *Sexual Politics* (1970), a work that studied structures of domination in male-female relationships.

level of penal responsibility, what position could be assumed by a supporter of Reich? — can he bring a charge, involve himself in an act of repression?

FOUCAULT   Yet both of you, as women, were immediately upset at the idea that one should say: rape belongs to the realm of physical violence and must simply be treated as such.

M.-O.F.   Especially when children, little girls, are involved.

D.C.   In the case of Roman Polanski, in the USA, where there was a question of oral, anal, and vaginal sex with a thirteen-year-old girl, the girl did not seem to have undergone a trauma. She rang up a friend of hers to talk about it all — but her sister was listening behind the door and so the whole business of the Polanski trial was set in motion. There was no wound there, the "trauma" came from certain social "ideal formations." The girl seems to have enjoyed her experiences.

FOUCAULT   She seems to have been a consenting party. And that brings me to the second question I'd like to ask you. Rape can all the same be defined fairly easily — not only as non-consent, but as refusal of physical access. On the other hand, there is the problem, for boys as well as girls — because, legally, rape of boys doesn't exist — of the child that is seduced. Or who begins to seduce you. Is it possible to propose a law that says: one may have with a consenting child, a child who doesn't refuse, any kind of relations — this does not concern the law?

D.C.   A digression: two years ago in England, five women were condemned — with a suspended sentence — for the rape of a man. But, for many men, that would be paradise, wouldn't it?

FOUCAULT   This is the question that concerns children. There are children who throw themselves at an adult at the age of ten — so? There are children who consent, who would be delighted, aren't there?

M.-O.F.   One shuts one's eyes to activities between children. When an adult is involved, there is no longer equality or a balance of discoveries and responsibilities. There's an inequality that is difficult to define.

FOUCAULT   I'd be tempted to say: from the moment that the child doesn't refuse, there is no reason to punish any act.

But one thing struck me yesterday when I was talking to members of the Board of Magistrates. One of them was putting forward very radical points of view: it was the one, in fact, who was saying that rape didn't have to be punished as rape, that it was quite simply an act of violence. On the subject of children, he also began to take a very radical position. But at one point he suddenly jumped and said: But, I have to admit, if I saw someone touching my kids!

Then there are cases involving an adult who is in a position of authority in relation to the child — as parent, guardian, teacher, or doctor. There again one would be tempted to say: it isn't true that one can get a child to do what it doesn't really want to, simply by exercising authority. And yet — there is the important problem of parents, especially of step-fathers, which is very common.

J.-P.F.   There's a curious thing about the Versailles affair . . .

FOUCAULT   . . . and he was a doctor . . . (plus two teachers!).

J.-P.F.   . . . about "child seduction" — I've taken a fairly close look at what the law actually says on these matters. Curiously enough it has raised the age threshold step by step. Under Louis-Philippe, it was eleven, then Napoleon III raised it to thirteen.[17]

FOUCAULT Until 1960, when the law moved in the direction of repression. The Code of 1810 made no mention of sexual offenses: it was the only European legal code in which homosexuality was not condemned. Gradually we have seen these offences — *attentat à la pudeur, public outrage* — reappear under Louis-Philippe in 1832, then under the Second Empire about 1860. Then there was a whole lot of legislation between 1885 and 1905. There was more under Pétain, even later. Then, in 1960, the situation went further with a law involving an increase of penalties when *"l'outrage public à la pudeur"* (in other words, making love in the open air) was committed by two men or two women: the penalty was doubled. So, in 1960, under De Gaulle, two women or two men kissing in

17. Louis-Philippe (1773–1850). Accepted the French crown as "citizen king" after the Revolution of 1830. A victim of political corruption, his regime degenerated into one of reactionary violence [L.D.K.].

public were punished more severely than if a man and a woman were involved. Between eighteen months and three years — rather than between six months and two years. (The minimum had tripled.) So we have to be very careful! We have to look at things very closely . . .

These laws have been brought in fairly recently.

J.-P.F.   Can't the Napoleonic legislation be regarded as an inheritance of the French Revolution, itself a break with earlier legislation?[18]

FOUCAULT   Earlier? There were some highly incommensurate penalties. Being burnt at the stake for homosexuals, for example — though this was implemented only twice or three times in the eighteenth century, and in cases regarded as rather "serious." There were severe laws against adultery, etc. All the late eighteenth-century reformers laid down the principle that the private life — that form of the private life — had nothing to do with legislation.

J.-P.F.   Beccaria . . .

FOUCAULT   Beccaria, Brissot . . . Brissot said some wonderful things about homosexuals . . . [19] To the effect that they had already been punished "by their own ridiculousness" not to need additional punishment . . .

J.-P.F.   When was that?

FOUCAULT   In 1787–88. The Revolutionary laws dropped practically all sexual crimes. Indeed I think that Napoleonic society, which in certain respects was very rigid, was ultimately a fairly tolerant one.

J.-P.F.   This turning of sex into discourse as a general process over a long period, which you describe admirably in *La volonté de savoir*, seems to undergo an interruption when we get to the realities of contemporary Soviet society. It hasn't happened there yet. Even among the dissidents, there is almost a reinforcement of this silence on sexuality, which is

18. On March 24, 1726 . . . "Etienne Deschauffours was declared duly convicted of the crimes of sodomy mentioned during the trial . . . The said Deschaufflours was condemned to be burnt alive on the Place de Grève, his ashes scattered to the winds, his possessions confiscated and handed over the the King" (*Histoire de la folie*, p. 101).

19. Cesare Marchese de Beccaria (1735–94). Italian politician who attacked capital punishment and torture and in its place opted for crime prevention through education. Jacques Pierre Brissot de Warville (1745–93). French jurist and revolutionary politician who expounded a theory of criminal laws [L.D.K.].

quite extraordinary. The typical case is Parajanov, for example, who suffers from an insuperable taboo.

FOUCAULT   Indeed you can't get a single Soviet dissident to say anything about Parajanov.

J.-P.F.   The other aspect is that in the descriptions, which are nevertheless secret ones, of the places of confinement, whether in the psychiatric hospitals or simply in prisons, the Gulag and others, there is the same total silence. There is no mention of it either by the great narrator of the Gulag. He talks about everything else: police, transport, politicians, the religious, criminals. On sex — nothing. The same taboo is extended — if not reinforced — among the dissidents.

Compared with the period of Alexandra Kollontai in the Russian Revolution, which so scandalized the good, bourgeois reporters of the time, it's really quite astonishing.

FOUCAULT   In the long term, taken over a long period, this process of growth in the discourse on sexuality — sexuality turned into discourse — is visible; but with periods of backtracking.

In the Soviet Union, in so far as we are probably seeing a sort of depoliticization, involving a looser grip of the political apparatus on individuals, those phenomena of uncoupling, of irony, which you mentioned a little while back (and which Paul Thorez told you about), new forms of supervision will be put in place. The purely political context, guaranteed by the single party, will be relayed by other levels of authority. At that point, psychiatry, which is already playing its familiar role, but also psychology, psychoanalysis . . . will start to function fully. The first Congress of Psychoanalysis in the Soviet Union is to be held next October: all the psychoanalysts will be foreigners, but they are being brought in. Why bring them in, if not because it is suspected that what they have to say may be of some use? And I'm sure they are being brought in as "sexologists." That's to say, there's a real need — which is probably not very clearly realized. I don't think there's a little Machiavelli behind all that. Fundamentally, there is a need felt for a "normalization" of the individual's behavior, a need to take charge of the individual's behavior through forms of authority that are no longer the administrative and police authorities of the KGB, but something much more subtle.

M.-O.F.　They must be talking a lot about it already . . . Indeed those invited to the congress have specifically asked that the presumed author of the "Psychiatric Guide for Political Dissidents," who is still being held . . .

J.-P.F.　Semion Gluzman.

M.-O.F.　. . . should be present at this Congress in October. This cropped up at the press conference in February, with Fainberg, Bukovsky, Pliuch, and Gorbanevskanya.

J.-P.F.　I think it was Cyril Kupernik who formulated this request.

FOUCAULT　I'd say that, on this matter, the dissidents are probably right, from a tactical point of view. For what is threatening, in the present situation, is probably a "discourse on sexuality" that would soon become the discourse of general psychiatrization . . . A socialist society in which individuals' sexuality is a problem of public health doesn't seem to me to be at all a contradiction in terms. It doesn't seem to me to be a structural impossibility. And I don't believe there's a necessary connection between socialism and prudishness. I can very well imagine a "socialism" appearing in which people's sexuality is . . .

J.-P.F.　. . . a public function?

FOUCAULT　People are held in place by simple means, whether housing conditions, mutual observation, several families sharing one kitchen or one bathroom.

M.-O.F.　But one can arrange to meet people on the steamboats going up the Moskva . . .

FOUCAULT　When people have their own space and consequently find it easier to escape or ignore the political apparatus, or to hide from it, how will they be caught? They'll be caught on the couch, in psychotherapy, etc . . .

M.Z.　But if we turn the problem round — to the subject of children — if one considers rape as being of the same nature as a punch in the face, would it be possible to regard things from the point of view of "moral prejudice"?

J.-P.F.　We're back to civil responsibility.

FOUCAULT　. . . damages, pretium doloris: there are certainly categories of this kind. What does it *mean*, if one says: the rapist will no longer be put in prison, that has no sense — he will be told to pay a hundred thousand francs in damages? Can we say that?

M.Z. I wasn't thinking in terms of money. I was just wondering how one might leave a door open to *recognize* the act of violence, so that it doesn't become ordinary.

FOUCAULT Like a car accident.

M.Z. Yes. Something about that bothers me — the connection with what adults can do to children. And a situation in which children would no longer have any legal way of defending themselves. There is something missing. If one regards the act simply like a punch in the face — doesn't that allow anyone to rape a child?

FOUCAULT You know, as well as the legislation concerning the rape of a child, the "legal protection" given to children is an instrument put into the hands of *parents*. It's usually used to solve their problems with other adults.

M.Z. Exactly.

FOUCAULT Otherwise one leaves it to government, some bureaucratic organization or other, the authority to decide on the mode of protection necessary to the child.

M.Z. No, that's impossible.

FOUCAULT Couldn't the social worker make the decisions?

M.Z. No, that would be quite impossible.

FOUCAULT People may ask why I've allowed myself to get involved in this — why I've agreed to ask these questions . . . But, in the end, I've become rather irritated by an attitude, which for a long time was mine, too, and which I no longer subscribe to, which consists in saying: our problem is to denounce and to criticize; let them get on with their legislation and their reforms. That doesn't seem to me the right attitude.

M.-O.F. Is it because of this reform in penal law that is being prepared, concerning rape and the protection of children, that the gutter press is carrying out such a campaign about the "child martyrs"?

FOUCAULT It seems obvious to me.

M.-O.F.   But this campaign is misdirected, because "modern parents" haven't suddenly become monsters. The child-adult relationship must be seen in a changing historical context: children used to be the responsibility of the community — or of the enlarged community family, as David has shown. Now the loneliness of a young couple with their children in a council flat, on a housing estate, leads precisely to the situation of the "child martyrs," a whole series of tensions — including child rape.

J.-P.F.   The pressure of the family and of its conflicts increases as the extent of that family contracts: this is what David's description has shown.

D.C.   Yes, the community was a place of (relatively) free exchanges. Including those between children and adults.

Sexual exchanges.

But how are we to reconstruct such a community in the context of advanced capitalism?

12

Iran: The Spirit of a World Without Spirit

Foucault praises the Iranian revolution as an exemplary manifestation of a collective will that could not be thought of as emanating from categories such as class struggle or economic oppression. For the revolution to be politically operative, Foucault claims, the Shi'ite opposition to the Shah had to entail a radical transformation in the subjectivity of the people. The spiritual politics of Islam enabled this change to take place, realizing the Marxist axiom that religion ostensibly constitutes the spirit of a world without spirit. This interview with Claire Brière and Pierre Blanchet, "The Spirit of a World without Spirit," originally appeared in Brière and Blanchet, Iran: la révolution au nom de Dieu (Paris: Seuil, 1979), 227–41. The translation is by Alan Sheridan.

C.B. Could we begin with the simplest question? like a lot of others, like you, I have been fascinated by what has happened in Iran. Why?

FOUCAULT I would like to go back at once to another, perhaps less important question, but one that may provide a way in: what is it about what has happened in Iran that a whole lot of people, on the left and on the right, find somewhat irritating? The Iran affair and the way in which it has taken place have not aroused the same kind of untroubled sympathy as Portugal, for example, or Nicaragua. I'm not saying that Nicaragua, in the middle of summer, at a time when people are tanning themselves in the sun, aroused a great deal of interest, but in the case of Iran, I soon felt a small, epidermic reaction what was not one of immediate sympathy. To take an example: there was this journalist you know very well. At Tehran she wrote an article that was published in Paris and, in the last sentence in which she spoke of the Islamic revolt, she found that the adjective "fanatic," which she had certainly not written, had been crudely added. This strikes me as being fairly typical of the irritations that the Iranian movement has provoked.

P.B.   There are several possible attitudes to Iran. There's the attitude of the classic, orthodox, extreme left. I'd cite above all the Communist League, which supports Iran and the whole of the extreme left, various Marxist-Leninist groups, which say: they are religious rebels, but that doesn't really matter. Religion is only a shield. Therefore we can support them unhesitatingly, it's a classic anti-imperialist struggle, like that in Vietnam, led by a religious man, Khomeini, but one who might be a Marxist-Leninist. To read *L'Humanité*, one might think that the PC had the same attitude as the LCR.[1] On the other hand, the attitude of the more moderate left, whether the PS or that of the more marginal left around the newspaper *Libération*, is one of irritation from the outset. They would say more or less two things. Firstly: religion is the veil, an archaism, a regression at least as far as women are concerned; the second, which cannot be denied, because one feels it: if ever the religious come to power and apply their program, should we not fear a new dictatorship?

FOUCAULT   It might be said that, behind these two irritations, there is another, or perhaps an astonishment, a sort of unease when confronted by a phenomenon that is, for our political mentality, very curious. It is a phenomenon that may be called revolutionary in the very broad sense of the term, since it concerns the uprising of a whole nation against a power that oppresses it. Now we recognize a revolution when we can observe two dynamics: one is that of the contradictions in that society, that of the class struggle or of social confrontations. Then there is a political dynamics, that is to say, the presence of a vanguard, class, party, or political

---

1.   *L'Humanité*. French daily newspaper founded in 1904 by Jean Jaurès as the official organ of the Socialist Party. After the 1920 schism within that party it subsequently became the newspaper of the French Communist party [L.D.K.].

ideology, in short, a spearhead that carries the whole nation with it. Now it seems to me that, in what is happening in Iran, one can recognize neither of those two dynamics that are for us distinctive signs and explicit marks of a revolutionary phenomenon. What, for us, is a revolutionary movement in which one cannot situate the internal contradictions of a society, and in which one cannot point out a vanguard either?

P.B.   At Tehran University, there were — I have met several of them — Marxists who were all conscious of living through a fantastic revolution. It was even much more than they had imagined, hoped for, dreamt for, dreamt about. Invariably, when asked what they thought, the Marxists replied: "It's a revolutionary situation, but there's no vanguard."

C.B.   The reaction I've heard most often about Iran is that people don't understand. When a movement is called revolutionary, people in the West, including ourselves, always have the notion of progress, of something that is about to be transformed in the direction of progress. All this is put into question by the religious phenomenon. Indeed, the wave of religious confrontation is based on notions that go back for thirteen centuries; it is with these that the Shah has been challenged, while, at the same time, advancing claims for social justice, etc., which seem to be in line with progressive thought or action. Now I don't know whether you managed, when you were in Iran, to determine, to grasp the nature of that enormous religious confrontation — I myself found it very difficult. The Iranians themselves are swimming in that ambiguity and have several levels of language, commitment, expression, etc. There is the guy who says "Long Live Khomeini," who is sincerely convinced about his religion; the guy who says "Long Live Khomeini," but I'm not particularly religious, Khomeini is just a symbol," the guy who says "I'm fairly religious, I like Khomeini, but I prefer Sharriat Madari," who is a very different kind of figure, there is the girl who puts on the *chador* to show that she is against the regime and another girl, partly secularized, partly Muslim, who doesn't put on the veil, but who will also say "I'm a Muslim and Long Live Khomeini" . . . , among all these people there are different levels of thought. And yet everybody shouts, at one and the same time, with great fevor, "Long Live Khomeini" and those different levels fall away.

FOUCAULT   I don't know whether you've read François Furet's book on the French Revolution.[2] It's a very intelligent book and might help us to sort out this confusion. He draws a distinction between the totality of the processes of economic and social transformation that began well before the revolution of 1789 and ended well after it, and the specificity of the Revolutionary event. That's to say, the specificity of what people experienced deep inside, but also of what they experienced in that sort of theater that they put together from day to day and which constituted the Revolution. I wonder whether this distinction might not be applied to some extent to Iran. It is true that Iranian society is shot through with contradictions that cannot in any way be denied, but it is certain that the revolutionary event that has been taking place for a year now, and which is at the same time an inner experience, a sort of constantly recommenced liturgy, a community experience, and so on, all that is certainly articulated onto the class struggle: but that doesn't find expression in an immediate, transparent way. So what role has religion, then, with the formidable grip that it has on people, the position that it has always held in relation to political power, its content, which make it a religion of combat and sacrifice, and so on? Not that of an ideology, which would help to mask contradictions or form a sort of sacred union between a great many divergent interests. It really has been the vocabulary, the ceremonial, the timeless drama into which one could fit the historical drama of a people that pitted its very existence against that of its sovereign.

P.B.   What struck me was the uprising of a whole population. I say *whole*. And if you take, for example, the demonstration of the Ashura, add up the figures: take away young children, the disabled, the old and a proportion of women who stayed at home. You will then see that the whole of Teheran was in the streets shouting "Death to the king," except the parasites who, really, lived off the regime. Even people who were with the regime for a very long time, who

2. François Furet (1927–   ). One of the practioners of the French New History. Author of *Penser la Revolution Française* (Paris: Gallimard, 1978) [L.D.K.].

were for a constitutional monarchy as little as a month before, were shouting "Death to the king." It was an astonishing, unique moment and one that must remain. Obviously, afterwards, things will settle down and different strata, different classes, will become visible.

FOUCAULT Among the things that characterize this revolutionary event, there is the fact that it has brought out — and few peoples in history have had this — an absolutely collective will. The collective will is a political myth with which jurists and philosophers try to analyze or to justify institutions, etc. It's a theoretical tool: nobody has ever seen the "collective will" and, personally, I thought that the collective will was like God, like the soul, something one would never encounter. I don't know whether you agree with me, but we met, in Tehran and throughout Iran, the collective will of a people. Well, you have to salute it, it doesn't happen every day. Furthermore (and here one can speak of Khomeini's political sense), this collective will has been given one object, one target and one only, namely the departure of the Shah. This collective will, which, in our theories, is always general, has found for itself, in Iran, an absolutely clear, particular aim, and has thus erupted into history. Of course, in the independence struggles, in the anti-colonial wars, one finds similar phenomena. In Iran the national sentiment has been extremely vigorous: the rejection of submission to foreigners, disgust at the looting of national resources, the rejection of a dependent foreign policy, American interference, which was visible everywhere, have been determinants in the Shah's being perceived as a Western agent. But national feeling has, in my opinion, been only one of the elements of a still more radical rejection: the rejection by a people, not only of foreigners, but of everything that had constituted, for years, for centuries, its political destiny.

P.B. We went to China in 1967, at the height of the Lin Piao period, and, at that time, too, we had the feeling that there was the same type of collective will. In any case, something very strong was taking place, a very deep desire on the part of the whole Chinese people, for example, concerning the relationship between town and country, intellectuals and manual workers, that is to say, about all those questions that have now been settled in China in the usual, traditional way. At Peking, we had the feeling that the Chinese were forming a people "in fusion." Afterwards, we came to realize that we'd been taken in to some extent, the Chinese, too. It's true that, to an extent, we took ourselves in. And that's why, sometimes, we hesitate to allow ourselves to be carried away by Iran. In any case, there is something similar in the charisma of Mao Tse-tung and of Khomeini, there is something similar in the way the young Islamic militants speak of Khomeini and the way the Red Guards spoke of Mao.

FOUCAULT   All the same, the Cultural Revolution was certainly presented as a struggle between certain elements of the population and certain others, certain elements in the party and certain others, or between the population and the party, etc. Now what struck me in Iran is that there is no struggle between different elements. What gives it such beauty, and at the same time such gravity, is that there is only one confrontation: between the entire people and the state threatening it with its weapons and police. One didn't have to go to extremes, one found them there at once, on the one side, the entire will of the people, on the other the machine guns. The people demonstrated, the tanks arrived. The demonstrations were repeated and the machine-guns fired yet again. And this occurred in an almost identical way, with, of course, an intensification each time, but without any change of form or nature. It's the repetition of the demonstration. The readers of Western newspapers must have tired of it fairly soon. Oh, another demonstration in Iran! But I believe the demonstration, in its very repetition, had an intense political meaning. The very word *demonstration* must be taken literally: a people was tirelessly *demonstrating* its will. Of course, it was not only because of the demonstration that the Shah left. But one cannot deny that it was because of an endlessly demonstrated rejection. There was in these demonstrations a link between collective action, religious ritual, and an expression of public right. It's rather like in Greek tragedy where the collective ceremony and the reenactment of the principles of right go hand in hand. In the streets of Tehran there was an act, a political and juridical act, carried out collectively within religious rituals — an act of deposing the sovereign.

P.B. On the question of the collective will, what struck me — I was both spellbound by Iran and, sometimes, too, somewhat irritated — is when, for example, the students came and said: "We are all the same, we are all one, we are all for the Koran, we are all Muslims, there's no difference between us. Make sure you write that, that we're all the same." Yet we knew perfectly well that there were differences, we knew perfectly well, for example, that the intellectuals, a section of the *bazaaris*, and the middle classes were afraid to go too far. And yet they followed. That's what needs explaining.

FOUCAULT Of course. There's a very remarkable fact in what is happening in Iran. There was a government that was certainly one of the best endowed with weapons, the best served by a large army that was astonishingly faithful compared with what one might think, there was a police that was certainly not very efficient, but whose violence and cruelty often made up for a lack of subtlety: it was, moreover, a regime directly supported by the United States; lastly, it had the backing of the whole world, of the countries large and small that surrounded it. In a sense, it had everything going for it, plus, of course, oil, which guaranteed the state an income that it could use as it wished. Yet, despite all this, a people rose up in revolt: it rose up, of course, in a context of crisis, of economic difficulties, etc., but the economic difficulties in Iran at that time were not sufficiently great for people to take to the streets, in their hundreds of thousands, in their millions, and face the machine-guns bare-chested. That's the phenomenon that we have to talk about.

P.B. In comparative terms, it may well be that our own economic difficulties are greater than those in Iran at the time.

FOUCAULT Perhaps. Yet, whatever the economic difficulties, we still have to explain why there were people who rose up and said: we're not having any more of this. In rising up, the Iranians said to themselves — and this perhaps is the soul of the uprising: "Of course, we have to change this regime and get rid of this man, we have to change this corrupt administration, we have to change the whole country, the political organization, the economic system, the foreign policy. But, above all, we have to change ourselves. Our way of being, our relationship with others, with things, with eternity, with God, etc., must be completely changed and there will only be a true revolution if this radical change in our experience takes place." I believe that it is here that Islam played a role. It may be that one or other of its obligations, one or other of its codes exerted a certain fascination. But, above all, in relation to the way of life that was theirs, religion for them was like the promise and guarantee of finding something that would radically change their subjectivity. Shi'ism is precisely a form of Island that, with its teaching and esoteric content, distinguishes between what is mere external obedience to the code and what is the profound spiritual life; when I say that they were looking to Islam for a change in their subjectivity, this is quite compatible with the fact that traditional Islamic practice was already there and already gave them their identity; in this way they had of living the Islamic religion as a revolutionary force there was something other than the desire to obey the law more faithfully, there was the desire to renew their entire existence by going back to a spiritual experience that they thought they could find within Shi'ite Islam itself. People always quote Marx and the opium of the people. The sentence that immediately preceded that statement and which is never quoted says that religion is the spirit of a world without spirit. Let's say, then, that Islam, in that year of 1978, was not the opium of the people precisely because it was the spirit of a world without a spirit.

C.B.   By way of illustrating what you just said — "A demonstration there is really a demonstration" — I think we should use the word *witness*. People are always talking about Hussein in Iran. Now who is Hussein? A "demonstrator," a witness — a martyr — who, by his suffering, demonstrates against evil and whose death is more glorious than the lives of his victor. The people who demonstrated with their bare hands were also witnesses. They bore witness to the crimes of the Shah, of SAVAK, the cruelty of the regime that they wanted to get rid of, of the evil that this regime personified.

P.B.   There seems to me to be a problem when one speaks of Hussein. Hussein was a martyr, he's dead. By endlessly shouting Martyr, Martyr, the Iranian population got rid of the Shah. It's incredible and unprecedented. But what can happen now? Everybody isn't just going to shout Martyr,

Martyr until everybody dies and there's a military coup d'état. With the Shah out of the way, the movement will necessarily split apart.

FOUCAULT   There'll come a moment when the phenomenon that we are trying to apprehend and which has so fascinated us — the revolutionary experience itself — will die out. There was literally a light that lit up in all of them and which bathed all of them at the same time. That will die out. At that point, different political forces, different tendencies will appear, there'll be compromises, there'll be this or that, I have no idea who will come out on top and I don't think there are many people who can say now. It will disappear. There'll be processes at another level, another reality in a way. What I meant is that what we witnessed was not the result of an alliance, for example, between various political groups. Nor was it the result of a compromise between social classes that, in the end, each giving into the other on this or that, came to an agreement to claim this or that thing. Not at all. Something quite different has happened. A phenomenon has traversed the entire people and will one day stop. At that moment, all that will remain are the different political calculations that each individual had had in his head the whole time. Let's take the activist in some political group. When he was taking part in one of those demonstrations, he was double: he had his political calculation, which was this or that, and at the same time he was an individual caught up in that revolutionary movement, or rather that Iranian who had risen up against his king. And the two things did not come into contact, he did not rise up against his king because his party had made this or that calculation.

C.B.   One of the significant examples of this movement is what has happened in the case of the Kurds. The Kurds, a majority of whom are Sunnis, and whose autonomist tendencies have long been known, have used the language of this uprising, of this movement. Everybody thought they would be against it, whereas they have supported it, saying: "Of course we are Sunnis, but above all we are Muslims." When people spoke to them of their Kurdish specificity, their reaction was almost one of anger, or rejection. "What! We are Kurds!" they replied to you in Kurdish and the interpreter had to translate from Kurdish, "No, not at all, we are Iranians above all, and we share all the problems of Iran, we want the king to go." The slogans in Kurdistan were exactly the same as those in Tehran or Mashad. "Long Live Khomeini," "Death to the Shah."

FOUCAULT I knew some Iranians in Paris, and what struck me about a lot of them was their fear. Fear that it would be known that they were consorting with left-wing people, fear that the agents of SAVAK might learn that they were reading this or that book, and so on. When I arrived in Iran, immediately after the September massacres, I said to myself that I was going to find a terrorized city, because there had been four thousand dead. Now I can't say that I found happy people, but there was an absence of fear and an intensity of courage, or rather, the intensity that people were capable of when danger, though still not removed, had already been transcended. In their revolution they had already transcended the danger posed by the machine-gun that constantly faced all of them.

P.B. Were the Kurds still with the Shi'ites? Was the National Front still with the religious? Was the intelligentsia still following Khomeini? If there are twenty thousand dead and the army reacts, if there's a civil war lurking below the surface or an authoritarian Islamic Republic, there's a risk that we'll see some curious swings back. It will be said, for example, that Khomeini forced the hand of the National Front. It will be said that Khomeini did not wish to respect the wishes of the middle classes and intelligentsia for compromise. All these things are either true or false.

FOUCAULT That's right. It will be true and, at the same time, not true. The other day, someone said to me: everything you think about Iran isn't true, and you don't realize that there are communists everywhere. But I do know this. I know that in fact there are a lot of people who belong to communist or Marxist-Leninist organizations — there's no denying that. But what I liked about your articles was that they didn't try to break up this phenomenon into its constituent elements, they tried to leave it as a single beam of light, even though we know that it is made up of several beams. That's the risk and the interest in talking about Iran.

P.B.   Let me give you an example. One evening, we went out after the curfew with a very Westernized, forty-year-old woman, who had lived in London and was now living in a house in northern Tehran. One evening, during the pre-Moharram period, she came to where we were living, in a working-class district. Shots were being fired on every side. We took her into the backstreets, to see the army, to see the ordinary people, the shouts from the rooftops . . . It was the first time she had been in that district on foot. It was the first time she had spoken with such ordinary people, people who cried out *Allah O Akbar*. She was completely overcome, embarrassed that she was not wearing a *chador*, not because she was afraid that someone might throw vitriol in her face, but because she wanted to be like the other women. It wasn't so much the episode of the *chador* that is important, but what those people said to us. They spoke in a very religious way and always said at the end: "May God keep you" and other such religious expressions. She replied in the same way, with the same language. She said to us: this is the first time I have ever spoken like that. She was very moved.

FOUCAULT   Yet, one day, all this will become, for historians, a rallying of the upper classes to a popular, left-wing movement, etc. That will be an analytical truth. I believe it is one of the reasons why one feels a certain unease when one comes back from Iran and people, wanting to understand, ask one for an analytical schema of an already constituted reality.

C.B.   I'm thinking of another interpretative grid that we Western journalists have often had. This movement has followed such an odd logic that, on several occasions, Western observers have ignored it. The day of the National Front strike, in November, which had been a failure. Or the fortieth day of mourning of Black Friday. Black Friday had been terrible. One could imagine how the fortieth day of mourning would be very moving, very painful. Now, on the fortieth day, many shops were reopened and people didn't seem particularly sad. Yet the movement began again with its own logic, its own rhythm, its own breathing. It seemed to me that in Iran, despite the hectic rhythm at Tehran, the movement followed a rhythm that might be compared with that of a man — they walked like a single man — who breathes, gets tired, gets his breath back, resumes the attack, but really with a collective rhythm. On that fortieth day of mourning, there was no great demonstration of mourning. After the massacre in Jaleh Square, the Iranians were getting their breath back. The movement was relaunched by the astonishing contagion of the strikes that began about that time. Then there was the start of the new academic year, the angry reaction of the Tehran population, which set fire to Western symbols.

FOUCAULT   Another thing that struck me as odd was the way the weapon of oil was used. If there was one immediately sensitive spot it was oil, which was both the cause of the evil and the absolute weapon. One day we may know what happened. It certainly seems that the strike and its tactics had not been calculated in advance. On the spot, without their being any order coming from above, at a given moment, the workers went on strike, coordinating among themselves, from town to town, in an absolutely free way. Indeed it wasn't a strike in the strict sense of a cessation of work and an interruption of production. It was clearly the affirmation that the oil belonged to the Iranian people and not to the Shah or to his clients or partners. It was a strike in favor of national reappropriation.

C.B.   Then, on the contrary, for it would not be honest to be silent about it, it must be said that when I, an individual, a foreign journalist, a woman, was confronted by this oneness, this common will, I felt an extraordinary shock, mentally and physically. It was as if that oneness required that everyone conform to it. In a sense, it was woe betide anyone who did not conform. We all had problems of this kind in Iran. Hence, perhaps, the reticence that people often feel in Europe. An uprising is all very fine, yes, but . . .

FOUCAULT   There were demonstrations, verbal at least, of violent anti-semitism. There were demonstrations of xenophobia and directed not only at the Americans, but also at foreign workers who had come to work in Iran.

P.B.   This is indeed the other side of the unity that certain people may find offensive. For example, once, one of our photographers got punched in the face several times because he was thought to be an American. "No, I'm French," he protested. The demonstrators then embraced him and said: "Above all, don't say anything about this in the press." I'm thinking, too, of the demonstrators' imperious demands: "Make sure you say that there were so many thousand victims, so many million demonstrators in the streets."

C.B. That's another problem: it's the problem of a different culture, a different attitude to the truth. Besides it's part of the struggle. When your hands are empty, if you pile up the dead, real and imaginary, you ward off fear, and you become all the more convincing.

FOUCAULT They don't have the same regime of truth as ours, which, it has to be said, is very special, even if it has become almost universal. The Greeks had their own. The Arabs of the Mahgreb have another. And in Iran it is largely modelled on a religion that has an exoteric form and an esoteric content. That is to say, everything that is said under the explicit form of the law also refers to another meaning. So not only is saying one thing that means another not a condemnable ambiguity, it is, on the contrary, a necessary and highly prized additional level of meaning. It's often the case that people say something that, at the factual level, isn't true, but which refers to another, deeper meaning, which cannot be assimilated in terms of precision and observation . . .

C.B. That doesn't bother me. But I am irritated when I am told over and over again that all minorities will be respected and when, at the same time, they aren't being respected. I have one particularly strong memory — and I am determined all the same that it will appear somewhere — of the September demonstration when, as a woman, I was veiled. I was wearing a *chador*. They tried to stop me getting into the truck with the other reporters. I'd had enough of walking. When I was in the truck, the demonstrators who were around us tried to stop me standing up. Then some guy starting yelling — it was hateful — because I was wearing sandals without socks: I got an enormous impression of intolerance. Yet there were about fifty people around us saying: "She's a reporter, she has to be in the procession, there's no reason why she can't be in the truck." But when people speak to you about Jews — it's true that there was a lot of anti-semitic talk — that they will tolerate them only if they don't support Israel, when anonymous notes are sent out, the credibility of the movement is somewhat affected. It's the strength of the Movement to be a single unity. As soon as it perceives slight differences, it feels threatened. I believe the intolerance is there — and necessary.

FOUCAULT What has given the Iranian movement its intensity has been a double register. On the one hand, a collective will that has been very strongly expressed politically and, on the other hand, the desire for a radical change in ordinary life. But this double affirmation can only be based on traditions, institutions that carry a charge of chauvinism, nationalism, exclusiveness, which have a very powerful attraction for individuals. To confront so fearsome an armed power, one mustn't feel alone, nor begin with nothing. Apart from the problem of the immediate succession to the Shah, there is another question that interests me at least as much: will this unitary movement, which, for a year now has stirred up a people faced with machine-guns, have the strength to cross its own frontiers and go beyond the things on which, for a time, it has based itself. Are those limits, are those supports going to disappear once the initial enthusiasm wanes, or are they, on the contrary, going to take root and become stronger? Many here and some in Iran are waiting for and hoping for the moment when secularization will at last come back to the fore and reveal the good, old type of revolution we have always known. I wonder how far they will be taken along this strange, unique road, in which they seek, against the stubbornness of their destiny, against everything they have been for centuries, "something quite different."

The Ethics of Sexuality

13

The Battle for Chastity

The following text analyzes Cassian's notion of the battle for chastity in monastic life against the spirit of fornication in both the Institutiones *and Conferences. Fornication, the consequence of pride, is studied as having its own position in the table of vices. Not only is it rooted in the flesh but it is also created by the images born from the movements of the mind. Beyond the sphere of carnal passion and physical relationships, Cassian characterizes this struggle against fornication as one that is essentially non-sexual. Pollution functions as the yardstick of concupiscence in that it helps measure the role played by the will in its generation. This battle is described as a "chastity-oriented asceticism" that enacts a process of subjectivization in which self-knowledge is articulated as a form of truth. This text originally appeared in a special issue of* Communications *35 (1982) ["Sexualités occidentales] edited by Philippe Ariès and André Bejin where it was presented as an extract from the forthcoming third volume of the* History of Sexuality. *In fact it doesn't appear there and it is most likely to be part of the unpublished volume 4,* Les Aveux de la Chair *(Confessions of the Flesh). The English version, translated by Anthony Forster, originally appeared in* Western Sexuality *(Oxford: Basil Blackwell, 1985).*

The battle for chastity is discussed in detail by Cassian in the sixth chapter of the *Institutiones,* "Concerning the spirit of fornication," and in several of his *Conferences:* the fourth on "the lusts of the flesh and of the spirit," the fifth on "the eight principal vices," the twelfth on "chastity" and the twenty-second on "night visions." It ranks second in a list of eight battles,[1] in the shape of a fight against the spirit of fornication. As for fornication itself it is subdivided into three categories.[2] On the face of it a very unjuridical list if one compares it with the catalogue of sins that are to be found when the medieval Church organizes the sacrament of penance on the lines of a penal code. But Cassian's specifications obviously have a different meaning.

Let us first examine the place of fornication among the other sinful tendencies. Cassian arranges his eight sins in a particular order. He sets up pairs of vices that seem linked in some specifically close way:[3] pride and vainglory, sloth and accidie, avarice and wrath. Fornication is coupled with greed, for several reasons. They are two "natural" vices, innate and hence very difficult to cure. They are also the two vices that involve the participation of the body, not only in their growth but also in achieving their object; and finally they also have a direct causal connection — over-indulgence in food and drink fuels the urge to commit fornication.[4] In addition, the spirit of fornication occupies a position of peculiar importance among the other vices, either because it is closely bound with greed, or simply by its very nature.

First the causal chain. Cassian emphasizes the fact that the vices do not exist in isolation, even though an individual may be particularly affected by one vice or another.[5] There is a causal link that binds them all together. It begins with greed, which arises in the body and inflames the spirit of fornication: these two engender avarice, understood as an attachment to worldly wealth, which in turn leads to rivalries, quarrelling, and wrath. The result is despondency and sorrow, provoking the sin of accidie and total disgust with monastic life. Such a progression implies that one will never be able to conquer a vice unless one can conquer the one on which it leans: "The

---

1. The seven others are greed, avarice, wrath, sloth, accidie, vainglory and pride.

2. See below, p. 17.

3. *Conferences*, V, 10.

4. *Institutions*, V and *Conferences*. V.

5. *Conferences*, V. 13–14.

defeat of the first weakens the one that depends on it; victory over the former leads to the collapse of the latter without further effort." Like the others, the greed-fornication pair, like "a huge tree whose shadow stretches afar," has to be uprooted. Hence the importance for the ascetic of fasting as a way of conquering greed and suppressing fornication. Therein lies the basis of the practice of asceticism, for it is the first link in the causal chain.

The spirit of fornication is seen as being in an odd relationship to the last vices on the list, and especially pride. In fact, for Cassian, pride and vainglory do not form part of the causal chain of other vices. Far from being generated by them they result from victory over them:[6] "carnal pride," i.e. flaunting one's fasts, one's chastity, one's poverty etc. before other people, and "spiritual pride," which makes one think that one's progress is all due to one's own merits.[7] One vice that springs from the defeat of another means a fall that is that much greater. And fornication, the most disgraceful of all the vices, the one that is most shameful, is the consequence of pride — a chastisement, but also a temptation, the proof that God sends to the presumptuous mortal to remind him that he is always threatened by the weakness of the flesh if the grace of God does not come to his help. "Because someone has for long exulted in the pureness of his heart and his body, it naturally follows . . . that in the back of his mind he rather prides himself on it . . . so it is a good thing for the Lord to desert him, for his own good. The pureness which has been making him so self-assured begins to worry him, and in the midst of his spiritual well-being he finds himself faltering."[8] When the soul has only itself to combat, the wheel comes full circle, the battle begins again and the prickings of the flesh are felt anew, showing the inevitable continuance of the struggle and the threat of a perpetual recurrence.

Finally, fornication has, as compared with other vices, an

6. *Conferences*, V. 10.

7. *Institutions*, XII, 2.

8. *Conferences*, XII, 6. For examples of lapses into pride and presumptuousness, see *Conferences* II, 13; and especially *Institutions*, XII, 20 and 21, where offenses against humility are punished by the most humiliating temptation, that of a desire *contra usum naturae*.

ontological particularity which gives it a special ascetic importance. Like greed it is rooted in the body, and impossible to beat without chastisement. While wrath or despondency can be fought only in the mind, fornication cannot be eradicated without "mortifying the flesh, by vigils, fasts and back-breaking labor."[9] This still does not exclude the battle the mind has to wage against itself, since fornication may be born of thoughts, images and memories. "When the Devil, with subtle cunning, has insinuated into our hearts the memory of a woman, beginning with our mother, our sisters, or certain pious women, we should as quickly as possible expel these memories for fear that, if we linger on them too long, the tempter may seize the opportunity to lead us unwittingly to think about other women."[10] Nevertheless there is one fundamental difference between fornication and greed. The fight against the latter has to be carried on with a certain restraint, since one cannot give up all food: "The requirements of life have to be provided for . . . for fear lest the body, deprived through our own error, may lose the strength to carry out the necessary spiritual exercises."[11] This natural propensity for eating has to be kept at arm's length, treated unemotionally, but not abolished. It has its own legitimacy; to repudiate it totally, that is to say to the point of death, would be to burden one's soul with a crime. On the other hand there are no holds barred in the fight against the spirit of fornication; everything that can direct our steps to it must be eradicated and no call of nature can be allowed to justify the satisfaction of a need in his domain. This is an appetite whose suppression does not lead to our bodily death, and it has to be totally eradicated. Of the eight sins fornication is the only one which is at once innate, natural, physical in origin, and needing to be as totally destroyed as the vices of the soul, such as avarice and pride. There has to be severe mortification therefore, which lets us live in our bodies while releasing us from the flesh. "Depart from this flesh while living in the body."[12] It is into this region beyond nature, but

9. *Conferences*, V, 4.

10. *Institutions*, VI, 13.

11. *Institutions*, V, 8.

12. *Institutions*, VI, 6.

in our earthly lives, that the fight against fornication leads us. It "drags us from the slough of the earth." It causes us to live in this world a life which is not of this world. Because this mortification is the harshest, it promises the most to us in this world below: "rooted in the flesh," it offers "the citizenship which the saints have the promise of possessing once they are delivered from the corruption of the flesh."[13]

Thus one sees how fornication, although just one of the elements in the table of vices, has its own special position, heading the causal chain, and is the sin chiefly responsible for backsliding and spiritual turmoil, at one of the most difficult and decisive points in the struggle for an ascetic life.

In his fifth *Conference* Cassian divides fornication into three varieties. The first consists of the "joining together of the two sexes" (*commixtio sexus utriusque*); the second takes place "without contact with the woman" (*absque femineo tactu*) — the damnable sin of Onan; the third is "conceived in the mind and the thoughts."[14] Almost the same distinction is repeated in the twelfth *Conference*: "carnal conjunction" (*carnalis commixtio*), which Cassian calls *fornicatio* in its restricted sense; next uncleanness, *immunditia*, which takes place without contact with a woman, while one is either sleeping or awake, and which is due to "the negligence of an unwatchful mind"; finally there is *libido*, which develops in "the dark corners of the soul" without "physical passion" (*sine passione corporis*).[15] These distinctions are important, for they alone help one to understand what Cassian meant by the general term *fornicatio*, to which he gives no definition elsewhere. But they are particularly important for the way he uses these three categories — in a way that differs so much from what one finds in earlier texts.

There already existed a traditional trilogy of the sins of the flesh: adultery, fornication (meaning sexual relations outside marriage) and "the corruption of children." At least these are the three categories to be found in the *Didache*: "Thou shalt not commit adultery; thou shalt not commit

13. *Institutions*, VI, 6.

14. *Conferences*, V, 11.

15. *Conferences*, XII, 2.

fornication; thou shalt not seduce young boys."[16] And these are what we find in the "Epistle of St Barnabas": "Do not commit fornication or adultery; do not corrupt the young."[17] We often find later that only the first two precepts are imposed, fornication covering all sexual offenses, and adultery covering those which infringe the marriage vows.[18] But in any case these were habitually accompanied by precepts about covetousness in thought or sight or anything that might lead one to commit a forbidden sexual act: "Refrain from covetousness, for it leads to fornication; abstain from obscene talk and brazen looks, for all this sort of thing leads to adultery."[19]

Cassian's analysis has two special features: one is that he does not deal separately with adultery but places it with fornication in its limited sense, and the other is that he devotes attention mostly to the other two categories. Nowhere in the various texts in which he speaks of the battle for chastity does he refer to actual sexual relations. Nowhere are the various sins set out dependent on actual sexual relations — the partner with whom it was committed, his or her age, or possible degree of consanguinity. Not one of the categories that in the Middle Ages were to be built up into a great code of sins is to be found here. Doubtless Cassian, who was addressing an audience of monks who had taken vows to renounce all sexual relations, felt he could skip these preliminaries. One notices, however, that on one very important aspect of celibacy, where Basil of Caesarea and Chrysostom had given explicit advice,[20] Cassian does make discreet allusion: "Let no one, especially when among young folk, remain alone with another, even for a short time, or

16. *Didache*, II, 2.

17. *Epistle of St Barnabas*, XIX, 4. Earlier on, dealing with forbidden foods, the same text interprets the ban on eating hyena flesh as forbidding adultery, of hare as forbidding the seduction of children, of weasel as forbidding oral sex.

18. For instance St Augusting, *Sermon*, 56.

19. *Didache*, III, 3.

20. Basil of Caesarea, *Exhortation to renounce the World*, 5. "Eschew all dealing, all relations with young men of your own age. Avoid them as you would fire. Many, alas, are those who through mixing with them, have been consigned by the Enemy to burn eternally in hell-fire." Cf. the precautions laid down in *The Great Precepts* (34) and *The Short Precepts* (220). See also John Chrysostom, *Adversus oppugnatores vitae monasticae*.

withdraw with him or take him by the hand."[21] He carries on his discussion as if he is only interested in his last two categories (about what goes on without sexual relationship or physical passion), as if he was passing over fornication as a physical union of two individuals and only devoting serious attention to behavior which up till then had been severely censured only when leading up to real sexual acts.

But even though Cassian's analysis ignores physical sex, and its sphere of action is quite solitary and secluded, his reasoning is not purely negative. The whole essence of the fight for chastity is that it aims at a target which has nothing to do with actions or relationships; it concerns a different reality to that of a sexual connection between two individuals. A passage in the twelfth *Conference* reveals the nature of this reality. In it Cassian describes the six stages that mark the advance towards chastity. The object of the description is not to define chastity itself, but to pick out the negative signs by which one can trace progress towards it — the various signs of impurity which disappear one by one — and so get an idea of what one has to contend with in the fight for chastity.

First sign of progress: when the monk awakes he is not "smitten by a carnal impulse" — *impugnatione carnali non eliditur*, i.e. the mind is no longer troubled by physical reactions over which the will has no control.

Second stage: if "voluptuous thoughts" (*voluptariae cogitationes*) should arise in the monk's mind, he does not let it dwell on them. He can stop thinking about things that have arisen in his mind involuntarily and in spite of himself.[22]

Third stage: when a glimpse of the world outside can no longer arouse lustful feelings, and one can look upon a woman without any feeling of desire.

Fourth stage: one no longer on one's waking hours feels any, even the most innocent, movement of the flesh. Does Cassian mean that there *is* no movement of the flesh, and that

---

21. *Institutions*, II, 15. Those who infringe this rule commit a grave offense and are under suspicion (*conjurationis pravique consilii*). Are these words hinting at amorous behavior, or are they simply aimed at the danger of members of the same community showing particular favor to one another? Similar recommendations are to be found in *Institutions*, IV, 16.

22. The word used by Cassian for dwelling on such thoughts is *immorari*. Later, *delectatio morosa* has an important place in the medieval sexual ethic.

therefore one has total control over one's own body? Probably not, since elsewhere he often insists on the persistence of involuntary bodily movements. The term he uses, *perferre*, signifies no doubt that such movements are not capable of affecting the mind, which thus does not suffer from them.

Fifth stage: "If the subject of a discourse or the logical consequence of a reading involves the idea of human procreation, the mind does not allow itself to be touched by the remotest thought of sexual pleasure, but contemplates the act in a mood of calmness and purity, as a simple function, a necessary adjunct to the prolongation of the human race, and departs no more affected by the recollection of it than if it had been thinking about brickmaking or some other trade."

Finally, the last stage is reached when our sleep is not troubled by the vision of a seductive woman. Even though we may not think it a sin to be subject to such illusions, it is however a sign that some lustful feeling still lurks in the depths of our being.[23]

Amid all this description of the different symptoms of fornication, gradually fading out as one approaches the state of chastity, there is no mention of relationships with others, no acts, not even any intention of committing one. In fact there is no fornication in the strict sense of the word. This microcosm of the solitary life lacks the two major elements on which are centred the sexual ethic not only of the philosophers of the ancient world, but also that of a Christian like Clement of Alexandria (at least in Epistle II of his *Pedagogus*), namely the sexual union of two individuals (*sunousia*) and the pleasure of the act (*aphrodisia*). Cassian is interested in the movements of the body and the mind, images, feelings, memories, faces in dreams, the spontaneous movements of thoughts, the consenting (or refusing) will, waking and sleeping. Now two opposing poles appear, not, one has to realize, those of mind versus body. They are, firstly, the involuntary pole, which consists either of physical movements or of feelings evoked by memories and images that survive from the past and ferment in the mind, besieging and enticing the will, and, secondly, the pole of the will itself, which accepts or repels, averts its eyes or allows itself to be

23. *Conferences*, XII, 7.

ensnared, holds back or consents. On the one side then bodily and mental reflexes that bypass the mind and, becoming infected with impurity, may proceed to corruption, and on the other side an internal play of thoughts. Here we find the two kinds of "fornication" as broadly defined by Cassian, to which he confines the whole of his analysis, leaving aside the question of physical sex. His theme is *immunditia*, something which catches the mind, waking or sleeping, off its guard and can lead to pollution, without any contact with another; and the *libido*, which develops in the dark corners of the mind. In this connection Cassian reminds us that *libido* has the same origin as *libet* (it pleases).[24]

The spiritual battle and the advance towards chastity, whose six stages are described by Cassian, can thus be seen as a task of dissociation. We are now far away from the rationing of pleasure and its strict limitation to permissible actions; far away too from the idea of as drastic a separation as possible between mind and body. But what does concern us is a never-ending struggle over the movements of our thoughts (whether they extend or reflect those of our body, or whether they motivate them), over its simplest manifestations, over the factors that can activate it. The aim is that the subject should never be affected in his effort by the obscurest or the most seemingly "unwilled" presence of will. The sex stages that lead to chastity represent steps towards the disinvolvement of the will. The first step is to exclude its involvement in bodily reactions; then exclude it from the imagination (not to linger on what crops up in one's mind); then exclude it from the action of the senses (cease to be conscious of bodily movements); then exclude it from figurative involvement (cease to think of things as possible objects of desire); and finally oneiric involvement (the desires that may be stirred by images that appear, albeit spontaneously, in dreams). This sort of involvement, of which the wilful act or the explicit will to commit an act, are the most visible form, Cassian calls *concupiscence*. This is the enemy in the spiritual battle, and this is the effort of dissociation and disinvolvement that has to be made.

Here is the reason why, all through this battle against the

24. *Conferences*, V, 11, and XII, 2. Cf. above.

spirit of fornication and for chastity, the sole fundamental problem is that of pollution — whether as something that is subservient to the will and a possible form of self-indulgence, or as something happening spontaneously and involuntarily in sleep or dreams. So important is this that Cassian makes the absence of erotic dreams and nocturnal pollution a sign that one has reached the pinnacle of chastity. He often returns to this topic: "The proof that one has achieved this state of purity will be that no apparition will beguile us when resting or stretched out in sleep,"[25] or again "This is the sum of integrity and the final proof: that we are not visited by voluptuous thoughts during sleep and that we should be unaware of the pollutions to which we are subjected by nature."[26] The whole of the twenty-second *Conference* is devoted to the question of "nocturnal pollutions" and "the necessity of using all our strength to be delivered from them." And on various occasions Cassian calls to mind holy characters like Serenus, who had attained such a high degree of virtue that they were never troubled by inconveniences of this kind.[27]

Obviously, in a rule of life where renunciation of all sexual relations was absolutely basic, it was quite logical that this topic should assume such importance. One is reminded of the importance, in groups inspired by Pythagorean ideas, accorded to the phenomena of sleep and dreams for what they reveal about the quality of existence, and to the self-purification that was supposed to guarantee its serenity. Above all one must realize that nocturnal pollution raised problems where ritual purity was concerned, and it was precisely these problems which prompted the twenty-second *Conference*: can one draw near to the "holy altars" and partake of the bread and wine when one has suffered nocturnal defilement?[28] But even if all these reasons can explain such preoccupations among the theoreticians of monastic life, they cannot account for the absolutely central position occupied by

25. *Institutions*, VI, 10.

26. *Institutions*, VI, 20.

27. *Conferences*, VII, 1. XII, 7. Other allusions to this theme in *Institutions*, II, 13.

28. *Conferences*, XXII, 5.

the question of voluntary/involuntary pollution in the whole discussion of the battle for chastity. Pollution was not simply the object of a stricter ban than anything else, or harder to control. It was a yardstick of concupiscence in that it helped to decide — in the light of what formed its background, initiated it and finally unleashed it — the part played by the will in forming these images, feelings and memories in the mind. The monk concentrates his whole energy on never letting his will be involved in this reaction, which goes from the body to the mind and from the mind to the body, and over which the will may have a hold, either to encourage it or halt it through mental activity. The first five stages of the advance towards chastity constitute increasingly subtle disengagements of the will from the increasingly restricted reactions that may bring on this pollution.

There remains the final stage, attainable by holiness: absence of "absolutely" involuntary pollutions during sleep. Again Cassian points out that these pollutions are not necessarily all involuntary. Over-eating and impure thoughts during the day all show that one is willing, if not intending, to have them. He makes a distinction between the type of dream that accompanies them, and the degree of impurity of the images. Anyone who is taken by surprise would be wrong to blame his body or sleep: "It is a sign of the corruption that festers within, and not just a product of the night. Buried in the depth of the soul, the corruption has come to the surface during sleep, revealing the hidden fever of passions with which we have become infected by glutting ourselves all day long on unhealthy emotions."[29] Finally there is the pollution that is totally involuntary, devoid of the pleasure that implies consent, without even the slightest trace of a dream image. Doubtless this is the goal attainable by the ascetic who has practised with sufficient rigor; the pollution is only a "residue," in which the person concerned plays no part. "We have to repress the reactions of our minds and the emotions of our bodies until the flesh can satisfy the demands of nature without giving rise to any pleasurable feelings, getting rid of the excess of our bodily humors without any unhealthy urges and without having to plunge back into the battle for our

29. *Institutions*, VI, 11.

chastity."[30] Since this is a supra-natural phenomenon, only a supra-natural power can give us this freedom, spiritual grace. This is why non-pollution is the sign of holiness, the stamp of the highest chastity possible, a blessing one may hope for but not attain.

For his part man must do no less than keep ceaseless watch over his thoughts and bodily movements day and night — during the night for the benefit of the day and during the day in thinking of the approaching night. "As purity and vigilance during the day dispose one to be chaste during the night, so too nocturnal vigilance replenishes the strength of the heart to observe chastity during the day."[31] This vigilance means exerting the sort of "discrimination" that lies at the heart of the self-analysis developed in active spirituality. The work of the miller sorting out his grain, the centurion picking his troops, the money-changer who weighs coins before accepting or refusing them — this is how the monk must unceasingly treat his own thoughts, so as to identify those that may bring temptation. Such an effort will allow him to sort out his thoughts according to their origin, to distinguish them by their quality and to separate the objects they represent from the pleasure they can evoke. This is an endless task of analysis that one has to apply to oneself and, by the duty of confession, to our relations with others.[32] Neither the idea of the inseparability of chastity and "fornication" affirmed by Cassian, nor the way in which he analyzes them nor the different elements that, according to him, inhere in them, nor the connections he establishes between them — pollution, libido, concupiscence — can be understood without reference to the techniques of self-analysis which characterize monastic life and the spiritual battle that is fought across it.

---

30. *Institutions*, VI, 22.

31. *Institutions*, VI, 23.

32. Cf. in the twenty-second *Conferences* (6) the case of a consultation over a monk, who each time he was going to communion suffered a nocturnal visitation and dared not participate in the holy mysteries. The "spiritual physicians" after an interrogation and discussions diagnosed that it was the Devil who sent these visitations so as to prevent the monk from attending the desired communion. To abstain was to fall into the Devil's trap; to communicate in spite of everything was to defeat him. Once this decision had been taken the Devil appeared no more.

Do we find that, between Tertullian and Cassian, prohibitions have been intensified, an even greater importance attached to absolute continence, and the sexual act increasingly stigmatized? Whatever the answer, this is not the way the question should be framed. The organization of monasticism and the dimorphism that developed between monastic and secular life brought about important changes in the problem of sexual renunciation. They brought with them the development of very complex techniques of self-analysis. So, in the very manner in which sex was renounced there appeared a rule of life and a mode of analysis which, in spite of obvious continuities, showed important differences with the past. With Tertullian the state of virginity implied the external and internal posture of one who has renounced the world and has adopted the rules governing appearance, behavior and general conduct that this renunciation involves. In the mystique of virginity which developed after the thirteenth century the rigor of this renunciation (in line with the theme, already found in Tertullian, of union with Christ) transforms the negative aspect of continence into the promise of spiritual marriage. With Cassian, who describes rather than innovates, there occurs a sort of double action, a withdrawal that also reveals hidden depths within.

This has nothing to do with the internalization of a whole list of forbidden things, merely substituting the prohibition of the intention for that of the act itself. It is rather the opening up of an area (whose importance has already been stressed by the writings of Gregory of Nyssa and, especially, of Basil of Ancyra) which is that of thought, operating erratically and spontaneously, with its images, memories and perceptions, with movements and impressions transmitted from the body to the mind and the mind to the body. This has nothing to do with a code of permitted or forbidden actions, but is a whole technique for analyzing and diagnosing thought, its origins, its qualities, its dangers, its potential for temptation and all the dark forces that can lurk behind the mask it may assume. Given the objective of expelling for good everything impure or conducive to impurity, this can only be achieved by eternal vigilance, a suspiciousness directed every moment against one's thought, an endless self-questioning to flush out any secret fornication lurking in the inmost recesses of the mind.

In this chastity-oriented asceticism one can see a process of "subjectivization" which has nothing to do with a sexual ethic based on physical self-control. But two things stand out. This subjectivization is linked with a process of self-knowledge which makes the obligation to seek and state the truth about oneself an indispensable and permanent condition of this asceticism; and if there is subjectivization, it also involves an indeterminate objectivization of the self by the self-indeterminate in the sense that one must be forever extending as far as possible the range of one's thoughts, however insignificant and innocent they may appear to be. Morever, this subjectivization, in its quest for the truth about oneself, functions through complex relations with others, and in many ways. One has to rid oneself of the power of the Other, the Enemy, who hides behind seeming likenesses of oneself, and eternal warfare has to be waged against this Other, which one cannot win without the help of the Almighty, who is mightier than he. Finally, confession to others, submission to their advice and permanent obedience to one's superiors is essential in this battle.

These new fashions in monastic sexual mores, the build-up of a new relationship between the subject and the truth, and the establishment of complex relations of obedience to the other self all form part of a whole whose coherence is well illustrated in Cassian's text. No new point of departure is involved. Going back in time before Christianity, one may find many of these elements in embryonic form and sometimes fully shaped in ancient philosophy — Stoic or Neo-Platonic, for instance. Moreover Cassian himself presents in a systematic way (how far he makes his own contribution is another question which need not concern us here) a sum of experience which he asserts to be that of eastern monasticism. In any case study of a text of this kind shows that it hardly makes sense to talk about a "Christian sexual ethic," still less about a "Judaeo-Christian" one. So far as consideration of sexual behavior was concerned, some fairly involved thinking went on between the Hellenistic period and St Augustine. Certain important events stand out such as the guidelines for conscience laid down by the Stoics and the Cynics, the organization of monasticism, and many others. On the other hand the coming of Christianity, considered as a massive rupture with earlier moralities and the dominant introduction of a quite different one, is barely noticeable. As P. Brown says, in speaking of Christianity as part of our reading of the giant mass of antiquity, the topography of the parting of the waters is hard to pin down.

14

The Return of Morality

The return to morality represents an effort to rediscover in antiquity a form of thought which seeks an unmitigated convergence between freedom and truth and which has not yet been contaminated by Christianity. By transforming sexuality into a moral experience the Greeks, according to Foucault, were able to examine the problem of individual conduct. Foucault here coins the term "subjectivization", a procedure from which subjectivity is constituted as a possibility derived from self-conscious selection. This was Foucault's last interview. It was conducted by Gilles Barbadette and André Scala on the occasion of the French publication of volumes 2 and 3 of The History of Sexuality *[L'Usage des plaisirs and* Le Souci de soi *(Paris: Gallimard, 1984)], and was published in* Les Nouvelles *on June 28, 1984. This English translation was done by Thomas Levin and Isabelle Lorenz for* Raritan *(Summer 1985).*

G.B. AND A.S.   What strikes us upon reading your latest books is a clear, pure, and smooth writing, very different from the style we were used to. Why this change?

FOUCAULT   I am in the process of rereading the manuscripts dealing with the beginning of Christianity which I wrote for this history of morality (one reason for the delay in the appearance of these books is that the order in which they are coming out is the opposite of that in which they were written). Rereading these long abandoned manuscripts I rediscover the same resistance to a style as in *The Order of Things, Madness and Civilization,* or in *Raymond Roussel.* I must say that this causes a problem for me because the rupture did not occur progressively. It was very abrupt. Starting in 1975–76, I completely abandoned this style because I intended to write a history of the subject which would not be a history of an event that came about one day and of which the genesis and outcome should have been told.

G.B. AND A.S.   In detaching yourself from a certain style, have you not become more of a philosopher than you ever were before?

FOUCAULT   I admit it! The philosophical study I performed in *The Order of Things, Madness and Civilization,* and even in *Discipline and Punish* was essentially based on a certain use of a philosophical vocabulary, game, and experience, to which I was, moreover, completely devoted. However, while admitting this, it is certain that now I am trying to detach myself from this form of philosophy; but I do this precisely in order to use it as a field of experience to be studied, mapped out, and organized so that this period, which to some people might seem to be a radical non-philosophy is, at the same time, a more radical way of thinking the philosophical experience.

G.B. AND A.S.   It seems that you make certain things more explicit which could only be read between the lines in your previous books.

FOUCAULT   I must say that I would not put it that way. It seems to me that in *Madness and Civilization, The Order of Things* and also in *Discipline and Punish* a lot of things which were implicit could not be rendered explicit due to the manner in which I posed the problems. I tried to locate three major types of problems: the problem of truth, the problem of power, and the problem of individual conduct. These three domains of experience can only be understood in relation to each other, not independently. What bothered me about the previous books is that I considered the first two experiences without taking the third one into account. By bringing to light this third experience, it seemed to provide a kind of guiding thread which, in order to justify itself, did not need to resort to somewhat rhetorical methods of avoiding one of the three fundamental domains of experience.

G.B. AND A.S.   The question of style also involves the

question of existence. How can one make the style of life into a major philosophical problem?

FOUCAULT   That's a difficult question. I am not sure I am able to give a response. I do in fact believe that the question of style was central to experience in antiquity — stylization of the relation to oneself, style of conduct, stylization of the relation to others. Antiquity never stopped posing the question of whether it was possible to define a style common to these different domains of conduct. In fact, the discovery of such a style could probably have led to a definition of the subject. The unity of a "style of morality" began to be thought of only during the Roman Empire in the second and third centuries, and it was thought of immediately in terms of code and truth.

G.B. AND A.S.   A style of existence, that's admirable. The Greeks — did you find them admirable?

FOUCAULT   No.

G.B. AND A.S.   Neither exemplary nor admirable?

FOUCAULT   No.

G.B. AND A.S.   What did you think of them?

FOUCAULT   Not very much. They immediately stumbled upon what I consider to be the contradiction of the mortality of antiquity between the relentless search for a certain style of existence on the one hand and the effort to make it available to all on the other. While the Greeks probably approached this style more or less obscurely with Seneca [?] and Epictetus, it found expression only within the framework of a religious style. All of antiquity seems to me to have been a "profound error." [*Laughter*]

G.B. AND A.S.   You are not the only one to introduce the notion of style in history. Peter Brown has done so in *The Making of Late Antiquity*.[1]

FOUCAULT   My usage of "style" is to a large extent borrowed from Peter Brown. But what I am going to say now, which does not relate to what he has written, does not involve him in any way. To me, this notion of style seems very

---

1. Peter Brown, *The Making of Late Antiquity* (Cambridge: Harvard University Press, 1978) [L.D.K.].

important in the history of the morality of antiquity. A moment ago I spoke badly of this morality; I could now try to speak well of it. At first, the morality of antiquity addressed itself only to a very small number of individuals; it did not require everybody to obey the same pattern of behavior. It concerned only a very small minority of the people, even of the free people. There were several forms of freedom; the freedom of the head of state or of the leader of the army had nothing to do with the freedom of the wise man. Then this morality expanded. At the time of Seneca or even more so at the time of Marcus Aurelius, it might have been valid for everybody, but there was never a question of making it an obligation for all. Morality was a matter of individual choice; anyone could come and share in it. It is nevertheless very difficult to know who did participate in it during antiquity or under the Roman Empire. We are thus very far from the moral conformities, the structures of which are elaborated by sociologists and historians by appealing to a hypothetical average population. What Peter Brown and I try to do allows us to isolate individuals, who in their uniqueness have played a role in the morality of antiquity or in Christianity. We are at the very beginning of these studies of style, and it would be interesting to see how this notion was transmitted from the fourth century B.C. to the first of our era.

G.B. AND A.S. The morality of a philosopher of antiquity cannot be studied without at the same time taking into account all of his philosophy. In particular, with regard to the Stoics, one feels that precisely because Marcus Aurelius had neither physics nor logic, his morality tended more towards what you call Code rather than towards what you call Ethics.

FOUCAULT If I understand correctly, you are making this long evolution into the result of a loss. You seem to see in Plato, Aristotle, and the early Stoics a philosophy particularly balanced between the conceptions of truth, politics, and private life. Little by little, from the third century B.C. to the second century of our era, people would have dropped interrogations of truth and political power and would have asked themselves questions about morality. Indeed, from Socrates to Aristotle, philosophical reflection in general constitutes the matrix of a theory of knowledge, politics, and individual conduct. And then political theory entered a period of regression because the city of antiquity disappeared and was replaced by the great monarchies which followed Alexander. For more complicated reasons which, however, seem to be related, the conception of truth also began to regress. Finally one ended up with the following: in the first century some people said that philosophy should by no means concern itself with truth in general but rather with useful truths such as politics and, above all, morality. Here we have the grand scene of the philosophy of antiquity: exactly during his time off from political activity Seneca began to practice philosophy. He was exiled; he regained power; he exercised this power until he returned to a semiexile and died in complete exile. It is during these periods that philosophical discourse took on all its meaning for him. This very important and essential phenomenon is, if you will, the misfortune of the philosóphy of antiquity or, in any case, the historical starting point from which philosophy became a form of thought which would be found again in Christianity.

G.B. AND A.S.   On several occasions you seem to turn writing into a privileged practice of the self. Is writing central to the "culture of the self"?

FOUCAULT   It is true that the question of the self and writing of the self has not been central but always very important in the formation of the self. Let's take Plato for example, leaving aside Socrates, whom we only know through Plato. The least one could say of Plato is that he neither cultivated the practice of the self as a written practice nor as a practice of memory or of editing the self based on one's memories. While Plato wrote a considerable amount on a number of political, moral and metaphysical problems, the texts in the Platonic debate which give evidence of the relation to the self seem relatively restrained. This is also true for Aristotle. On the other hand, beginning in the first century of our era, one sees a great number of writings which follow a model of writing as a relation to the self (recommendations, advice and counseling given to students, etc.). In the Roman Empire young people were taught to behave themselves properly during the lessons which were given to them; subsequently, but only subsequently, they were taught how to formulate their questions. They were then taught how to give their opinions, how to formulate these opinions in the form of lessons and ultimately in didactic form. We have proof of this in the texts of Seneca, Epictetus, and Marcus Aurelius. I would not entirely agree that one could say that the morality of antiquity was, throughout its history, a morality of the attention to the self; rather, it became a morality of the self at a certain moment. Christianity introduced some perversions, some quite considerable modifications, when it organized extremely extensive penetential functions which involved taking account of oneself, telling about oneself to another, but without anything being written. On the other hand, at the same time or shortly afterwards, Christianity developed a spiritual movement connecting individual experiences — for example the practice of the diary — which made it possible to gauge or in any case to estimate the reactions of each person.

G.B. AND A.S.   There are, it seems, enormous differences between the modern practices of the self and those of the Greeks. Are they in no way related to each other?

FOUCAULT   In no way? Yes and no. From a strictly philosophical point of view the morality of Greek antiquity and contemporary morality have nothing in common. On the other hand, if one considers these respective moralities in terms of what they prescribe, intimate, and advise, they are extraordinarily close. It is important to point out the proximity and the difference, and, through their interplay, to show how the same advice given by ancient morality can function differently in a contemporary style of morality.

G.B. AND A.S.   It would seem that we have a very different experience of sexuality from that which you attribute to the Greeks. Do they have a place, as we do, for amorous delirium, the loss of the self? Does their eroticism communicate with what is alien or unknown?

FOUCAULT   I cannot respond to you in general. I will respond as a philosopher, that is, to the extent that what I have learned is from texts which are philosophical. It definitely seems to me that in these texts dating from the fourth century B.C. to the second century of our era there is hardly any conception of love which would have been

qualified to represent the experiences you are talking about —
experiences of madness or of great amorous passion.

G.B. AND A.S.   Not even in Plato's *Phaedrus*?

FOUCAULT   Oh no! I don't think so! One would have to
look closer, but it seems to me that in the *Phaedrus* there are
people who, after an amorous experience, disregard the
prevailing and longstanding tradition of their time. This
tradition based the erotic on a manner of "courtship" in order
to attain the type of knowledge which would allow them to
love each other on the one hand and, on the other, to have
the appropriate attitude towards the law and the obligations
imposed on the citizens. You begin to see in Ovid the
emergence of the amorous delirium at the moment when you
have the possibility and the beginning of an experience in
which the individual in some sense completely loses his head,
no longer knows who he is, ignores his identity, and lives his
amorous experience as a perpetual forgetting of the self. What
we have here is a later experience which absolutely does not
correspond to that of Plato or Aristotle.

G.B. AND A.S.   Up till now we were accustomed to locating
you in the historical space which runs from the Classical era to
the end of the nineteenth century. But here you are where no
one expected you — in antiquity! Is there a return to the
Greeks today?

FOUCAULT   We must be careful. It is true that there is a
return to some form of Greek experience; but this return is a
return to morality. Let us not forget that this Greek morality
has its origin in the fifth century B.C. and that Greek
philosophy transformed itself little by little into a morality in
which we recognize ourselves today. It must be said,
however, that in this morality we forget what its fundamental
accompaniment was in the fourth century: political philosophy and philosophy itself.

G.B. AND A.S.   But isn't the return to the Greeks the
symptom of a crisis of thought much like what might have
been the case in the Renaissance, at the time of the religious
schism and much later after the French Revolution?

FOUCAULT   This is very likely. Christianity has long
represented a certain form of philosophy. Then there were
periodic efforts to rediscover in antiquity a form of thought

not contaminated by Christianity. In this regularly repeated return to the Greeks there is certainly a sort of nostalgia, an attempt to retrieve an original form of thought and an effort to conceive the Greek world outside of Christian phenomena. In the sixteenth century it was a matter of rediscovering through Christianity a sort of Greco-Christian philosophy. Beginning with Hegel and Schelling, this took the form of an attempt to recover the philosophy of the Greeks while bypassing Christianity — here I'm speaking of the early Hegel — an attempt which one finds again in Nietzsche. Trying to rethink the Greeks today does not consist of setting off Greek morality as the domain of morality par excellence which one would need for self-reflection. The point is rather to see to it that European thinking can take up Greek thinking again as an experience which took place once and with regard to which one can be completely free.

G.B. AND A.S. Hegel's and Nietzsche's return to the Greeks put into play the relations between history and philosophy. For Hegel it was a matter of basing historical thought on philosophical knowledge. For you, on the contrary, as for Nietzsche, there is between history and philosophy both a genealogy and a kind of self-alienation. Does your return to the Greeks participate in a weakening of the ground on which we think and live? What did you want to destroy?

FOUCAULT I did not want to destroy anything! But I believe that in this "fishing around" that one undertakes with the Greeks, one must absolutely not impose limits on oneself nor establish in advance a sort of program which would allow one to say: this part of the Greeks I accept; this other part I reject. All of Greek experience can be taken up in nearly the same manner by each time taking into account differences of context and by indicating those aspects of the experience which could perhaps be salvaged and those which could, on the contrary, be abandoned.

G.B. AND A.S. In what you describe, you have found a point of convergence between an experience of freedom and of truth. There is at least one philosopher for whom the relation between freedom and truth was the beginning of occidental thought. This philosopher is Heidegger who, on this basis, established the possibility of an ahistorical discourse. Whereas previously you had Hegel and Marx in your line of sight, did you not have Heidegger in mind here?

FOUCAULT   Certainly. For me Heidegger has always been the essential philosopher. I began by reading Hegel, then Marx, and I set out to read Heidegger in 1951 or 1952; then in 1952 or 1953 — I don't remember any more — I read Nietzsche. I still have here the notes that I took when I was reading Heidegger. I've got tons of them! And they are much more important than the ones I took on Hegel or Marx. My entire philosophical development was determined by my reading of Heidegger. I nevertheless recognize that Nietzsche outweighed him. I do not know Heidegger well enough: I hardly know *Being and Time* nor what has been published recently. My knowledge of Nietzsche certainly is better than my knowledge of Heidegger. Nevertheless, these are the two fundamental experiences I have had. It is possible that if I had not read Heidegger, I would not have read Nietzsche. I had tried to read Nietzsche in the fifties but Nietzsche alone did not appeal to me — whereas Nietzsche and Heidegger: that was a philosophical shock! But I have never written anything on Heidegger, and I wrote only a very small article on Nietzsche; these are nevertheless the two authors I have read the most. I think it is important to have a small number of authors with whom one thinks, with whom one works, but about whom one does not write. Perhaps I will write about them one day, but at such a time they will no longer be instruments of thought for me. In the end, for me there are three categories of philosophers: the philosophers that I don't know; the philosophers I know and of whom I have spoken; and the philosophers I know and about whom I don't speak.

G.B. AND A.S.   Isn't this precisely the source of misunderstandings which surround your work?

FOUCAULT   Do you mean to say that my fundamental Nietzscheanism might be at the origin of different misunderstandings? Here you are asking me a question which embarrasses me, since I am in the worst position of anyone of whom it would be asked. The question addresses itself to those who themselves pose questions! I can only respond by saying that I am simply Nietzschean, and I try to see, on a number of points, and to the extent that it is possible, with the aid of Nietzsche's texts — but also with anti-Nietzschean theses (which are nevertheless Nietzschean!) — what can be done in this or that domain. I'm not looking for anything else but I'm really searching for that.

G.B. AND A.S.   Your books often say something different from what their titles announce. Aren't you playing a double game of surprise and deception with the reader?

FOUCAULT   It is quite likely that the works which I have written do not correspond exactly to the titles I have given them. It's clumsy of me, but once I choose a title I keep it. I write a book; I rework it; I discover new problematics; but the book retains its title. There is another reason. In the books that I write I try to circumscribe a type of problem which has not been circumscribed before. As a result, under these circumstances I need to be able to bring out a certain kind of problem at the end of the book which cannot be reformulated in the title. Here you have the two reasons why there is this sort of "game" between the title and the work. One should undoubtedly either tell me that these books don't make sense with these titles and that their titles should in fact be changed, or one should realize that there is a kind of gap which opens up between the title of the book and its content. This shifting should be considered as the distance which I myself effected in the course of writing the book.

G.B. AND A.S.   To accomplish your Nietzschean project of genealogies you have had to straddle various disciplines and extract the knowledge of the institutions which were running them. But is the power of these institutions so intimidating that you insist on saying that you are doing "studies of history and not those of a historian" and that you are neither a "Hellenist nor a Latinist"?

FOUCAULT   Yes, I will repeat this because sooner or later someone will say it — I can even tell you who! I am not a Hellenist; I am not a Latinist. I know some Latin and some Greek too, although not as much. Recently I have studied them again in order to ask some questions which can be recognized by Hellenists and Latinists on the one hand, while on the other hand they can be structured like truly philosophical problems.

G.B. AND A.S.   You repeat: I have changed; I did not do what I had announced. Why announce it then?

FOUCAULT   It is true that when I wrote the first volume of *The History of Sexuality* seven or eight years ago, I absolutely had intended to write historical studies on sexuality starting with the sixteenth century and to analyze the evolution of this knowledge up to the nineteenth century. And while I was doing this project, I noticed that it was not working out. An important problem remained: why had we made sexuality into a moral experience? So I locked myself up, abandoned everything I had written on the seventeenth century, and started to work my way back — first to the fifth century in order to look at the beginnings of the Christian experience, then to the period immediately preceding it, the end of antiquity. Finally I finished three years ago with the study of sexuality in the fifth and fourth centuries B.C. You'll say to me: was it simple absentmindedness on your part at the beginning or a secret desire that you were hiding and would have revealed at the end? I really don't know. I must admit that I do not even want to know. My experience, as I see it now, is that I probably could only produce this *History of Sexuality* adequately by retracing what happened in antiquity to see how sexuality was manipulated, lived, and modified by a certain number of actors.

G.B. AND A.S.   In the introduction to *L'Usage des plaisirs* you expose the fundamental problem of your history of sexuality: how do individuals constitute themselves as subjects of desire and pleasure? This question of the subject is, you say, what turned your work in a new direction. But your preceding books seemed to ruin the sovereignty of the subject. Is this not a return to an unanswerable question which would be for you the ordeal of an endless toil?

FOUCAULT   Endless toil, that's for sure: it is just exactly what I ran up against and what I wanted to do, since my problem was to define not the moment at which something like the subject would appear but rather the combination of processes by which the subject exists with its different problems and obstacles and through forms which are far from being completed. Thus, the point was to reintroduce the problem of the subject which I had more or less left aside in my first studies and to try and follow the developments or difficulties throughout its history. There is perhaps a bit of trickery in saying things this way, but in fact what I really wanted to do was to show how the problem of the subject did not cease to exist throughout this question of sexuality, which in its diversity does not cease to encounter and multiply it.

G.B. AND A.S.   Is this subject for you the condition of possibility of experience?

FOUCAULT   Absolutely not. It is experience which is the rationalization of a process, itself provisional, which results in a subject, or rather, in subjects. I will call subjectivization the procedure by which one obtains the constitution of a subject, or more precisely, of a subjectivity which is of course only one of the given possibilities of organization of a self-consciousness.

G.B. AND A.S.   When one reads your work, one gets the impression that there is probably no theory of the subject among the Greeks. But could they have given a definition of the subject which would have been lost in Christianity?

FOUCAULT   I do not believe that an experience of the subject should be reconstituted where it did not find formulation. I am much closer to things than that. And because no Greek thinker ever found a definition of the subject and never searched for one, I would simply say that there is no subject. Which does not mean that the Greeks did not strive to define the conditions in which an experience would take place — an experience not of the subject but of the individual, to the extent that the individual wants to constitute itself as its own master. What was missing in classical antiquity was the problematization of the constitution of the self as subject. Beginning with Christianity we have the opposite: an appropriation of morality by the theory of the subject. But a moral experience essentially centered on the subject no longer seems satisfactory to me today. Because of this, certain questions pose themselves to us in the same terms as they were posed in antiquity. The search for styles of existence as different from each other as possible seems to me to be one of the points on which particular groups in the past may have inaugurated searches we are engaged in today. The search for a form of morality acceptable to everybody in the sense that everyone should submit to it, strikes me as catastrophic. But it would be a misunderstanding to want to base modern morality on the morality of antiquity without considering the morality of Christianity. If I undertook such a long study, it was precisely to try to uncover how what we call the morality of Christianity was encrusted in European morality, not since the beginning of the Christian world but since the morality of antiquity.

G.B. AND A.S.   Insofar as you do not affirm any universal truths, but instead raise paradoxes in thought and make out of philosophy a permanent question, are you a skeptical thinker?

FOUCAULT   Absolutely. The only thing I would not accept in the skeptical program is the attempt the skeptics made to reach a certain number of results in a given order — because skepticism has never been total skepticism! It tried to raise problems in certain areas and to legitimate within other fields notions actually considered valid within other areas; secondly, it seems to me that for the skeptics, the ideal was to be optimists knowing relatively little about things, but knowing what they knew in a very secure and unimpeachable way. Instead, what I am aiming for is a use of philosophy which may enable us to limit the areas of knowledge.

15

The Concern for Truth

Foucault explains here his desire to write the history of the relations between thought and truth in Antiquity as a reflection on sexual behavior. In the analysis put forth in L'Usage des plaisirs and Le Souci de soi sexual activity is problematized as a moral dilemma inasmuch as the issues of desire and pleasure constitute an object of thought in the quest for a personal ethics. This technology of the self generates an aesthetics of existence or an art of living in which the exemplary individual — who is quintessentially male — must be master of himself and others. The ethical dimension of Foucault's most recent research enables him to rethink the role and function of the intellectual in contemporary society. "The Concern for Truth: an interview by Francois Ewald" appeared in Magazine littéraire 207 (May 1984), 18–23. The translation is by Alan Sheridan.

F.E. *La Volonté de savoir* was published as the first volume in a forthcoming History of sexuality. The second volume appeared eight years later and was based on a quite different plan from the one originally envisaged.

FOUCAULT I changed my mind. When a piece of work is not also an attempt to change what one thinks and even what one is, it is not very amusing. I did begin to write two books in accordance with my original plan, but I very soon got bored. It was unwise of me to embark on such a project and run counter to my usual practice.

F.E. Why did you do it then?

FOUCAULT Out of laziness. I dreamt that the day would come when I would know in advance what I would want to say and all I would have to do would be to say it. It was a symptom of the aging process. I imagined that I had at last reached an age when all one has to do is to unroll what is in one's head. It was at the same time a kind of presumption and a way of giving up. But, for me, to work is to try to think something other than what one thought before.

F.E.   But your readers believed in it.

FOUCAULT   I feel some scruples for and quite a lot of confidence in my readers. The reader is like a listener at a lecture. He can tell perfectly well when one has done one's work and when one is talking off the top of one's head. If the reader is disappointed, it will not be because I have just repeated what I said before.

F.E.   L'Usage des plaisirs and Le Souci de soi are presented, in the first instance, as the work of a positivist historian, a systematization of the sexual morals of Antiquity. Is that so?

FOUCAULT   They are certainly the work of a historian, with the proviso that these books, like the others, belong to the history of thought. The history of thought means not just the history of ideas or of representations, but also an attempt to answer this question: how is a particular body of knowledge able to be constituted? How can thought, insofar as it is related to truth, have a history? That is the question that is posed. I am trying to respond to a precise problem: the birth of a morality, a morality in so far as it is a reflection on sexuality, on desire, on pleasure.

It should be clearly understood that I am not writing a history of morals, of behavior, a social history of sexual practices, but a history of the way in which pleasures, desires, and sexual behavior were problematized, reflected upon, and conceived in Antiquity in relation to a certain art of living. It is clear that this art of living was practiced only by a small group of people. It would be ridiculous to think that what Seneca, Epictetus, or Musonius Rufus had to say about sexual behavior represented in any way the general practice of the Greeks and Romans. But I do believe that the fact that those things were said about sexuality, that they constituted a tradition that is to be found again, transposed, metamorphosed, and profoundly revised in Christianity, constitutes a historical fact. Thought, too, has a history; thought is a historical fact, even if it has many other dimensions than the historical. In this respect, these books are very similar to the ones I wrote on madness and penal history. In *Surveiller et punir*, I had no intention of writing the history of the prison as an institution: that would have required a quite different kind of research and a different type of analysis. On the other hand, I did ask myself how the conception of punishment had the history that it did at the end of the eighteenth century and at the beginning of the nineteenth. What I am trying to do is to write the history of the relations between thought and truth; the history of thought as such is thought about truth. All those who say that, for me, truth doesn't exist are being simplistic.

F.E.   Nevertheless, in *L'Usage des plaisirs* and *Le Souci de soi* truth does take on a very different form from the one it had in earlier works: that painful form of subjection, of objectification.

FOUCAULT   The notion common to all the work that I have done since *Histoire de la folie* is that of problematization, though it must be said that I never isolated this notion sufficiently. But one always finds what is essential after the event; the most general things are those that appear last. It is the ransom and reward for all work in which theoretical questions are elaborated on the basis of a particular empirical field. In *Histoire de la folie* the question was how and why, at a given moment, madness was problematized through a certain institutional practice and a certain apparatus of knowledge. Similarly, in *Surveiller et punir*, I was trying to analyze the changes in the problematization of the relations between crime and punishment through penal practices and penitentiary institutions in the late eighteenth and early nineteenth centuries. How is sexual activity now problematized?

Problematization doesn't mean representation of a pre-existing object, nor the creation by discourse of an object that doesn't exist. It is the totality of discursive or non-discursive practices that introduces something into the play of true and false and constitutes it as an object for thought (whether in the form of moral reflection, scientific knowledge, political analysis, etc.).

F.E.   *L'Usage des plaisirs* and *Le Souci de soi* have no doubt emerged from the same problematic. Yet they seem very different from the earlier books.

FOUCAULT   Yes, I have changed direction. When I was dealing with madness I set out from the "problem" that it may have constituted in a certain social, political, and epistemological context: the problem that madness poses for others. Here I set out from the problem that sexual behavior might pose for individuals themselves (or at least to men in Antiquity). In the first case, I had to find out how madmen were "controlled"; in the second, how one "controls" oneself. Though I should add that in the case of madness, I did try to approach, from that starting point, the constitution of the experience of oneself as mad, in the context of mental illness, psychiatric practice, and the mental institution. Here I would like to show how self-control is integrated into the practice of controlling others. They are, in short, two opposite ways of approaching the same question: how is an "experience" formed in which the relationship to oneself and the relationship to others are linked together?

F.E.   It seems to me that the reader will experience two kinds of strangeness. The first in relation to you yourself, to what he expects of you . . .

FOUCAULT   Excellent. I accept this difference entirely. That's the game I am playing.

F.E.   The second kind of strangeness concerns sexuality, the relations between what you describe and our own experience of sexuality.

FOUCAULT   I really don't think one should exaggerate this sense of strangeness. It is true that there is a certain received wisdom about Antiquity, and that the morality of Antiquity is often represented as "tolerant," liberal, and accommodating. But many people are perfectly well aware that in Antiquity there was an austere, rigorous morality. It's a well-known fact that the Stoics were in favor of marriage and conjugal fidelity. By bringing out this "severe" aspect of philosophical morality, I am not saying anything extraordinary.

F.E.   I meant the strangeness in relation to the themes that are so familiar to us in the analysis of sexuality: those of law and prohibition.

FOUCAULT   It's a paradox that surprised me, too, even though I had suspected as much in *La volonté de savoir*, when I stated the hypothesis that one could not analyze the constitution of a body of knowledge about sexuality simply on the basis of mechanisms of repression. What struck me about Antiquity was that the points of most active reflection on the subject of sexual pleasure were not at all the points representing the traditionally accepted forms of prohibition. On the contrary, it was where sexuality was most free that the moralists of Antiquity pursued their questions with greatest intensity and succeeded in formulating the most rigorous doctrines. Let us take the simplest example: the status of married women prohibited them from any sexual relationship outside marriage; yet there is hardly any philosophical reflection or theoretical concern with this "monopoly." On the other hand, men were quite free to love boys (within certain bounds) and it was on this kind of love that a whole conception of self-control, abstinence, and the non-sexual relationship was elaborated. It is not, therefore, prohibition that accounts for the forms of problematization.

F.E.   It seems to me that you were going further, that you were setting up an opposition between, on the one hand, the categories of "law" and "prohibition" and, on the other, those of "the art of living," "techniques of self," "stylization of existence."

FOUCAULT   I could, using methods and schemata of thought that are fairly common at the moment, have said that certain prohibitions were actually posed as such and that other, more diffuse ones were expressed in the form of morality. It seems to me that it was more suited to the areas I was dealing with and the documents at my disposal to conceive of this morality in the very form in which contemporaries had reflected upon it, i.e., in the form of an *art of existence* or, rather, a *technique of life*. It was a question of knowing how to govern one's own life in order to give it the most beautiful possible form (in the eyes of others, of oneself, and of the future generations for which one might serve as an example). That is *what* I tried to reconstitute: the formation and development of a practice of self whose aim was to constitute oneself as the worker of the beauty of one's own life.

F.E.   The categories of "art of living" and "techniques of self" do not have as their sole domain of validity the sexual experience of the Greeks and Romans.

FOUCAULT   I don't think there can be a morality without a number of practices of self. It may be that these practices of self are associated with a lot of systematic, constricting codal structures. It may even be that they almost fade away in the face of this set of rules, which is then presented as the essence of a morality. But it may also be that they constitute the most important and most active focus of morality and that it is around them that reflection develops. The practices of self take on the form of an art of self, relatively independent of moral legislation. Christianity certainly reinforced in moral reflection the principle of law and codal structure, even if the practices of asceticism continued to give great importance to the practices of self.

F.E.   Our own, modern experience of sexuality begins, therefore, with Christianity.

FOUCAULT   Early Christianity brought several important changes to the asceticism of Antiquity: it intensified the form of law, but it also diverted the practices of self towards the hermeneutics of self and the deciphering of oneself as a subject of desire. The articulation of law and desire seems to be fairly characteristic of Christianity.

F.E.   The description of the disciplines in *Surveiller et punir* had accustomed us to the most minute prescriptions. It is odd that the prescriptions of sexual morality in Antiquity in no way fall short of them from this point of view.

FOUCAULT   You have to go into detail. In Antiquity people were very attentive to the elements of conduct and they wanted everybody to pay attention to them. But the modes of attention were not the same as those that came to be known later. Thus the sexual act itself, its morphology, the way in which one seeks and obtains one's pleasure, the "object" of desire, do not seem to have been a very important theoretical problem in Antiquity. On the other hand, what was an object of preoccupation was the intensity of sexual activity, its rhythm, the moment chosen; it was also the active or passive role that one played in the relationship. Thus one finds hundreds of details concerning sexual acts in relation to the seasons, the hours of the day, periods of rest and exercise, or the way in which a boy should behave if he is to have a good reputation, but none of those catalogues of permitted and forbidden acts that were to be so important in Christian pastoral practice.

F.E.   The various practices you describe, in relation to the body, to women, and to boys each seems to have been conceived on its own, without being linked together in a rigorous system. That is another difference in relation to your earlier book.

FOUCAULT   Reading one account of my work, I learnt that I had summed up the whole experience of madness in the classical age by the practice of confinement. How *Histoire de la folie* is constructed on the thesis that there were at least two distinct experiences of madness: one was that of confinement, the other that of a medical practice with a long history behind it. There is nothing extraordinary in the fact that one can have different (simultaneous as well as successive) experiences of the same thing.

F.E.   The architecture of your recent books reminds me rather of the contents page of the *Nicomachaean Ethics*. You examine each practice one after the other. What is the link, then, between the relationship to the body, the relationship to the home and wife, and the relationship to the boy?

FOUCAULT   A certain style of morality that is *self-control*. Sexual activity is represented, perceived as violence, and therefore problematized from the point of view of the difficulty there is in controlling it. Hubris is fundamental. In this ethics, one must constitute for oneself rules of conduct by which one will be able to ensure that self-control that may itself be ordered on three different principles: 1. the relationship to the body and the problem of health; 2. the relationship to women, that is to say, to woman in general and to one's wife in particular, in so far as the conjugal couple forms part of the same household; 3. the relationship to those very special individuals who may one day become free citizens, namely, youths. In these three domains, self-control assumes three different forms; there is no one single domain that would unify them all, as was to appear with the notions of flesh and sexuality. Among the great transformations that Christianity was to bring was the notion that the ethics of the flesh was as valid for women as for men. In the ancient morality, on the other hand, self-control is a problem only for the individual who must be master of himself and master of others and not for those who must obey others. That is why this ethics concerns only men and does not have exactly the same form when applied to relations with one's own body, with one's wife, or with boys.

F.E.   After these books, the question of sexual liberation seems to be devoid of meaning.

FOUCAULT   It may be said that in Antiquity one is dealing with a desire for rules, a desire for form, a search for austerity. How was it formed? Is that desire for austerity anything more than the expression of a fundamental prohibition? Or, on the contrary, was it not the matrix, from which certain general forms of prohibition were later derived?

F.E.   So you are proposing a complete reversal of the traditional way of considering the question of the relations between sexuality and prohibition?

FOUCAULT   In Greece, there were fundamental prohibitions. The prohibition of incest, for instance. But they were of very little interest to philosophers and moralists, compared with the overriding concern with retaining self-control. When Xenophon gives the reasons why incest is forbidden, he explains that if one married one's mother the difference in age would be such that the children could be neither beautiful nor healthy.

F.E.   Yet Sophocles seems to have said something different.

FOUCAULT   The interesting thing is that this serious, important prohibition could be at the heart of a tragedy. It is not, however, at the center of moral reflection.

F.E.   Why turn your attention to those periods, which, some will say, are so very far from our own?

FOUCAULT   I set out from a problem expressed in the terms current today and I try to work out its genealogy. Genealogy means that I begin my analysis from a question posed in the present.

F.E.   What, then, is the question posed in the present here?

FOUCAULT   For a long time many people imagined that the strictness of the sexual codes, in the form that we know them, was indispensable to so-called "capitalist" societies. Yet the lifting of the codes and the dislocation of prohibitions have probably been carried out more easily than people thought they would (which certainly seems to indicate that their purpose was not what it was believed to be); and the problem of an ethics as a form to be given to one's behavior and life has arisen once more. In sum, people were wrong when they believed that all morality resided in prohibition and that the listing of these prohibitions in itself solved the question of ethics.

F.E. Did you write these books for the liberation movement?

FOUCAULT Not for, but in terms of, a contemporary situation.

F.E. You remarked about *Surveiller et punir* that it was your "first book." Could one not use the term yet again with the publication of *L'Usage des plaisirs* and *Le Souci de soi*?

FOUCAULT Writing a book is, in a way, to abolish the previous one. In the end you realize that what you have done is — it may come either as a comfort or a disappointment — fairly close to what you have already written.

F.E. You speak of "detaching yourself from yourself." What is the significance of so strange a desire?

FOUCAULT What can the ethics of an intellectual be — I claim this title of intellectual, though, at the present time, it seems to make certain people sick — if not this: to make oneself permanently capable of detaching oneself from oneself (which is the opposite of the attitude of conversion)? If I had wanted to be exclusively an academic, it would no doubt have been wiser to choose one field and one alone to work in, accepting a given problematic and trying either to implement it or to alter it in certain respects. I could then have written books like the ones envisaged in *La Volonté de savoir*, six volumes of a history of sexuality, knowing in advance what I wanted to do and where I hoped to arrive. To be at once an academic and an intellectual is to try to manipulate a type of knowledge and analysis that is taught and received in the universities in such a way as to alter not only others' thoughts, but also one's own. This work of altering one's own thought and that of others seems to me to be the intellectual's raison d'être.

F.E.   Sartre, for example, tended to have the image of an intellectual who had spent his life developing a fundamental intuition. This desire to "detach yourself from yourself" certainly seems peculiar to you.

FOUCAULT   I don't know whether there is anything peculiar to me about it. But what I am sure of is that this change does not take the form of a sudden illumination in which "one's eyes are opened," nor of a permeability to all the movements at work in the present; I would like it to be an elaboration of self by self, a studious transformation, a slow, arduous process of change, guided by a constant concern for truth.

F.E.   The earlier books produced an image of you as the thinker of confinement, of subjected, constrained, disciplined subjects. L'Usage des plaisirs and Le Souci de soi offer up the quite different image of free subjects. It would seem that there is an important change in your own thinking here.

FOUCAULT   We must go back to the problem of the relations between knowledge and power. I know that, as far as the general public is concerned, I am the guy who said that knowledge merged with power, that it was no more than a thin mask thrown over the structures of domination and that those structures were always ones of oppression, confinement, and so on. The first point is so absurd as to be laughable. If I had said, or meant, that knowledge was power, I would have said so, and, having said so, I would have had nothing more to say, since, having made them identical, I don't see why I would have taken the trouble to show the different relations between them. What I set out to show was how certain forms of power that were of the same type could give rise to bodies of knowledge that were extremely different both in their object and in their structure. Let's take the problem of the structure of the hospital: it gave rise to confinement of a psychiatric type, to which corresponded the formation of a body of psychiatric knowledge whose epistemological structure may leave one fairly skeptical. But in another book, Naissance de la clinique, I tried to show how, in that same hospital structure, there developed a body of anatomo-pathological knowledge that was the foundation of a medicine possessing a quite different potential for scientific development. We have, then, power structures, fairly closely related institutional forms — psychiatric confinement, medical hospitalization — that are bound up with different forms of knowledge, between which it is possible to draw up a system of relations based not on cause and effect, still less on identity, but on conditions. Those who say that for me knowledge is the mask of power seem to me to be quite incapable of understanding. It is hardly worth answering them.

F.E.   But which, nevertheless, you find sufficiently useful to do now.

FOUCAULT   Which indeed I find important to do now.

F.E.   Your last two books mark a sort of movement from politics to ethics. People are certainly now going to expect an answer from you to the question: What must one do? What must one want?

FOUCAULT   The role of an intellectual is not to tell others what they have to do. By what right would he do so? And remember all the prophecies, promises, injunctions, and programs that intellectuals have managed to formulate over the last two centuries and whose effects we can now see. The work of an intellectual is not to shape others' political will; it is, through the analyses that he carries out in his own field, to question over and over again what is postulated as self-evident, to disturb people's mental habits, the way they do and think things, to dissipate what is familiar and accepted, to reexamine rules and institutions and on the basis of this re-problematization (in which he carries out his specific task as an intellectual) to participate in the formation of a political will (in which he has his role as citizen to play).

F.E.   Intellectuals have recently been criticized a great deal for their silence.

FOUCAULT   Quite wrongly, even, though I don't wish to enter into this controversy, the starting point of which was a lie. On the other hand, the very fact of this campaign is not entirely devoid of interest. One must ask oneself why the Socialists and the government have launched it or relaunched it, running the risk of revealing between themselves and a whole body of left-wing opinion a split that did not serve their purposes. Superficially, for some, there was of course the dressing up as a statement of what was actually an injunction: "You are saying nothing" meaning "Since we don't want to hear you, shut up." But, more seriously, there was, in this reproach, something like a request and a complaint: "Say some of the things we so much want to hear. During the whole period when we had such difficulty handling our electoral alliance with the Communists, there was obviously no question of saying anything that did not stem from a 'socialist' orthodoxy acceptable to them. There were enough bones of contention between them and us not to add that one to them. So, during that period, your job was to keep quiet and let us dismiss you, in the interests of our alliance, as the 'little left,' 'American' or 'Californian left.' But once we were in government, we needed you to speak up. We wanted you to provide a form of discourse possessing a double function: it would have manifested the secure base for a body of left-wing opinion around us (we would have preferred fidelity, but we would have settled for a more independent stance); but there would also have been a need to speak about a certain economic and political reality, which we used to take care to keep out of our own discourse. We needed others beside us to maintain a discourse on the rationality of the government that would be neither the lying discourse of our alliance, nor the bare, unvarnished discourse of our right-wing adversaries (the one we are using today). "We wanted to bring you back into the game; but you deserted us in the middle of the ford and there you are sitting on the bank." To which the intellectuals might reply: "When we urged you to change your discourse, you condemned us in the name of your most worn-out slogans. And now you are changing direction, under pressure of a reality that you are not capable of perceiving, you are asking us to provide you, not with the thought that might enable you to confront it, but with a discourse that would conceal your change. The trouble lies not, as has been said, in the fact that intellectuals ceased to be Marxists as soon as the Communists got to power, it lies in the fact that the scruples of your alliance prevented you, when it would have been useful, to carry out with the intellectuals the work of thought that would have made you capable of governing, of governing in a different way than with your faded slogans and with the unrejuvenated techniques of the others."

F.E. Is there a common approach in the various interventions that you have made in politics and in particular in relation to Poland?

FOUCAULT Let's try to pose a few questions in terms of truth and error. When our Foreign Minister said that Jaruzelski's coup was a matter that concerned only Poland, was this true? Is it true that Europe is of so little importance that its division and the Communist domination that is practiced behind an arbitrary line does not concern us? Is it true that the refusal of elementary trade-union freedom in a socialist country is a matter of no importance in a country ruled by Socialists and Communists? If it is true that the presence of Communists in the government has no influence on the major decisions of foreign policy, what is one to think of this government and of the alliance on which it rests? These questions certainly do not define a policy; but they are the questions to which those who do define policy ought to address themselves.

F.E. Does the role that you give yourself in politics correspond to that principle of "free speech" which you have made the theme of your lectures over the last two years?

FOUCAULT Nothing is more inconsistent than a political regime that is indifferent to truth; but nothing is more dangerous than a political system that claims to lay down the truth. The function of "telling the truth" must not take the form of law, just as it would be pointless to believe that it resides by right in the spontaneous interplay of communication. The task of telling the truth is an endless labor: to respect it in all its complexity is an obligation which no power can do without — except by imposing the silence of slavery.

The Politics of Sexuality

16

Sexual Morality and the Law

Michel Foucault, Guy Hocquenghem, and Jean Danet discuss here the legal aspects of sexual relations between adults and children. They argue that the decency/indecency paradigm that has been articulated by jurists, doctors, and psychologists since the nineteenth century has functioned not so much to punish offenses, but rather to target individuals whose sexuality reaches criminal proportions because it is thought to endanger an entire segment of the population. This text is the transcription of the program "Dialogues" broadcast by France-Culture, April 4, 1978 (Producer: Roger Pillaudin). It was published as "La loi de la pudeur" in Recherches *37 (April 1979), 69–82. The translation is by Alan Sheridan.*

FOUCAULT   All three of us agreed to take part in this broadcast (it was agreed in principle several months ago) for the following reason. Things had evolved on such a wide front, in such an overwhelming and at first sight apparently irreversible way, that many of us began to hope that the legal regime imposed on the sexual practices of our contemporaries would at last be relaxed and broken up. This regime is not as old as all that, since the penal code of 1810[1] said very little about sexuality, as if sexuality was not the business of the law; and it was only during the nineteenth century and above all in the twentieth, at the time of Pétain or of the Mirguet

---

1. Penal Code of 1810: — Part of the Napoleonic code. This group of 485 articles defines crimes, offenses, and misdemeanors as well as the resulting punishments. Promulgated February 12, 1810 [L.D.K.].

amendment (1960),[2] that legislation on sexuality became increasingly oppressive. But, over the last ten years or so, a movement in public opinion and sexual morals has been discernible in favor of reconsidering this legal regime. There was even set up a Commission for the Reform of Penal Law, whose task it was, to revise a number of fundamental articles in the penal code. And this commission has actually admitted, with, I must say, great seriousness, not only the possibility, but the need to change most of the articles in our present legislation concerning sexual behavior. This commission, which has now been sitting for several months, considered this reform of the sexual legislation last May and June. I believe that the proposals it expected to make were what may be called liberal. However, it would seem that for several months now, a movement in the opposite direction has begun to emerge. It is a disturbing movement — firstly, because it is occurring not only in France. Take, for example, what is happening in the United States, with Anita Bryant's campaign against homosexuals, which has almost gone so far as to call for murder. It's a phenomenon observable in France. But in France we see it through a number of particular, specific facts, which we shall talk about later (Jean Danet and Guy Hocquenghem will certainly provide examples), but ones that seem to show that in both police and legal practice we are returning to tougher and stricter positions. And this movement, observable in police and legal practice, is unfortunately supported very often by press campaigns, or by a system of information carried out in the press. It is therefore in this situation, that of an overall movement tending to liberalism, followed by a phenomenon of reaction, of slowing down, perhaps even the beginnings of a reverse process, that we are holding our discussion this evening.

G.H.   Six months ago we launched a petition demanding the abrogation of a number of articles in the law, in particular those concerning relations between adults and minors, those forbidding the incitement of minors to "debauchery," and the

---

2. Mirguet amendment: Promulgated July 18, 1960 as amendment to article 38 of the 1958 French constitution (October 4, 1958). It declared the necessity to fight against all threats to public hygiene and specifically names tuberculosis, cancer, alcoholism, prostitution and homosexuality as objects of attack [L.D.K.].

decriminalization of relations between minors and adults below the age of fifteen. A lot of people signed it, people belonging to a wide range of political positions, from the Communist Party to Mme Dolto.[3] So it's a petition that has been signed by a lot of people who are suspect neither of being particularly pedophiles themselves nor even of entertaining extravagant political views. We felt that a certain movement was beginning to emerge, and this movement was confirmed by the evidence submitted to the commission reforming the penal code. What we can now see, then, is not only that this kind of movement is something of a liberal illusion, but that in fact it does not amount to a profound transformation in the legal system, either in the way a case is investigated or in the way it is judged in court. But, furthermore, at the level of public opinion, at the level of the mass media, the newspapers, radio, television, etc., it is rather the opposite that is beginning to take place, with new arguments being used. These new arguments are essentially about childhood, that is to say, about the exploitation of popular sentiment and its spontaneous horror of anything that links sex with the child. Thus an article in the *Nouvel Observateur* begins with a few remarks to the effect that "pornography involving children is the ultimate American nightmare and no doubt the most terrible in a country fertile in scandals." When someone says that child pornography is the most terrible of present-day scandals, one cannot but be struck by the disproportion between this — child pornography, which is not even prostitution — and everything that is happening in the world today — what the Blacks have to put up with in the United States, for instance. This whole campaign about pornography, about prostitution, about all those social phenomena, which are in any case controversial (nobody here is advocating child pornography or prostitution), only leads to one fundamental question: it's worse when children are consenting and worse still if it is neither pornographic, nor paid for, etc. In other words, the entire

---

3. Françoise Dolto (1908–). French clinical psychoanalyst whose research on children focuses particularly on the theoretical aspects of early maladjustment [L.D.K.].

criminalizing context serves only to bring out the kernel of the accusation: you want to make love with consenting children. It serves only to stress the traditional prohibition and to stress in a new way, with new arguments, the traditional prohibition on sexual relations without violence, without money, without any form of prostitution, that may take place between majors and minors.

J.D.   We already know that some psychiatrists consider that sexual relations between children and adults are always traumatizing. And that if a child doesn't remember them, it is because they remain in his unconscious, but in any case the child is marked for ever, the child will become emotionally disturbed. So what takes place with the intervention of psychiatrists in court is a manipulation of the children's consent, a manipulation of their words. Then there is another use, a fairly recent one, I think, of repressive legislation, which should be noted because it may be used by the legal system as a temporary tactic to fill in the gaps. Indeed in the traditional disciplinary institutions — prisons, schools, and asylums — the nurses, teachers, and so on followed a very strict regimen. Their superiors kept as close a watch on *them* as on the inmates. On the other hand, in the new agencies of social control, control through hierarchy is much more difficult. Indeed we may well wonder whether we are not witnessing a use of common-law legislation; incitement of a minor to commit an immoral act, for example, can be used against social workers and teachers. And I would point out in passing that Villerot is a teacher, that Gallien was a doctor, even if the acts did not take place at a time when he was practicing his profession; that in 1976, in Nantes, a teacher was tried for inciting minors to immoral acts, when what in fact he had done was to supply contraceptives to the boys and girls in his charge. So the common law appears to have been used this time to repress teachers and social workers who were not carrying out their task of social control as their respective hierarchies wished. Between 1830 and 1860, we already see laws directed specifically at teachers: certain judgments stated this explicitly. Article 334 of the Penal Code — which applied to certain persons — teachers, for example — and concerned the incitement of minors to commit immoral acts, was invoked in a case that did not involve a teacher. So we can see the extent to which such legislation is ultimately looking for places where perverts likely to corrupt young people might slip in. The judges were obsessed with this. They were unable to come up with a definition of the perversions. Medicine and psychiatry were to do it for them. In the mid-nineteenth century they had one obsession: if the pervert was everywhere, then they must start tracking him down in the most dangerous institutions, the institutions at risk, among the populations at risk, though the term had not yet been invented. If it has been possible to believe for a time that there was to be a withdrawal of legislation, it was not because we thought we were living in a liberal period but because we knew that more subtle forms of sexual supervision would be set up — and perhaps the apparent freedom that camouflaged these more subtle, more diffuse social controls was going to extend beyond the field of the juridical and the penal. This is not always necessarily the case, and it is quite possible to believe that traditional repressive laws will function side-by-side with much more subtle forms of control, a hitherto unknown form of sexology that would invade all institutions, including educational ones.

FOUCAULT   Indeed it seems to me that we have reached an important point. It is true that we are witnessing a real change: it is probably not true that this change will be favorable to any real alleviation of the legislation on sexuality. As Jean Danet has shown, a very large body of legislation was gradually promulgated, though not without difficulty, throughout the nineteenth century. But this legislation was characterized by the odd fact that it was never capable of saying exactly what it was punishing. *Attentats* (attacks) were punished; and *attentat* was never defined. *Outrages* (outrageous acts) were punished; nobody ever said what an *outrage* was. The law was intended to defend *pudeur* (decency); nobody ever knew what *pudeur* was. In practice, whenever a legislative intervention into the sphere of sexuality had to be justified, the law on *pudeur* was always invoked. And it may be said that all the legislation on sexuality introduced since the nineteenth century in France is a set of laws on *pudeur*. It is certainly a fact that this legislative apparatus, aimed at an undefined object, was never used except in cases when it was considered to be tactically useful. Indeed there has been a whole campaign against teachers. There was a time when it was used against the clergy. There was a use of this legislation to regulate the phenomenon of child prostitution, so important throughout the nineteenth century between 1830 and 1880. We are now aware that this instrument, which possessed the advantage of flexibility, since its object was undefined, could no longer survive when these notions of *pudeur*, *outrage*, and *attentat* were seen as belonging to a particular system of value, culture, and discourse; in the pornographic explosion and the profits that it involves, in this new atmosphere, it is no longer possible to use these words and to make the law function on this basis. But what is emerging and indeed why I believe it was important to speak about the problem of children, what is emerging is a new penal system, a new legislative system, whose function is not so much to punish offenses against these general laws concerning decency, as to protect populations and parts of populations regarded as particularly vulnerable. In other words, the legislator will not justify the measures that he is proposing by saying: the universal decency of mankind must be defended. What he will say is: there are people for whom others' sexuality may become a permanent danger. In this category are, of course, children, who may find themselves at the mercy of an adult sexuality that is alien to them and may well be harmful to them. Hence there is a legislation that appeals to this notion of a vulnerable population, a "high-risk population," as they say, and to a whole body of psychiatric and psychological knowledge imbibed from psychoanalysis — it doesn't really matter whether the psychoanalysis is good or bad — and this will give the psychiatrists the right to intervene twice. Firstly, in general terms, to say: yes, of course, children do have sexuality, we can't go back to those old notions about children being pure and not knowing what sexuality is. But we psychologists or psychoanalysts or psychiatrists, or teachers, we know perfectly well that children's sexuality is a specific sexuality, with its own forms, its own periods of maturation, its own highpoints, its specific drives, and its own latency periods, too. This sexuality of the child is a territory with its own geography that the adult must not enter. It is virgin territory, sexual territory, of course, but territory that must preserve its virginity. The adult will therefore intervene as guarantor of that specificity of child sexuality in order to protect it. And, on the other hand, in each particular case, he will say: this is an instance of an adult bringing his own sexuality into the child's sexuality. It could be that the child, with his own sexuality, may have desired that adult, he may even have consented, he may even have made the first moves. We may even agree that it was he who seduced the adult; but we specialists with our psychological knowledge know perfectly well that even the seducing child runs a risk, in every case, of being damaged and traumatized by the fact that he or she has had sexual dealings with an adult. Consequently, the child must be protected from his own desires, even when his desires orientate him towards an adult. The psychiatrist is the one who will be able to say: I can predict that a trauma of this degree of importance will occur as a result of this or that type of sexual relation. It is therefore within the new legislative framework — basically intended to protect certain vulnerable sections of the population, with the establishment of a new medical power — that a conception of sexuality and above all of the relations between child and adult sexuality will be based; and it is one that is extremely questionable.

G.H.   There is a whole mixture of notions that makes it possible to fabricate this notion of crime or *attentat à la pudeur* offence against decency), a highly complex mixture, which we do not have time here to discuss at length, but which comprises both the religious prohibitions concerning sodomy and the completely new notions, to which Michel Foucault has just referred, about what people think they know of the total difference between the world of the child and the world of the adult. But the overall tendency of today is indisputably not only to fabricate a type of crime that is quite simply the erotic or sensual relationship between a child and an adult, but also, since this may be isolated in the form of a crime, to create a certain category of the population defined by the fact that it tends to indulge in those pleasures. There then exists a particular category of the pervert, in the strict sense, of monsters whose aim in life is to practice sex with children. Indeed they become perverts and intolerable monsters since the crime as such is recognized and constituted, and now strengthened by the whole psychoanalytical and sociological arsenal. What we are doing is constructing an entirely new type of criminal, a criminal so inconceivably horrible that his crime goes beyond any explanation, any victim. It is rather like that kind of legal monster, the term *attentat sans violence*: an attack without violence that is unprovable in any case and leaves no trace, since even the anuscope is unable to find the slightest lesion that might legitimate in some way or other the notion of violence. Thus, in a way, *outrage public à la pudeur* also realizes this, insofar as the offense in question does not require a public in order to be committed. In the case of *attentat sans violence*, the offense in which the police have been unable to find anything, nothing at all, in that case, the criminal is simply a criminal because he is a criminal, because he has those tastes. It is what used to be called a crime of opinion. Take the cast of Parajanov. When a delegation arrived in Paris to see the representative of the Soviet embassy to hand in a protest, the Soviet representative replied: in fact you don't really know why he was condemned; he was condemned for raping a child. This representative read the press: he knew very well that this term inspired more fear than any other. The constitution of this type of criminal, the constitution of this individual perverse enough to do a thing that hitherto had always been done without anybody thinking it right to stick his nose into it, is an extremely grave step from a political point of view. Even if it has not reached the same dimensions as the campaigns against the terrorists, there are nevertheless several hundred cases going before the courts each year. And this campaign suggests that a certain section of the population must henceforth be regarded a priori as criminals, may be pursued in operations of the "help the police" type, and this is what happened in the case of Villerot. The police report notes with interest that the population took part in the search, that people used their cars to look for the satyr. In a way the movement feeds upon itself. The crime vanishes, nobody is concerned any longer to know whether in fact a crime was committed or not, whether someone has been hurt or not. No one is even concerned any more whether there was actually a victim. The crime feeds totally upon itself in a manhunt, by the identification, the isolation of the category of individuals regarded as pedophiles. It culminates in that sort of call for a lynching sent out nowadays by the gutter press.

J.D.   It is true that lawyers defending these cases have a lot of problems. But I should like to say something specifically about such problems. In cases like the Croissant affair, the terrorists' lawyers were regarded immediately as dangerous accomplices of the terrorists.[4] Anyone who came into contact with the affair became implicated. Similarly, the defense of someone found guilty of an indecent act with a minor, especially in the provinces, has extremely serious problems, because many lawyers simply cannot take on such a defense, avoid doing so, and prefer to be appointed by the court. For, in a way, anyone who defends a pedophile may be suspected of having some sympathy for that cause. Even judges think to themselves: if he defends them, it's because he isn't really so much against it himself. It's a serious matter, though it's almost laughable really, though it's a fact known to anyone who has had to deal with such cases whether in the provinces or in Paris: it is extremely difficult both for the lawyer to defend such a case and even sometimes to find a lawyer willing to do so. A lawyer will be quite happy to defend someone accused of murdering ten old ladies. That doesn't bother him in the least. But to defend someone who has touched some kid's cock for a second, that's a real problem. That is part of the whole set up around this new sort of criminal, the adult who has erotic relations with children.

I apologize for referring to history once again, but I think in this matter one can usefully refer to what happened in the nineteenth and early twentieth centuries. As we have seen, when an open letter to the commission for the reform of the penal code was published and signatures placed at the bottom of this letter, it was seen that a number of psychologists, sexologists, and psychiatrists had signed. What they were demanding, then, was the decriminalization of immoral acts with minors over the age of fifteen, a different regime for immoral acts with minors between fifteen and eighteen, abolition of the offense of *outrage public* etc., etc. The fact that psychiatrists and psychologists demanded that the law be brought up to date on this point did not mean that they were on the side of those who were subjected to such repression.

4.   Klaus Croissant: The lawyer of the German terrorist group Baader. He sought asylum in France but was the victim of extradition to Germany in 1978. Foucault took on the cause of Croissant and wrote many articles on his behalf in the *Nouvel observateur* [L.D.R.].

What I mean is, just because one is involved in a struggle against some authority, in this instance, the legal authorities, this does not mean one is on the side of those who are subjected to it. This is proved by the example of Germany, where from the nineteenth century onwards, from 1870, a whole movement protested against a law that was aimed at homosexuals, paragraph 175 of the German penal code. It was not even a habitual crime. There was no need to be an acknowledged homosexual; a single homosexual act was enough, whatever it may be. So a whole movement developed, made up of homosexuals, but also of doctors and psychiatrists, to demand the abolition of this law. But if one reads the literature published by these doctors and psychiatrists it becomes absolutely clear that they expected only one thing from the abolition of this law, namely, to be able to take over the perverts for themselves and to be able to treat them with all the knowledge that they claimed to have acquired since around 1860. With Morel's "Treatise On Degeneracy" what we have is the setting up of a whole nosography of the perversions; and these psychiatrists were demanding in fact that the perverts be handed over to them, that the law should give up any dealings it may have with sexuality, which it speaks of so badly, in so unscientific a way, and that they should be able to treat cases in a perhaps less aggressive, less systematic, less blind way than the law; they alone could say in each case who was guilty, who was sick, and calmly decide what measures were to be taken.[5] I'm not saying that things were reproduced in the same way, but it is interesting to see how the two authorities could be in competition to get hold of that population of perverts.

FOUCAULT   I'm certainly not going to sum up everything that has been said. I think Hocquenghem has shown very clearly what was developing in relation to the strata of the population that had to be "protected." On the other hand, there is childhood, which by its very nature is in danger and must be protected against every possible danger, and therefore any possible act or attack. Then, on the other hand,

5. Bénédict-Auguste Morel (1809–1873). He studied the institution of the insane asylum in Europe and reformulated the coercive procedures used against the mentally ill [L.D.K.].

there are dangerous individuals, who are generally adults of course, so that sexuality, in the new system that is being set up, will take on quite a different appearance from the one it used to have. In the past, laws prohibited a number of acts, indeed acts so numerous one was never quite sure what they were, but, nevertheless, it was acts that the law concerned itself with. Certain forms of behavior were condemned. Now what we are defining and, therefore, what will be found by the intervention of the law, the judge, and the doctor, are dangerous individuals. We're going to have a society of dangers, with, on the one side, those who are in danger and, on the other, those who are dangerous. And sexuality will no longer be a kind of behavior hedged in by precise prohibitions, but a kind of roaming danger, a sort of omnipresent phantom, a phantom that will be played out between men and women, children and adults, and possibly between adults themselves, etc. Sexuality will become a threat in all social relations, in all relations between members of different age groups, in all relations between individuals. It is on this shadow, this phantom, this fear that the authorities would try to get a grip through an apparently generous and, at least general, legislation and through a series of particular interventions that would probably be made by the legal institutions, with the support of the medical institutions. And what we will have there is a new regime for the supervision of sexuality; but in the second half of the twentieth century it may well be decriminalized, but only to appear in the form of a danger, a universal danger, and this represents a considerable change. I would say that the danger lay there.

DISCUSSION

P.H.   I would simply like to mention a work that appeared about ten years ago, but which seems to me to be rather important in the present context. It is a work on the personality of exhibitionists. On the one hand, then, there is this classification that leads to excluding a certain type of exhibitionist from what I would call the system of psychoanalytic reeducation and, on the other hand, it consists in fact in returning, but in rather different ways, apparently to the notion of the born criminal. I would just like to quote this sentence from the book, because it seems to me significant and I shall then say why: "The exhibitionist perversion is a category of exhibitionistic perverts — exhibitionistic perversion corresponds here to a phenomenon of radical amputation from part of the instincts, and this amputation takes place at a stage that is neither genital nor non-genital in sexual development, but in that still mysterious area where personality and instinct seem to me to be potential."

Yes, we are back to Lombroso's notion of the born criminal, which the author himself had just quoted.[6] It is really something that is there before birth, something that appears to be in the embryo; and if I mention the embryo it is because at the present time we are seeing a strong return of certain old methods, though perhaps wrapped up in new forms: methods such as psycho-surgery, in which, for example, homosexuals, pedophiles, and rapists might be operated on in the brain. On the other hand, certain genetic manipulations are being carried out: we had proof of this quite recently, especially in East Germany. All this seems to me very disturbing. Of course, it is pure repression. But, on the other hand, it is also evidence of a certain use of the critique of psychoanalysis that is in a sense quite reactionary, I would say, in inverted commas.

The expert referred to in the text I have quoted is called Jacques Stephani, a psychiatrist in Bordeaux who has contributed to the study of the exhibitionist personality. The expert actually says that the judge must act as one element in a process of therapeutic reeducation, except in the extreme case where the subject is regarded as beyond rehabilitation. This is the moral madman, Lombroso's born criminal. Indeed this idea that legislation, the legal system, the penal system, even medicine must concern themselves essentially with dangers, with dangerous individuals rather than acts, dates more or less from Lombroso and so it is not at all surprising if one finds Lombroso's ideas coming back into fashion. Society has to defend itself against dangerous individuals. There are individuals by nature, by heredity, by genetic code, etc. [Question.] I would just like to ask Guy Hocquenghem, who

6. Cesare Lombroso (1836–1909). Italian founder of the science of criminology. Postulated a theory that distinguishes "normal" individuals from criminal types [L.D.K.].

has established for us pertinent data concerning some examples of the repression associated today with this type of act, how can we create strategic alliances to overcome this dilemma? The natural allies of this type of movement — which are, let's say, the progressive groups — are somewhat reticent about getting mixed up in this sort of business. Movements such as the women's movement are focusing their activities on such problems as rape and are succeeding in increasing the penalization of such acts.

G.H.   We were very careful in the text of the Open Letter to the Penal Code. We took great care to speak exclusively of *attentat à la pudeur sans violence* (an indecent act not involving violence) and *incitation de mineur à la débauche* (incitement of a minor to commit an indecent act). We were extremely careful not to touch, in any way, on the problem of rape, which is totally different. Now I agree with you on one thing, and that is that we have all seen the television program on rape and were all shocked by the reactions it aroused in France, some of which even went so far as telephone calls demanding the chemical castration of the rapists. There are two problems here. There is the problem of rape in the strict sense, on which the women's movement and women in general have expressed themselves perfectly clearly, but there is the other problem of the reactions at the level of public opinion. One triggers off secondary effects of man-hunting, lynching, or moral mobilization.

J.D.   I should like to add something in reply to the same question. When we say that the problem of consent is quite central in matters concerned with pedophilia, we are not, of course, saying that consent is always there. But — and this is where one may separate the attitude of the law with regard to rape and with regard to pedophilia — with regard to rape, judges consider that there is a presumption of consent on the part of the women and that the opposite has to be demonstrated. Whereas where pedophilia is concerned, it's the opposite. It's considered that there is a presumption of non-consent, a presumption of violence, even in a case where no charge of *attentat à la pudeur avec violence* (an indecent act with violence) has been made, that is, in a case in which the charge used is that of *attentat à la pudeur sans violence*, with consenting pleasure — because it has to be said that *attentat à la pudeur sans violence* is the repressive, legal translation of consenting pleasure. We must certainly see how the system of proof is manipulated in opposite ways in the case of rape of women and in the case of indecent assault on a minor.

[Question.] Public opinion, including enlightened opinion such as that of the doctors of the Institute of Sexology, asked at what age there can said to be definite consent. It's a big problem.

FOUCAULT   . . . Yes, it is difficult to lay down barriers. Consent is one thing; it is a quite different thing when we are dealing with the likelihood of a child being believed when, speaking of his sexual relations, his affections, his tender feelings, or his contacts (the sexual adjective is often an embarrassment here, because it does not correspond to reality), a child's ability to explain what his feelings are, what actually happened, how far he is believed, these are quite different things. Now, where children are concerned, they are supposed to have a sexuality that can never be directed towards an adult, and that's that. Secondly, it is supposed that they are not capable of talking about themselves, of being sufficiently lucid about themselves. They are unable to express their feelings. Therefore they are not believed. They are thought to be incapable of sexuality and they are not thought to be capable of speaking about it. But, after all, listening to a child, hearing him speak, hearing him explain what his relations actually are with someone, adult or not, provided one listens with enough sympathy, must allow one to establish more or less what degree of violence if any was used or what degree of consent was given. And to suppose that a child is incapable of explaining what happened and incapable of giving his consent are two abuses that are intolerable, quite unacceptable.

[Question.] If you were a legislator, you would fix no limit and you would leave it to the judges to decide whether or not an indecent act was committed with or without consent? Is that your position?

FOUCAULT   In any case, an age barrier laid down by law does not have much sense. Again, the child may be trusted to say whether or not he was subjected to violence. An examining magistrate, a liberal, told me once when we were discussing this question: after all, there are eighteen-year-old girls who are practically forced to make love with their fathers or their stepfathers; they may be eighteen, but it's an intolerable system of constraint. And one, moreover, that they feel as intolerable, if only people are willing to listen to them and put them in conditions in which they can say what they feel.

G.H.   On the one hand, we didn't put any age limit in our text. In any case, we don't regard ourselves as legislators, but simply as a movement of opinion that demands the abolition of certain pieces of legislation. Our role isn't to make up new ones. As far as this question of consent is concerned, I prefer the terms used by Michel Foucault: listen to what the child says and give it a certain credence. This notion of consent is a trap, in any case. What is sure is that the legal form of an intersexual consent is nonsense. No one signs a contract before making love.

FOUCAULT   Consent is a contractual notion.

G.H.   It's a purely contractual notion. When we say that children are "consenting" in these cases, all we intend to say is this: in any case, there was no violence, or organized manipulation in order to gain affective or erotic relations. It's an important point, all the more important for the children because it's an ambiguous victory in that to get a judge to organize a ceremony in which the children come and say that they were actually consenting is an ambiguous victory. The public affirmation of consent to such acts is extremely difficult, as we know. Everybody — judges, doctors, the defendant — knows that the child was consenting, but nobody says anything, because, apart from anything else, there's no way it can be introduced. It's not the effect of a prohibition by law: it's really impossible to express a very complete relationship between a child and an adult — a relation that is progressive, long, goes through all kinds of stages, which are not all exclusively sexual, through all kinds of affective contacts. To express this in terms of legal consent is an absurdity. In any case, if one listens to what a child says and if he says "I didn't mind," that doesn't have the legal value of a consent. But I'm also very mistrustful of that formal recognition of consent on the part of a minor, because I know it will never be obtained and is meaningless in any case.

17

Sexual Choice, Sexual Act: Foucault and Homosexuality

This interview reveals Foucault's concerns about the strategic role played by sexual preference within a legal and social framework. In evoking the "grammar" of modern homosexual experience Foucault asserts that the condemnation of gay culture has led to an intensification of the sex act itself to the detriment of amorous courtship. Gayness encourages the elaboration of unforeseen relations which explore the internal possibilities of sexuality, a phenomenon that ultimately threatens the heterosexual population. This is the edited transcript of an interview conducted and translated by James O'Higgins. It appeared as pages 10–24 of a special issue of Salmagundi, *58–59 (Fall 1982-Winter 1983), on "Homosexuality: Sacrilege, Vision, Politics."*

J.O'H. Let me begin by asking you to respond to John Boswell's recent book on the history of homosexuality from the beginning of the Christian era through the middle ages.[1]

1. John Boswell, *Christianity, Social Tolerance and Homosexuality: Gay People in Western Europe from the Christian Era to the Fourteenth Century* (Chicago: University of Chicago Press, 1980). According to Boswell the urban culture of Roman society did not distinguish homosexuals from others. The literature of the early Christian church also did not oppose gay behavior. But hostility to the sexuality of gay people became more evident at the time of the dissolution of the Roman state and its urban centers. The eleventh century brought a renaissance of urban life and with it the reappearance of a more visible gay culture which was only to be threatened a century later by theological and legal prejudices. The intolerance of the late Middle Ages continued to have an effect on European culture for centuries to come. To understand the nature of gay relationships Boswell insists that they must be studied within temporal boundaries according to the customs of their day [L.D.K.].

As an historian yourself, do you find his methodology valid? To what extent do you think the conclusions he draws contribute to a better understanding of the contemporary homosexual experience?

FOUCAULT   This is certainly a very important study whose originality is already evident from the way in which it poses the question. Methodologically speaking, the rejection by Boswell of the categorical opposition between homosexual and heterosexual, which plays such a significant role in the way our culture conceives of homosexuality, represents an advance not only in scholarship but in cultural criticism as well. His introduction of the concept of "gay" (in the way he defines it) provides us both with a useful instrument of research and at the same time a better comprehension of how people actually conceive of themselves and their sexual behavior. On the level of investigative results, this methodology has led to the discovery that what has been called the repression of homosexuality does not date back to Christianity properly speaking, but developed within the Christian era at a much later date. In this type of analysis it is important to be aware of the way in which people conceived of their own sexuality. Sexual behavior is not, as is too often assumed, a superimposition of, on the one hand, desires which derive from natural instincts, and, on the other hand, of permissive or restrictive laws which tell us what we should or shouldn't do. Sexual behavior is more than that. It is also the consciousness one has of what one is doing, what one makes of the experience, and the value one attaches to it. It is in this sense that I think the concept "gay" contributes to a positive (rather than a purely negative) appreciation of the type of consciousness in which affection, love, desire, sexual rapport with people have a positive significance.

J.O'H.   I understand that your own recent work has led you to a study of sexuality as it was experienced in ancient Greece.

FOUCAULT   Yes, and precisely Boswell's book has provided me with a guide for what to look for in the meaning people attached to their sexual behavior.

J.O'H.   Does this focus on cultural context and people's discourse about their sexual behavior reflect a methodological decision to bypass the distinction between innate predisposition to homosexual behavior and social conditioning; or do you have any conviction one way or the other on this issue?

FOUCAULT   On this question I have absolutely nothing to say. "No comment."

J.O'H.   Does this mean you think the question is unanswerable, or bogus, or does it simply not interest you?

FOUCAULT   No, none of these. I just don't believe in talking about things that go beyond my expertise. It's not my problem and I don't like talking about things that are not really the object of my work. On this question I have only an opinion; since it is only an opinion it is without interest.

J.O'H.   But opinions can be interesting, don't you agree?

FOUCAULT   Sure, I could offer my opinion, but this would only make sense if everybody and anybody's opinions were also being consulted. I don't want to make use of a position of authority while I'm being interviewed to traffic in opinions.

J.O'H.   Fair enough. We'll shift direction then. Do you think it is legitimate to speak of a class consciousness in connection with homosexuals? Ought homosexuals to be encouraged to think of themselves as a class in the way that unskilled laborers or black people are encouraged to in some countries? How do you envision the political goals of homosexuals as a group?

FOUCAULT   In answer to the first question, I would say that the homosexual consciousness certainly goes beyond one's individual experience and includes an awareness of being a member of a particular social group. This is an undeniable fact that dates back to ancient times. Of course, this aspect of their collective consciousness changes over time and varies from place to place. It has, for instance, on different occasions taken the form of membership in a kind of secret society, membership in a cursed race, membership in a segment of humanity at once privileged and persecuted, all kinds of different modes of collective consciousness, just as, incidentally, the consciousness of unskilled laborers has undergone numerous transformations. It is true that more recently certain homosexuals have, following the political model, developed or tried to create a certain class consciousness. My impression is that this hasn't really been a success, whatever the political consequences it may have had, because homosexuals do not constitute a social class. This is not to say that one can't imagine a society in which homosexuals would constitute a social class. But in our present economic and social mode of organization I don't see this coming to pass.

As for the political goals of the homosexual movement, two points can be made. First, there is the question of freedom of sexual choice that must be faced. I say freedom of sexual *choice* and not freedom of sexual *acts* because there are sexual acts like rape which should not be permitted whether they involve a man and a woman or two men. I don't think we should have as our objective some sort of absolute freedom or total liberty of sexual action. However, where freedom of sexual choice is concerned one has to be absolutely intransigent. This includes the liberty of expression of that choice. By this I mean the liberty to manifest that choice or not to manifest it. Now, there has been considerable progress in this area on the level of legislation, certainly progress in the direction of tolerance, but there is still a lot of work to be done.

Second, a homosexual movement could adopt the objective of posing the question of the place in a given society which sexual choice, sexual behavior and the effects of sexual relations between people could have with regard to the individual. These questions are fundamentally obscure. Look, for example, at the confusion and equivocation that surround pornography, or the lack of elucidation which characterizes the question of the legal status which might be attached to the liaison between two people of the same sex. I don't mean that the legalization of marriage among homosexuals should be an objective; rather, that we are dealing here with a whole series of questions concerning the insertion and recognition — within a legal and social framework — of diverse relations among individuals which must be addressed.

J.O'H. I take it, then, that your point is that the homosexual movement should not only give itself the goal of enlarging legal permissiveness but should also be asking broader and deeper questions about the strategic roles played by sexual preferences and how they are perceived. Is it your point that the homosexual movement should not stop at liberalizing laws relating to personal sexual choice but should also be provoking society at large to rethink its own presuppositions regarding sexuality? In other words, it isn't that homosexuals are deviants who should be allowed to practice in peace, but rather that the whole conceptual scheme which categorizes homosexuals as deviants must be dismantled. This throws an interesting light on the question of homosexual educators. In the debate which arose in California, regarding the right of homosexuals to teach primary and secondary school, for example, those who argued against permitting homosexuals to teach were concerned not only with the likelihood of homosexuals constituting a threat to innocence in that they may be prone to seducing their students, but also that they might preach the gospel of homosexuality.

FOUCAULT The whole question, you see, has been wrongly formulated. Under no circumstances should the sexual choice of an individual determine the profession he is allowed, or forbidden, to practice. Sexual practices simply fall outside the pertinent factors related to the suitability for a given profession. "Yes," you might say, "but what if the profession is used by homosexuals to encourage others to become homosexual?"

Well, let me ask you this, do you believe that teachers who for years, for decades, for centuries, explained to children that homosexuality is intolerable; do you believe that the textbooks that purged literature and falsified history in order to exclude various types of sexual behavior, have not caused ravages at least as serious as a homosexual teacher who speaks about homosexuality and who can do no more harm than explain a given reality, a lived experience?

The fact that a teacher is a homosexual can only have electrifying and intense effects on the students to the extent that the rest of society refuses to admit the existence of homosexuality. A homosexual teacher should not present any more of a problem than a bald teacher, a male teacher in an all female school, a female teacher in an all male school, or an Arab teacher in a school in the 16th district in Paris.

As for the problem of a homosexual teacher who actively tries to seduce his students, all I can say is that in all pedagogical situations the possibility of this problem is present; one finds instances of this kind of behavior much more rampant among heterosexual teachers — for no other reason that that there are a lot more heterosexual teachers.

J.O'H. There is a growing tendency in American intellectual circles, particularly among radical feminists, to distinguish between male and female homosexuality. The basis of this distinction is two-fold. If the term homosexuality is taken to denote not merely a tendency toward affectional relations with members of the same sex but an inclination to find members of the same sex erotically attractive and gratifying, then it is worth insisting on the very different physical things that happen in the one encounter and the other. The second basis for the distinction is that lesbians seem in the main to want from other women what one finds in stable heterosexual relationships: support, affection, long-term commitment, and so on. If this is not the case with male homosexuals, then the difference may be said to be striking, if not fundamental. Do you think the distinction here a useful and viable one? Are there discernible reasons for the differences noted so insistently by many prominent radical feminists?

FOUCAULT [Laughs] All I can do is explode with laughter.

J.O'H. Is the question funny in a way I don't see, or stupid, or both?

FOUCAULT Well, it is certainly not stupid, but I find it very amusing, perhaps for reasons I couldn't give even if I wanted to. What I will say is that the distinction offered doesn't seem to me convincing, in terms of what I observe in the behavior of lesbian women. Beyond this, one would have to speak about the different pressures experienced by men and women who are coming out or are trying to make a life for themselves as homosexuals. I don't think that radical feminists in other countries are likely to see these questions quite in the way you ascribe to such women in American intellectual circles.

J.O'H. Freud argued in "Psychogenesis of a Case of

Hysteria in a Woman" that all homosexuals are liars.[2] We don't have to take this assertion seriously to ask whether there is not in homosexuality a tendency to dissimulation that might have led Freud to make his statement. If we substitute for the word "lie" such words as *metaphor* or *indirection*, may we not be coming closer to the heart of the homosexual style? Or is there any point in speaking of a homosexual style or sensibility? Richard Sennett, for one, has argued that there is no more a homosexual style than there is a heterosexual style. Is this your view as well?

FOUCAULT   Yes, I don't think it makes much sense to talk about a homosexual style. Even on the level of nature, the term homosexuality doesn't have much meaning. I'm reading right now, as a matter of fact, an interesting book which came out recently in the U.S. called *Proust and the Art of Love*.[3] The author shows us how difficult it is to give meaning to the proposition 'Proust was a homosexual.' It seems to me that it is finally an inadequate category. Inadequate, that is, in that we can't really classify behavior on the one hand, and the term can't restore a type of experience on the other. One could perhaps say there is a "gay style" or at least that there is an ongoing attempt to recreate a certain style of existence, a form of existence or art of living, which might be called "gay."

In answer to the question about dissimulation, it is true that, for instance, during the 19th century it was, to a certain degree, necessary to hide one's homosexuality. But to call homosexuals liars is equivalent to calling the resistors under a military occupation liars. It's like calling Jews "money lenders," when it was the only profession they were allowed to practice.

J.O'H.   Nevertheless, it does seem evident, at least on a sociological level, that there are certain characteristics one can discern in the gay style, certain generalizations which (your laughter a moment ago notwithstanding) recall such stereotypifications as promiscuity, anonymity between sexual partners, purely physical relationships, and so on.

2.   See *Standard Edition of the Complete Psychological Works of Sigmund Freud*, volume II, trans. James Strachey (London: Hogarth Press, 1955) [L.D.K.].

3.   J.C. Rivers, *Proust and the Art of Love: The Aesthetics of Sexuality in the Life, Times, and Art of Marcel Proust* (New York: Columbia University Press, 1980) [L.D.K.].

FOUCAULT   Yes, but it's not quite so simple. In a society like ours where homosexuality is repressed, and severely so, men enjoy a far greater degree of liberty than women. Men are permitted to make love much more often and under less restrictive conditions. Houses of prostitution exist to satisfy their sexual needs. Ironically, this has resulted in a certain permissiveness with regard to sexual practices between men. Sexual desire is considered more intense for men and therefore in greater need of release; so, along with brothels, one saw the emergence of baths where men could meet and have sex with each other. The Roman baths were exactly this, a place for heterosexuals to engage in sexual acts. It wasn't until the 16th century, I believe, that these baths were closed as places of unacceptable sexual debauchery. Thus even homosexuality benefited from a certain tolerance toward sexual practices, as long as it was limited to a simple physical encounter. And not only did homosexuality benefit from this situation but, by a curious twist — often typical of such strategies — it actually reversed the standards in such a way that homosexuals came to enjoy even more freedom in their physical relations than heterosexuals. The effect has been that homosexuals now have the luxury of knowing that in a certain number of countries — Holland, Denmark, the United States, and even as provincial a country as France — the opportunities for sexual encounters are enormous. There has been, you might say, a great increase in consumption on this level. But this is not necessarily a natural condition of homosexuality, a biological given.

J.O'H.   The American sociologist Philip Rieff, in an essay on Oscar Wilde entitled "The Impossible Culture," sees Wilde as a forerunner of modern culture.[4] The essay begins with an extensive quotation from the transcript of the trial of Oscar Wilde, and goes on to raise questions about the viability of a culture in which there are no prohibitions, and therefore no sense of vital transgression. Consider, if you will, the following:

"A culture survives the assault of sheer possibility against it only so far as the members of a culture learn, through their

4. Philip Rieff, "The Impossible Culture," *Salmagundi* 58–59 (Fall 1982-Winter 1983), 406–426 [L.D.K.].

membership, how to narrow the range of choices otherwise open."

"As culture sinks into the psyche and becomes character, what Wilde prized above all else is constrained: individuality. A culture in crisis favors the growth of individuality; deep down things no longer weigh so heavily to slow the surface play of experience. Hypothetically, if a culture could grow to full crisis, then everything would be expressed and nothing would be true."

"Sociologically, a truth is whatever militates against the human capacity to express everything. Repression is truth."

Is Rieff's response to Wilde and to the idea of culture Wilde embodied at all plausible?

FOUCAULT   I'm not sure I understand Professor Rieff's remarks. What does he mean, for instance, by "Repression is truth"?

J.O'H.   Actually, I think this idea is similar to claims you make in your own books about truth being the product of a system of exclusions, a network, or *episteme*, that defines what can and cannot be said.

FOUCAULT   Well, the important question here, it seems to me, is not whether a culture without restraints is possible or even desirable but whether the system of constraints in which a society functions leaves individuals the liberty to transform the system. Obviously constraints of any kind are going to be intolerable to certain segments of society. The necrophiliac finds it intolerable that graves are not accessible to him. But a system of constraint becomes truly intolerable when the individuals who are affected by it don't have the means of modifying it. This can happen when such a system becomes intangible as a result of its being considered a moral or religious imperative, or a necessary consequence of medical science. If Rieff means that the restrictions should be clear and well defined, I agree.

J.O'H.   Actually, Rieff would argue that a true culture is one in which the essential truths have been sunk so deep in everyone that there would be no need to articulate them. Clearly, in a society of law, one would need to make explicit a great variety of things that were not to be done, but the main credal assumptions would for the most part remain inaccessible to simple articulation. Part of the thrust of Rieff's work is directed against the idea that it is desirable to do away with credal assumptions in the name of a perfect liberty, and also the idea that restrictions are by definition what all must aim to clear away.

FOUCAULT There is no question that a society without restrictions is inconceivable, but I can only repeat myself in saying that these restrictions have to be within the reach of those affected by them so that they at least have the possibility of altering them. As to credal assumptions, I don't think that Rieff and I would agree on their value or on their meaning or on the devices by which they are taught.

J.O'H. You're no doubt right about that. In any case, we can move now from the legal and sociological spheres to the realm of letters. I would like to ask you to comment on the difference between the erotic as it appears in heterosexual literature and the manner in which sex emerges in homosexual literature. Sexual discourse, as it appears in the great heterosexual novels of our culture — I realize that the designation "heterosexual novels" is itself dubious — is characterized by a certain modesty and discretion that seems to add to the charm of the works. When heterosexual writers treat sex too explicitly it seems to lose some of the mysteriously evocative quality, some of the potency we find in novels like *Anna Karenina*. The point is made with great cogency in a number of essays by George Steiner, as a matter of fact. In contrast to the practice of the major heterosexual novelists, we have the example of various homosexual writers. I'm thinking for example of Cocteau's *The White Paper*, where he succeeds in retaining the poetic enchantment, which heterosexual writers achieve through veiled allusion, while depicting sexual acts in the most graphic terms.[5] Do you think such a difference does exist between these two types of literature, and if so, how would you account for it?

FOUCAULT That's a very interesting question. As I mentioned earlier, over the past few years I have been reading a lot of Latin and Greek texts that describe sexual practices both between men and between men and women; and I've been

5. Jean Cocteau, *Le Livre Blanc* (Paris: Editions des Quatre-Chemins, 1928). English translation with introduction by Margaret Crosland, London, Owen, 1969 [L.D.K.].

struck by the extreme prudishness of these texts (with certain exceptions, of course). Take an author like Lucin. Here we have an ancient writer who talks about homosexuality but in an almost bashful way. At the end of one of his dialogues, for instance, he evokes a scene where a man approaches a boy, puts his hand on the boy's knee, slides his hand under his tunic and caresses the boy's chest; then the hand moves down to the boy's stomach and suddenly the text stops there. Now I would attribute this prudishness, which generally characterizes homosexual literature in ancient times, to the greater freedom then enjoyed by men in their homosexual practices.

J.O'H.   I see. So the more free and open sexual practice is, the more one can afford to be reticent or oblique in talking about it. This would explain why homosexual literature is more explicit in our culture than heterosexual literature. But I'm still wondering how one could use this explanation to account for the fact that the former manages to achieve the same effect in the imagination of the reader as the latter achieves with the exact opposite tools.

FOUCAULT   Let me try to answer your question another way. The experience of heterosexuality, at least since the middle ages, has always consisted of two panels; on the one hand, the panel of courtship in which the man seduces the woman; and, on the other hand, the panel of sexual act itself. Now the great heterosexual literature of the west has had to do essentially with the panel of amorous courtship, that is, above all, with that which precedes the sexual act. All the work of intellectual and cultural refinement, all the aesthetic elaboration of the west, were aimed at courtship. This is the reason for the relative poverty of literary, cultural, and aesthetic appreciation of the sexual act as such.

In contrast, the modern homosexual experience has no relation at all to courtship. This was not the case in ancient Greece, however. For the Greeks, courtship between men was more important than between men and women. (Think of Socrates and Alcibiades.) But in western Christian culture homosexuality was banished and therefore had to concentrate all its energy on the act of sex itself. Homosexuals were not allowed to elaborate a system of courtship because the cultural expression necessary for such an elaboration was denied them. The wink on the street, the split-second decision to get it on, the speed with which homosexual relations are consummated: all these are products of an interdiction. So when a homosexual culture and literature began to develop it was natural for it to focus on the most ardent and heated aspect of homosexual relations.

J.O'H.   I'm reminded of Cassanova's famous expression that "the best moment in life is when one is climbing the stairs." One can hardly imagine a homosexual today making such a remark.

FOUCAULT   Exactly. Rather, he would say something like: "the best moment of love is when the lover leaves in the taxi."

J.O'H.   I can't help thinking that this describes more or less precisely Swann's relations with Odette in the first volume of Proust's great novel.

FOUCAULT   Well, yes, that is true. But though we are speaking there of a relationship between a man and a woman, we should have to take into account in describing it the nature of the imagination that conceived it.

J.O'H.   And we would also then have to take into account the pathological nature of the relationship as Proust himself conceives it.

FOUCAULT   The question of pathology I would as well omit in this context. I prefer simply to return to the observation with which I began this part of our exchange, namely, that for a homosexual, the best moment of love is likely to be when the lover leaves in the taxi. It is when the act is over and the boy is gone that one begins to dream about the warmth of his body, the quality of his smile, the tone of his voice. It is the recollection rather than the anticipation of the act that assumes a primary importance in homosexual relations. This is why the great homosexual writers of our culture (Cocteau, Genet, Burroughs) can write so elegantly about the sexual act itself, because the homosexual imagination is for the most part concerned with reminiscing about the act rather than anticipating it. And, as I said earlier, this is all due to very concrete and practical considerations and says nothing about the intrinsic nature of homosexuality.

J.O'H.   Do you think this has any bearing on the so-called

proliferation of perversions one sees today? I am speaking of phenomena like the S & M scene, golden showers, scatological amusements and the like. We know these practices have existed for some time but they seem much more openly practiced these days.

FOUCAULT   I would say they are much more widely practiced also.

J.O'H.   Do you think this general phenomenon and the fact that homosexuality is "coming out of the closet," making public its form of expression, have anything to do with each other?

FOUCAULT   I would advance the following hypothesis. In a civilization that for centuries considered the essence of the relation between two people to reside in the knowledge of whether one of the two parties was going to surrender to the other, all the interest and curiosity, the cunning and manipulation of people was aimed at getting the other to give in, to go to bed with them. Now when sexual encounters become extremely easy and numerous, as is the case with homosexuality nowadays, complications are only introduced after the fact. In this type of casual encounter it is only after making love that one becomes curious about the other person. Once the sexual act has been consummated you find yourself asking your partner, "By the way, what was your name?"

What you have, then, is a situation where all the energy and imagination, which in the heterosexual relationship were channelled into courtship, now become devoted to intensifying the act of sex itself. A whole new art of sexual practice develops which tries to explore all the internal possibilities of sexual conduct. You find emerging in places like San Francisco and New York what might be called laboratories of sexual experimentation. You might look upon this as the counterpart of the medieval courts where strict rules of proprietary courtship were defined.

It is because the sexual act has become so easy and available to homosexuals that it runs the risk of quickly becoming boring, so that every effort has to be made to innovate and create variations that will enhance the pleasure of the act.

J.O'H.   Yes, but why have these innovations taken the

specific form they have? Why the fascination with excretory functions, for instance?

FOUCAULT   I find the S & M phenomenon in general to be more surprising than that. That is to say, sexual relations are elaborated and developed by and through mythical relations. S & M is not a relationship between he (or she) who suffers and he (or she) who inflicts suffering, but between the master and the one on whom he exercises his mastery. What interests the practitioners of S & M is that the relationship is at the same time regulated and open. It resembles a chess game in the sense that one can win and the other lose. The master can lose in the S & M game if he finds he is unable to respond to the needs and trials of his victim. Conversely, the servant can lose if he fails to meet or can't stand meeting the challenge thrown at him by the master. This mixture of rules and openness has the effect of intensifying sexual relations by introducing a perpetual novelty, a perpetual tension and a perpetual uncertainty which the simple consummation of the act lacks. The idea is also to make use of every part of the body as a sexual instrument.

Actually this is related to the famous phrase *"animal triste post coitum."* Since in homosexuality coitus is given immediately the problem becomes "what can be done to guard against the onset of sadness?"

J.O'H.   Would you venture an explanation for the fact that bisexuality among women today seems to be much more readily accepted by men than bisexuality among men?

FOUCAULT   This probably has to do with the role women play in the imagination of heterosexual men. Women have always been seen by them as their exclusive property. To preserve this image a man had to prevent this woman from having too much contact with other men, so women were restricted to social contact with other women and more tolerance was exercised with regard to the physical rapport between women. By the same token, heterosexual men felt that if they practiced homosexuality with other men this would destroy what they think is their image in the eyes of their women. They think of themselves as existing in the minds of women as master. They think that the idea of their submitting to another man, of being under another man in the act of love, would destroy their image in the eyes of women. Men think that women can only experience pleasure in recognizing men as masters. Even the Greeks had a problem with being the passive partner in a love relationship. For a Greek nobleman to make love to a passive male slave was natural, since the slave was by nature an inferior. But when two Greek men of the same social class made love it was a real problem because neither felt he should humble himself before the other.

Today homosexuals still have this problem. Most homosexuals feel that the passive role is in some way demeaning. S & M has actually helped alleviate this problem somewhat.

J.O'H.   Is it your impression that the cultural forms growing up in the gay community are directed very largely to young people in that community?

FOUCAULT   I think that is largely the case, though I'm not sure there is much to make of it. Certainly, as a fifty-year old man, when I read certain publications produced by and for gays I find that I am not being taken into account at all, that I don't belong somehow. This is not something on the basis of which I would criticize such publications, which after all do what their writers and readers are interested in. But I can't help observing that there is a tendency among articulate gays to think of the major issues and questions of life-style as involving typically people in their twenties.

J.O'H.   I don't see why this might not constitute the basis of a criticism, not only of particular publications but of gay life generally.

FOUCAULT   I didn't say that one *might* not find grounds for criticism, only that I don't choose to or think it useful.

J.O'H.   Why not consider in this context the worship of the youthful male body as the very center of the standard homosexual fantasy, and go on to speak of the denial of ordinary life processes entailed in this, particularly aging and the decline of desire?

FOUCAULT   Look, these are not new ideas you're raising, and you know that. As to the worship of youthful bodies, I'm not convinced that it is peculiar at all to gays or in any way to be regarded as a pathology. And if that is the intention of your question, then I reject it. But I would also remind you that gays are not only involved in life processes, necessarily, but very much aware of them in most cases. Gay publications may not devote as much space as I would like to questions of gay friendship and to the meaning of relationship when there are no established codes or guidelines. But more and more gay people are having to face these questions for themselves. And you know, I think that what most bothers those who are not gay about gayness is the gay life-style, not sex acts themselves.

J.O'H. Are you referring to such things as gays fondling or caressing one another in public, or their wearing flashy clothing, or adopting clone outfits?

FOUCAULT These things are bound to disturb some people. But I was talking about the common fear that gays will develop relationships that are intense and satisfying even though they do not at all conform to the ideas of relationship held by others. It is the prospect that gays will create as yet unforeseen kinds of relationships that many people can not tolerate.

J.O'H. You are referring to relationships that don't involve possessiveness or fidelity — to name only two of the common factors that might be denied?

FOUCAULT If the relationships to be created are as yet unforeseeable, then we can't really say that this feature or that feature will be denied. But you can see how, in the military for example, love between men can develop and assert itself in circumstances where only dead habits and rules were supposed to prevail. And it is possible that changes in established routines will occur on a much broader scale as gays learn to express their feelings for one another in more various ways and develop new life-styles not resembling those that have been institutionalized.

J.O'H. Do you see it as your role to address the gay community especially on matters of general importance such as you have been raising?

FOUCAULT I am of course regularly involved in exchanges with other members of the gay community. We talk, we try to find ways of opening ourselves to one another. But I am wary of imposing my own views, or of setting down a plan or program. I don't want to discourage invention, don't want gay people to stop feeling that it is up to them to adjust their own relationships by discovering what is appropriate in their situations.

J.O'H. You don't think there is some special advice, or a special perspective, that a historian or archaeologist of culture like yourself can offer?

FOUCAULT It is always useful to understand the historical contingency of things, to see how and why things got to be as they are. But I am not the only person equipped to show these things, and I want to avoid suggesting that certain developments were necessary or unavoidable. Gays have to work out some of these matters themselves. Of course there are useful things I can contribute, but again, I want to avoid imposing my own scheme or plan.

J.O'H. Do you think that in general intellectuals are more tolerant towards, or receptive to, different modes of sexual behavior than other people? If so, is this due to a better understanding of human sexuality? If not, how do you think that you and other intellectuals can improve this situation? In what way can the rational discourse on sex best be reoriented?

FOUCAULT I think that where tolerance is concerned we allow ourselves a lot of illusions. Take incest, for example. Incest was a popular practice, and I mean by this, widely practiced among the populace, for a very long time. It was towards the end of the 19th century that various social pressures were directed against it. And it is clear that the great interdiction of incest is an invention of the intellectuals.

J.O'H. Are you referring to figures like Freud and Levi-Strauss or to the class of intellectuals as a whole?

FOUCAULT No, I'm not aiming at anyone in particular. I'm simply pointing out that if you look for studies by sociologists or anthropologists of the 19th century on incest you won't find any. Sure, there were some scattered medical reports and the like, but the practice of incest didn't really seem to pose a problem at the time.

It is perhaps true that in intellectual circles these things are talked about more openly but that is not necessarily a sign of greater tolerance. Sometimes it means the reverse. I remember ten or fifteen years ago, when I used to socialize within the bourgeois milieu, that it was rare indeed for an evening to go by without some discussion of homosexuality and pederasty — usually even before dessert. But these same people who spoke so openly about these matters were not likely to tolerate their sons being pederasts.

As for prescribing the direction rational discourse on sex should take, I prefer not to legislate such matters. For one thing, the expression "intellectual discourse on sex" is too vague. There are very stupid things said by sociologists, sexologists, psychiatrists, doctors and moralists and there are very intelligent things said by members of those same professions. I don't think it's a question of intellectual discourse on sex but a question of asinine discourse and intelligent discourse.

J.O'H.　And I take it that you have lately found a number of works that are moving in the right direction?

FOUCAULT　More, certainly, than I had any reason to expect I would some years ago. But the situation on the whole is still less than encouraging.

Notes on the
Power of Culture

18

The Functions of Literature

This dialogue on the nature of literature is a fragment of a longer interview conducted on June 20, 1975 with Roger-Pol Droit. It took place several months after the publication of Surveiller et punir *(February 1975) and one year prior to the publication of* La Volonté de savoir *(December 1976). Roger Pol-Droit and Michel Foucault had decided to collaborate on a book of interviews — an on-going dialogue — that would further develop some of Foucault's theoretical concepts and address other issues left unexplored in his previously published work. The project, however, was never completed. The following represents a small portion of the "sixth" tape that was subsequently edited by Roger-Pol Droit and published for the first time in* Le Monde, *September 16, 1986. The translation is by Alan Sheridan.*

R.-P.D. What place, what status, have literary texts in your research?

FOUCAULT In *Histoire de la folie* and *Les Mots et les choses*, I merely indicated them, pointed them out in passing. I was the kind of stroller who says: "Well, when you see that, you cannot but talk about *Le Neveu de Rameau*." But I accorded them no role in the actual economy of the process.

For me literature was something I observed, not something I analyzed, or reduced, or integrated into the very field of analysis. It was a rest, a thought on the way, a badge, a flag.

R.-P.D. You didn't want to make these texts express or reflect historical processes.

FOUCAULT   No . . . [silence, thought]. We must approach the question at another level.

No one has ever really analyzed how, out of the mass of things said, out of the totality of actual discourse, a number of these discourses (literary discourse, philosophical discourse) are given a particular sacralization and function.

It would seem that traditionally literary or philosophical discourses could be made to function as substitutes or as a general envelope for all other discourses. Literature had to stand for the rest. People wrote the history of what was said in the eighteenth century, via Fontenelle, or Voltaire, or Diderot, or *La Nouvelle Héloïse*, etc. Or they regard these texts as the expression of something that, ultimately, could not be formulated at a more everyday level.

In this respect, I moved from the expectative (pointing literature out when I happened to encounter it, without indicating its relations with the rest) to a frankly negative position, trying to bring out positively all the non-literary or parallel discourses that were actually produced at a given period, excluding literature itself. In *Surveiller et punir* I refer only to bad literature . . .

R.-P.D.   How is one to distinguish between the good and the bad?

FOUCAULT   That is precisely the question that will have to be confronted one day. On the one hand, we shall have to ask ourselves what exactly is this activity that consists in circulating fiction, poems, stories . . . in a society. We should also analyze a second operation: among all the narratives, why is it that a number of them are sacralized, made to function as "literature"? They are immediately taken up with an institution that was originally very different: the university institution. Now it is beginning to be identified with the literary institution.

There is a very visible slope in our culture. In the nineteenth century, the university was the element within which was constituted a so-called classical literature, and which was valued both as the sole basis of contemporary literature and as a criticism of that literature. Hence a very curious interplay occurs, in the nineteenth century, between literature and the university, between the writer and the professor.

And then, little by little, the two institutions, which, despite all their squabbles, were profoundly linked, tended to merge completely. We know perfectly well that today so-called avant-garde literature is read only by university teachers and their students. We know very well that nowadays a writer over thirty is surrounded by students writing their theses on his work. We know that writers live mainly by teaching and lecturing.

So here we already have the truth of something: the fact that literature functions as literature through an interplay of selection, sacralization, and institutional validation, of which the university is both the operator and the receiver.

R.-P.D. Are there criteria internal to the texts, or is it simply a matter of sacralization by the university institution?

FOUCAULT I don't know. I would simply like to say this: in order to break with a number of myths, including that of the expressive character of literature, it has been very important to pose this great principle that literature is concerned only with itself. If it is concerned with its author, it is so rather in terms of the death, silence, disappearance even of the person writing.

It does not matter whether one refers here to Blanchot or to Barthes. The main point is the importance of this principle: the intransitivity of literature. This was, indeed, the first step by which we were able to get rid of the idea that literature was the locus of every kind of traffic, or the point at which all traffic came to an end, the expression of totalities.

But it seems to me that this was still only a stage. For, by keeping analysis at this level, one runs the risk of not unravelling the totality of sacralizations of which literature has been the object. On the contrary, one runs the risk of sacralizing even more. And this is indeed what happened, right up until 1970. You will have seen how a number of themes originating in Blanchot or Barthes were used in a kind of exaltation, both ultra-lyrical and ultra-rationalizing, of literature as a structure of language capable of being analyzed in itself and on its own terms.

Political implications were absent from this exaltation. Some people were even able to say that literature in itself was so emancipated from all determinations that the very fact of writing was in itself subversive, that the writer, in the very gesture of writing, had an inalienable right to subversion! The writer was, therefore, a revolutionary and the more writing was writing, the more it sank into intransitivity, the more it produced, by that very fact, the movement of revolution! As you know, such things were, unfortunately, said . . .

In fact, the approach used by Blanchot and Barthes tended to a desacralization of literature, by breaking the links that placed it in a position of absolute expression. This rupture implied that the next movement would be to desacralize absolutely and to try to see how, in the general mass of what was said, it was possible at a given moment, in a particular mode, for that particular region of language to be constituted. It must not be asked to bear the decisions of a culture, but rather how it comes about that a culture decided to give it this very special, very strange position.

R.-P.D.   Why strange?

FOUCAULT   Our culture accords literature a place that in a sense, is extraordinarily limited: how many people read literature? What place does it really have in the general expansion of discourses?

But this same culture forces all its children, as they move towards culture, to pass through a whole ideology, a whole ideology of literature during their studies. There is a kind of paradox here.

And it is not unconnected with the declaration that literature is subversive. The fact that someone declares it to be so, in this or that literary review, is of no importance and has no effect. But if at the same moment the entire teaching profession, from primary school teachers to heads of university departments, tell you, explicitly or not, that if you are to find the great decisions of a culture, the points at which it changes direction, then you must turn to Diderot of Sade, or Hegel, or Rabelais — and you'll find it all there. At this level, there is an effect of mutual reinforcement. The so-called avant-garde groups and the great mass of university teachers are in agreement. This has led to a very heavy political blocage.

R.-P.D.   How have you escaped from this blocage?

FOUCAULT   My way of taking up the problem was, first, the book on Raymond Roussel and, then, the book on Pierre

Rivière.[1] Between the two, there is the same question: what is the threshold beyond which a discourse (whether that of a sick person, or a criminal, etc.) begins to function in the field known as literature?

In order to know what literature is, I would not want to study its internal structures. I would rather grasp the movement, the little process, by which a type of non-literary discourse, neglected, forgotten as soon as it was made, enters the literary field. What happens? What is triggered off? How is this discourse modified in its efforts by the fact that it is recognized as literary?

R.-P.D. Nevertheless you have devoted texts to literary works about which this question is not asked. I am thinking in particular of the articles you published in *Critique* on Blanchot, Klossowski, and Bataille.[2] If they were brought together in a single volume, they might provide an image of your itinerary very different from the one we are used to . . .

FOUCAULT Yes, but . . . [pause]. It would be fairly difficult to talk about them. Really, Blanchot, Klossowski, and Bataille, which were in the end the three authors who interested me particularly in the sixties, were for me much

---

1. Raymond Roussel (1877–1933). Experimental French writer best known for *Impressions d'Afrique* [1910] and *Locus Solus* [1914]. His work had an enormous impact on the surrealist movement because of his probing exploration of poetic language. Foucault's *Raymond Roussel* was published in 1963.

Pierre Rivière. Twenty-year-old Norman peasant convicted in 1836 of having murdered his pregnant mother, younger sister, and brother. On studying medical and legal documents Foucault discovered this case, organized a research seminar, and with the collaboration of others published a study, *Moi, Pierre Rivière, ayant égorgé ma mère, ma soeur et mon frère* (Paris: Gallimard-Juillard, 1973; New York: Pantheon, trans. Frank Jellinek, 1975), the centerpiece of which was an untouched memoir transcribed by the murderer [L.D.K.].

2. *Critique*. Pioneering journal in the development of contemporary critical thought founded by Georges Bataille and Jean Piel in 1946. In its early years it explored the relationship between art and religion, thereby contesting the narrow category in which literature had previously been assigned. More recently it has introduced sociological, thematic, and post-structural research.

Pierre Klossowski (1905–). Avant-garde French novelist whose works provoke anxiety from the staging of a violent desire which destroys prohibitions and liberates violent fantasies. Manifesting the influence of Georges Bataille, his most famous works are *Sade mon Prochain* (1947), *La Vocation suspendue* (1950), and *Le Baphomet* (1965). Michel Foucault is the author of an important article on Klossowski, "La prose d'Actéon," *Nouvelle revue française* 135 (March 1964) [L.D.K.].

more than literary works or discourses within literature. They were discourses outside philosophy.

R.-P.D. Meaning?

FOUCAULT Let's take Nietzsche, if you like. In relation to academic philosophical discourse, which has constantly referred him back to himself, Nietzsche represents the outer frontier. Of course, a whole line of Western philosophy may be found in Nietzsche. Plato, Spinoza, the eighteenth-century philosophers, Hegel . . . all this goes through Nietzsche. And yet, in relation to philosophy, Nietzsche has all the roughness, the rusticity, of the outsider, of the peasant from the mountains, that allows him, with a shrug of the shoulders and without it seeming in any way ridiculous, to say with a strength that one cannot ignore: "Come on, all that is rubbish . . ."

Ridding oneself of philosophy necessarily implies a similar lack of deference. You will not get out of it by staying within philosophy, by refining it as much as you can, by circumventing it with one's own discourse. No. It is by opposing it with a sort of astonished, joyful stupidity, a sort of uncomprehending burst of laughter, which, in the end, understands, or, in any case, shatters. Yes . . . it shatters rather than understands.

Insofar as I was, after all, an academic, a professor of philosophy, what remained of traditional philosophical discourse in the work that I had done on the subject of madness embarrassed me. There is a certain Hegelianism surviving there. It isn't necessarily enough to deal with such menial things as police reports, measures taken for confinement, the cries of madmen to escape from philosophy. For me Nietzsche, Bataille, Blanchot, Klossowski were ways of escaping from philosophy.

In Bataille's violence, in Blanchot's insidious, disturbing sweetness, in Klossowski's spirals, there was something that, while setting out from philosophy, brought it into play and into question, emerged from it, then went back into it . . . Something like Klossowski's theory of breathing is bound up, by I know not how many threads, with the whole of Western philosophy. And then by the presentation, the formulation, the way in which it functions in *Le Baphomet*, it completely emerges from it.

The Functions of Literature 313

These exits and entrances through the very wall of philosophy made permeable — therefore, in the end derisory — the frontier between the philosophical and the non-philosophical.

19

Contemporary Music and the Public

This discussion between Michel Foucault and Pierre Boulez evokes the relationship between music and other elements of culture. The accessibility of avant-garde music is rendered problematic by our nostalgia for the past and our inability to recognize and respond to the tonalitics of modern composition. Originally published in CNAC Magazine 15 (May-June 1983), the present text is an English translation by John Rahn that appeared in Perspectives of New Music 24 (Fall-Winter 1985), 6–12.

FOUCAULT It is often said that contemporary music has drifted off track; that it has had a strange fate; that it has attained a degree of complexity which makes it inaccessible; that its techniques have set it on paths which are leading it further and further away. But on the contrary, what is striking to me is the multiplicity of links and relations between music and all the other elements of culture. There are several ways in which this is apparent. On the one hand, music has been much more sensitive to technological changes, much more closely bound to them than most of the other arts (with the exception perhaps of cinema). On the other hand, the evolution of these musics after Debussy or Stravinsky presents remarkable correlations with the evolution of painting. What is more, the theoretical problems which music has posed for itself, the way in which it has reflected on its language, its structures, and its material, depend on a question which has, I believe, spanned the entire twentieth century: the question of "form" which was that of Cézanne or the cubists, which was that of Schoenberg, which was also that of the Russian formalists or the School of Prague.

I do not believe we should ask: with music at such a distance, how can we recapture it or repatriate it? But rather: this music which is so close, so consubstantial with all our culture, how does it happen that we feel it, as it were, projected afar and placed at an almost insurmountable distance?

P.B.   Is the contemporary music "circuit" so different from the various "circuits" employed by symphonic music, chamber music, opera, Baroque music, all circuits so partitioned, so specialized that it's possible to ask if there really is a general culture? Acquaintance through recordings should, in principle, bring down those walls whose economic necessity is understandable, but one notices, on the contrary, that recordings reinforce specialization of the public as well as the performers. In the very organization of concerts or other productions, the forces which different types of music rely on more or less exclude a common organisation, even a polyvalence. Classical or romantic repertory implies a standardized format tending to include exceptions to this rule only if the economy of the whole is not disturbed by them. Baroque music necessarily implies not only a limited group, but instruments in keeping with the music played, musicians who have acquired a specialized knowledge of interpretation, based on studies of texts and theoretical works of the past. Contemporary music implies an approach involving new instrumental techniques, new notations, an aptitude for adapting to new performance situations. One could continue this enumeration and thus show the difficulties to be surmounted in passing from one domain to another: difficulties of organization, of placing oneself in a different context, not to mention the difficulties of adapting places for such or such a kind of performance. Thus, there exists a tendency to form a larger or smaller society corresponding to each category of music, to establish a dangerously closed circuit among this society, its music, and its performers. Contemporary music does not escape this development; even if its attendance figures are proportionately weak, it does not escape the faults of musical society in general: it has its places, its rendezvous, its stars, its snobberies, its rivalries, its exclusivities; just like the other society, it has its market values, its quotes, its statistics. The different circles of music, if they are not Dante's, none the less reveal a prison system in which most feel at ease but whose constraints, on the contrary, painfully chafe others.

FOUCAULT One must take into consideration the fact that for a very long time music has been tied to social rites and unified by them: religious music, chamber music; in the nineteenth century, the link between music and theatrical production is opera (not to mention the political or cultural meanings which the latter had in Germany or in Italy) was also an integrative factor.

I believe that one cannot talk of the "cultural isolation" of contemporary music without soon correcting what one says of it by thinking about other circuits of music.

With rock, for example, one has a completely inverse phenomenon. Not only is rock music (much more than jazz used to be) an integral part of the life of many people, but it is a cultural initiator: to like rock, to like a certain kind of rock rather than another, is also a way of life, a manner of reacting; it is a whole set of tastes and attitudes.

Rock offers the possibility of a relation which is intense, strong, alive, "dramatic" (in that rock presents itself as a spectacle, that listening to it is an event and that it produces itself on stage), with a music that is itself impoverished, but through which the listener affirms himself; and with the other music, one has a frail, faraway, hothouse, problematical relation with an erudite music from which the cultivated public feels excluded.

One cannot speak of a single relation of contemporary culture to music in general, but of a tolerance, more or less benevolent, with respect to a plurality of musics. Each is granted the "right" to existence, and this right is perceived as an equality of worth. Each is worth as much as the group which practices it or recognizes it.

P.B. Will talking about musics in the plural and flaunting an eclectic ecumenicism solve the problem? It seems, on the contrary, that this will merely conjure it away — as do certain devotees of an advanced liberal society. All those musics are good, all those musics are nice. Ah! Pluralism! There's nothing like it for curing incomprehension. Love, each one of you in your corner, and each will love the others. Be liberal, be generous toward the tastes of others, and they will be generous to yours. Everything is good, nothing is bad; there aren't any values, but everyone is happy. This discourse, as liberating as it may wish to be, reinforces, on the contrary, the ghettos, comforts one's clear conscience for being in a ghetto, especially if from time to time one tours the ghettos of others. The economy is there to remind us, in case we get lost in this bland utopia: there are musics which bring in money and exist for commercial profit; there are musics that cost something, whose very concept has nothing to do with profit. No liberalism will erase this distinction.

FOUCAULT I have the impression that many of the elements that are supposed to provide access to music actually impoverish our relationship with it. There is a quantitative mechanism working here. A certain rarity of relation to music could preserve an ability to choose what one hears, and thus a flexibility in listening. But the more frequent this relation is (radio, records, cassettes), the more familiarities it creates; habits crystallize; the most frequent becomes the most acceptable, and soon the only thing perceivable. It produces a "tracing," as the neurologists say.

Clearly, the laws of the marketplace will readily apply to this simple mechanism. What is put at the disposition of the public is what the public hears. And what the public finds itself actually listening to, because it's offered up, reinforces a certain taste, underlines the limits of a well-defined listening capacity, defines more and more exclusively a schema for listening. Music had better satisfy this expectation, etc. So commercial productions, critics, concerts, everything that increases the contact of the public with music, risks making perception of the new more difficult.

Of course the process is not unequivocal. Certainly increasing familiarity with music also enlarges the listening capacity and gives access to possible differentiations, but this phenomenon risks being only marginal; it must in any case remain secondary to the main impact of experience, if there is no real effort to derail familiarities.

It goes without saying that I am not in favor of a rarefaction of the relation to music, but it must be understood that the everydayness of this relation, with all the economic stakes that are riding on it, can have this paradoxical effect of rigidifying tradition. It is not a matter of making access to music more rare, but of making its frequent appearances less devoted to habits and familiarities.

P.B. We ought to note that not only is there a focus on the past, but even on the past in the past, as far as the performer is concerned. And this is of course how one attains ecstasy while listening to the interpretation of a certain classical work by a performer who disappeared decades ago; but ecstasy will reach orgasmic heights when one can refer to a performance of 20 July 1947 or of 30 December 1938. One sees a pseudo-culture of documentation taking shape, based on the exquisite hour and fugitive moment, which reminds us at once of the fragility and of the durability of the performer become immortal, rivalling now the immortality of the masterpiece. All the mysteries of the Shroud of Turin, all the powers of modern magic, what more could you want as an alibi for reproduction as opposed to real production? Modernity itself is this technical superiority we possess over former eras in being able to recreate the event. Ah! If we only had the first performance of the Ninth, even — especially — with all its flaws, or if only we could make Mozart's own delicious difference between the Prague and Vienna versions of *Don Giovanni* . . . This historicizing carapace suffocates those who put it on, compresses them in an asphyxiating rigidity; the mephitic air they breathe constantly enfeebles their organism in relation to contemporary adventure. I imagine Fidelio glad to rest in his dungeon, or again I think of Plato's cave: a civilization of shadow and of shades.

FOUCAULT Certainly listening to music becomes more difficult as its composition frees itself from any kind of schemas, signals, perceivable cues for a repetitive structure.

In classical music, there is a certain transparency from the composition to the hearing. And even if many compositional features in Bach or Beethoven aren't recognizable by most listeners, there are always other features, important ones, which are accessible to them. But contemporary music, by trying to make each of its elements a unique event, makes any grasp or recognition by the listener difficult.

P.B. Is there really only lack of attention, indifference on the part of the listener toward contemporary music? Might not the complaints so often articulated be due to laziness, to inertia, to the pleasant sensation of remaining in known territory? Berg wrote, already half a century ago, a text entitled "Why is Schoenberg's music hard to understand?" The difficulties he described then are nearly the same as those we hear of now. Would they always have been the same? Probably, all novelty bruises the sensibilities of those unaccustomed to it. But it is believable that nowadays the communication of a work to a public presents some very specific difficulties. In classical and romantic music, which constitutes the principal resource of the familiar repertory, there are schemas which one obeys, which one can follow independently of the work itself, or rather which the work must necessarily exhibit. The movements of a symphony are defined in their form and in their character, even in their rhythmic life; they are distinct from one another, most of the time actually separated by a pause, sometimes tied by a transition that can be spotted. The vocabulary itself is based on "classified" chords, well-named: you don't have to analyze them to know what they are and what function they have. They have the efficacy and security of signals; they recur from one piece to another, always assuming the same appearance and the same functions. Progressively, these reassuring elements have disappeared from "serious" music. Evolution has gone in the direction of an ever more radical renewal, as much in the form of works as in their language. Musical works have tended to become unique events, which do have antecedents, but are not reducible to any guiding schema admitted, a priori, by all; this creates, certainly, a handicap for immediate comprehension. The listener is asked to familiarize himself with the course of the work and for this to listen to it a certain number of times. When the course of the work is familiar, comprehension of the work, perception of what it wants to express, can find a propitious terrain to bloom in. There are fewer and fewer chances for the first encounter to ignite perception and comprehension. There can be a spontaneous connection with it, through the force of the message, the quality of the writing, the beauty of the sound, the readability of the cues, but deep understanding can only come from repeated hearings, from remaking the course of the work, this repetition taking the place of an accepted schema such as was practiced previously.

The schemas — of vocabulary, of form — which had been evacuated from what is called serious music (sometimes called learned music) have taken refuge in certain popular forms, in the objects of musical consumption. There, one still creates according to the genres, the accepted typologies. Conservatism is not necessarily found where it is expected: it is undeniable that a certain conservatism of form and language is at the base of all the commercial productions adopted with great enthusiasm by generations who want to be anything but conservative. It is a paradox of our times that played or sung protest transmits itself by means of an eminently subornable vocabulary, which does not fail to make itself known: commercial success evacuates protest.

FOUCAULT And on this point there is perhaps a divergent evolution of music and painting in the twentieth century. Painting, since Cézanne, has tended to make itself transparent to the very act of painting: the act is made visible, insistent, definitively present in the picture, whether it be by the use of elementary signs, or by traces of its own dynamic. Contemporary music on the contrary offers to its hearing only the outer surface of its composition.

Hence there is something difficult and imperious in listening to this music. Hence the fact that each hearing presents itself as an event which the listener attends, and which he must accept. There are no cues which permit him to expect it and recognize it. He listens to it happen. This is a very difficult mode of attention, one which is in contradiction to the familiarities woven by repeated hearing of classical music.

The cultural insularity of music today is not simply the consequence of deficient pedagogy or propagation. It would be too facile to groan over the conservatories or complain about the record companies. Things are more serious. Contemporary music owes this unique situation to its very composition. In this sense, it is willed. It is not a music that tries to be familiar; it is fashioned to preserve its cutting edge. One may repeat it, but it does not repeat itself. In this sense, one cannot come back to it as to an object. It always pops up on frontiers.

P.B. Since it wants to be in such a perpetual situation of discovery — new domains of sensibility, experimentation with new material — is contemporary music condemned to remain a Kamchatka (Baudelaire, Saint-Beuve, remember?) reserved for the intrepid curiosity of infrequent explorers? It is remarkable that the most reticent listeners should be those who have acquired their musical culture exclusively in the stores of the past, indeed of a particular past; and the most open — only because they are the most ignorant? — are the listeners with a sustained interest in other means of expression, especially the plastic arts. The "foreigners" the most receptive? A dangerous connection which would tend to prove that current music would detach itself from the "true" musical culture in order to belong to a domain both vaster and more vague, where amateurism would preponderate, in critical judgment as in creation. Don't call that "music" — then we are willing to leave you your plaything; that is in the jurisdiction of a different appreciation, having nothing to do with the appreciation we reserve for true music, the music of the masters. When this argument has been made, even in its arrogant naiveté, it approaches an irrefutable truth. Judgment and taste are prisoners of categories, of pre-established schemas which are referred to at all costs. Not, as they would have us believe, that the distinction is between an aristocracy of sentiments, a notability of expression, and a chancy craft based on experimentation: thought versus tools. It is, rather, a matter of a listening that could not be modulated or adapted to different ways of inventing music. I certainly am not going to preach in favor of an ecumenicism of musics, which seems to me nothing but a supermarket aesthetic, a demagogy that dare not speak its name and decks itself with good intentions the better to camouflage the wretchedness of its compromise. Moreover, I do not reject the demands of quality in the sound as well as in the composition: aggression and provocation, *bricolage* and bluff are but insignificant and harmless palliatives. I am fully aware — thanks to many experiences, which could not have been more direct — that beyond a certain complexity perception finds itself disoriented in a hopelessly entangled chaos, that it gets bored and hangs up. This amounts to saying that I can keep my critical reactions and that my adherence is not automatically derived from the fact of "contemporaneity" itself. Certain modulations of hearing are already occurring, rather badly as a matter of fact, beyond particular historical limits. One doesn't listen to Baroque music — especially lesser works — as one listens to Wagner or Strauss; one doesn't listen to the polyphony of the Ars Nova as one listens to Debussy or Ravel. But in this latter case, how many listeners are ready to vary their "mode of being," musically speaking? And yet in order for musical culture, all musical culture, to be assimilable, there need only be this adaptation to criteria, and to conventions, which invention complies with according to the historical moment it occupies. This expansive respiration of the ages is at the opposite extreme from the asthmatic wheezings the fanatics make us hear from spectral reflections of the past in a tarnished mirror. A culture forges, sustains, and transmits itself in an adventure with a double face: sometimes the brutality, struggle, turmoil; sometimes meditation, nonviolence, silence. Whatever form the adventure may take — the most surprising is not always the noisiest, but the noisiest is not irremediably the most superficial — it is useless to ignore it, and still more useless to sequestrate it. One might go so far as to say there are probably uncomfortable periods when the coincidence of invention and convention is more difficult, when some aspect of invention seems absolutely to go beyond what we can tolerate or "reasonably" absorb; and that there are other periods when things relapse to a more immediately accessible order. The relations among all these phenomena — individual and collective — are so complex that applying rigorous parallelisms or groupings to them is impossible. One would rather be tempted to say: gentlemen, place your bets, and for the rest, trust in the *air du temps*. But, please, play! Play! Otherwise, what infinite secretions of boredom!

20

The Masked Philosopher

Between 1979 and 1984 the newspaper Le
Monde published a weekly series of interviews
with leading European intellectuals. On April 6–7,
1980 an interview between Christian
Delacampagne and Michel Foucault was published in which the latter opted for the mask of
anonymity — the philosopher declined to reveal
his name — in order to demystify the power
society ascribes to the "name" of the intellectual.
Foucault sets out to liberate the consumer of
culture from a critical discourse that is overdeter-
mined by the characters that dominate our
perceptions. This interview was reprinted in
Entretiens avec Le Monde, I, Philosophies (Paris:
La Découverte, 1984), 21–30. The translation is
by Alan Sheridan.

C.D.   Allow me to ask you first why you have chosen anonymity?

FOUCAULT   You know the story of the psychologists who went to make a little film-test in a village in darkest Africa. They then asked the spectators to tell the story in their own words. Well, only one thing interested them in this story involving three characters: the movement of the light and shadow through the trees.

In our societies, characters dominate our perceptions. Our attention tends to be arrested by the activities of faces that come and go, emerge and disappear.

Why did I suggest that we use anonymity? Out of nostalgia for a time when, being quite unknown, what I said had some chance of being heard. With the potential reader, the surface of contact was unrippled. The effects of the book might land in unexpected places and form shapes that I had never thought of. A name makes reading too easy.

I shall propose a game: that of the "year without a name." For a year books would be published without their authors' names. The critics would have to cope with a mass of entirely anonymous books. But, now I come to think of it, it's possible they would have nothing to do: all the authors would wait until the following year before publishing their books . . .

C.D. Do you think intellectuals today talk too much? That they encumber what they say with a lot of stuff, much of it irrelevant to what they really have to say?

FOUCAULT The word *intellectual* strikes me as odd. Personally, I've never met any intellectuals. I've met people who write novels, others who treat the sick. People who work in economics and others who write electronic music. I've met people who teach, people who paint, and people of whom I have never really understood what they do. But intellectuals, never.

On the other hand, I've met a lot of people who talk about "the intellectual." And, listening to them, I've got some idea of what such an animal could be. It's not difficult — he's quite personified. He's guilty about pretty well everything: about speaking out and about keeping silent, about doing nothing and about getting involved in everything . . . In short, the intellectual is raw material for a verdict, a sentence, a condemnation, an exclusion . . .

I don't find that intellectuals talk too much, since for me they don't exist. But I do find that more and more is being said about intellectuals, and I don't find it very reassuring.

I have an unfortunate habit. When people speak about this or that, I try to imagine what the result would be if translated into reality. When they "criticize" someone, when they "denounce" his ideas, when they "condemn" what he writes, I imagine them in the ideal situation in which they would have complete power over him. I take the words they use — *demolish, destroy, reduce to silence, bury* — and see what the effect would be if they were taken literally. And I catch a glimpse of the radiant city in which the intellectual would be in prison or, if he were also a theoretician, hanged, of course. We don't, it's true, live under a regime in which intellectuals are sent to the ricefields. But have you heard of a certain Toni Negri?[1] Isn't he in prison simply for being an intellectual?

C.D. So what has led you to hide behind anonymity? Is it the way in which philosophers, nowadays, exploit the publicity surrounding their names?

FOUCAULT That doesn't shock me in the least. In the corridors of my old lycée I used to see plaster busts of great men. And now at the bottom of the front pages of newspapers I see the photograph of some thinker or other. I don't know whether things have improved, from an aesthetic point of view. Economic rationality certainly . . .

I'm very moved by a letter that Kant wrote when he was already very old: he was in a hurry, he says, against old age and declining sight, and confused ideas, to finish one of his books for the Leipzig Fair. I mention this to show that it isn't of the slightest importance. With or without publicity, with or without a fair, a book is something quite special. I shall never be convinced that a book is bad because its author has been seen on television. But, of course, it isn't good for that reason alone either.

If I have chosen anonymity, it is not, therefore, to criticize this or that individual, which I never do. It's a way of addressing the potential reader, the only individual here who is of interest to me, more directly: "Since you don't know who I am, you will be more inclined to find out why I say what you read; just allow yourself to say, quite simply, it's true, it's false. I like it or I don't like it. Period."

C.D. But doesn't the public expect the critic to provide him with precise assessments as to the value of a work?

FOUCAULT I don't know whether the public does or does not expect the critic to judge works or authors. Judges were there, I think, before he was able to say what he wanted.

It seems that Courbet had a friend who used to wake up

---

1. Italian philosopher, ex-professor at the University of Padua; a leading intellectual influence in the extreme-left movement, Workers' Autonomy. Underwent four years and three months preventative detention for armed insurrection against the state, subversive association, and the formation of armed gangs. Was freed on July 8, 1983, after being elected a Radical deputy during his imprisonment. His parliamentary immunity was lifted by the Chamber of Deputies, new warrants for his arrest were issued, and he took refuge in France.

in the night yelling: "I want to judge, I want to judge." It's amazing how people like judging. Judgment is being passed everywhere, all the time. Perhaps it's one of the simplest things mankind has been given to do. And you know very well that the last man, when radiation has finally reduced his last enemy to ashes, will sit down behind some rickety table and begin the trial of the individual responsible.

I can't help but dream about a kind of criticism that would not try to judge, but to bring an oeuvre, a book, a sentence, an idea to life; it would light fires, watch the grass grow, listen to the wind, and catch the sea-foam in the breeze and scatter it. It would multiply, not judgments, but signs of existence; it would summon them, drag them from their sleep. Perhaps it would invent them sometimes — all the better. All the better. Criticism that hands down sentences sends me to sleep; I'd like a criticism of scintillating leaps of the imagination. It would not be sovereign or dressed in red. It would bear the lightning of possible storms.

C.D.   So there are so many things to tell people about, so much interesting work being done, that the mass media ought to talk about philosophy all the time . . .

FOUCAULT   It's true that there is a traditional discomfort between the "critics" and those who write books. The first feel misunderstood and the second think the first are trying to bring them to heel. But that's the game.

It seems to me that today the situation is rather special. We have institutions administering shortages, whereas we are in a situation of superabundance.

Everybody has noticed the over-excitement that often accompanies the publication (or reprinting) of some work that may in fact be quite interesting. But it is never presented as being anything less than the "subversion of all the codes," the "antithesis of contemporary culture," the "radical questioning of all our ways of thinking." One would be justified in thinking that its author must be some unknown fellow living on the fringes of society.

On the other hand, others must be banished into total oblivion, from which they must never be allowed to reemerge; they were only the froth of "mere fashion," a mere product of the cultural institution, and so forth.

A superficial, very Parisian phenomenon, it will be said. I see it rather as the effect of a deep-seated anxiety. The feeling of "no room," "him or me," "it's my turn now." We have to walk in line because of the extreme narrowness of the place where one can listen and make oneself heard.

Hence a sort of anxiety that finds expression in innumerable symptoms, some funny, some less so. Hence, too, on the part of those who write, a sense of impotence when confronted by the mass media, which they criticize for running the world of books and creating or destroying reputations at will. Hence, too, the feeling among the critics that they will not be heard unless they shout louder and pull a rabbit out of the hat each week. Hence, too, a pseudo-politicization, which masks, beneath the need to wage an "ideological struggle" or to root out "dangerous thoughts," a deep-seated anxiety that one will not be heard or read. Hence, too, the fantastic phobia for power: anybody who writes exerts a disturbing power upon which one must try to place limitations, if not actually to put an end to it. Hence, too, the declaration, repeated over and over, that everything nowadays is empty, desolate, uninteresting, unimportant: a declaration that obviously comes from those who, not doing anything themselves, consider that there are too many others who are.

C.D.   But don't you think that our period is really lacking in great writers and in minds capable of dealing with its problems?

FOUCAULT   No, I don't subscribe to the notion of a decadence, of a lack of writers, of the sterility of thought, of a gloomy future, lacking in prospects.

On the contrary, I believe that there is a plethora. What we are suffering from is not a void, but inadequate means for thinking about everything that is happening. There is an overabundance of things to be known: fundamental, terrible, wonderful, funny, insignificant, and crucial at the same time. And there is an enormous curiosity, a need, a desire to know. People are always complaining that the mass media stuff one's head with people. There is a certain misanthropy in this idea. On the contrary, I believe that people react; the more one convinces them, the more they question things. The mind isn't made of soft wax. It's a reactive substance. And the desire to know more, and to know it more deeply and to know other things increases as one tries to stuff peoples' heads.

If you accept that and if you add that there's a whole host of people being trained in the universities and elsewhere who could act as intermediaries between this mass of things and this thirst for knowledge, you will soon come to the conclusion that student unemployment is the most absurd thing imaginable. The problem is to multiply the channels, the bridges, the means of information, the radio and television networks, the newspapers.

Curiosity is a vice that has been stigmatized in turn by Christianity, by philosophy, and even by a certain conception of science. Curiosity is seen as futility. However, I like the word; it suggests something quite different to me. It evokes "care"; it evokes the care one takes of what exists and what might exist; a sharpened sense of reality, but one that is never immobilized before it; a readiness to find what surrounds us strange and odd; a certain determination to throw off familiar ways of thought and to look at the same things in a different way; a passion for seizing what is happening now and what is disappearing; a lack of respect for the traditional hierarchies of what is important and fundamental.

I dream of a new age of curiosity. We have the technical means; the desire is there; there is an infinity of things to know; the people capable of doing such work exist. So what is our problem? Too little: channels of communication that are too narrow, almost monopolistic, inadequate. We mustn't adopt a protectionist attitude, to stop "bad"information from invading and stifling the "good." We must rather increase the possibility for movement backwards and forwards. This would not lead, as people often fear, to uniformity and levelling down, but, on the contrary, to the simultaneous existence and differentiation of these various networks.

C.D.   I imagine that at this level the mass media and the universities, instead of continuing to oppose one another, might play complementary roles.

FOUCAULT   You remember Sylvain Lévi's wonderful saying: when you have one listener, it's teaching; when you have two, it's popularization. Books, universities, learned journals are also information media. One should refrain from calling a mass medium every channel of information to which one cannot or does not wish to gain access. The problem is to know how to exploit the differences, whether we ought to set up a reserve, a "cultural park," for delicate species of scholars threatened by the rapacious inroads of mass information, while the rest of the space would be a huge market for shoddy products. Such a division does not seem to me to correspond to reality. What's more, it isn't at all desirable. If useful differentiations are to be brought into play, there must not be any such division.

C.D.   Let's risk a few concrete propositions. If everything is going badly, where do we make a start?

FOUCAULT   But everything *isn't* going badly. In any case, I believe we shouldn't confuse useful criticism of things with repetitive jeremiads against people. As for concrete propositions, they can't just make an appearance like gadgets, unless certain general principles are accepted first. And the first of such general principles should be that the right to knowledge must not be reserved to a particular age-group or to certain categories of people, but that one must be able to exercise it constantly and in many different ways.

C.D.   Isn't this desire for knowledge somewhat ambiguous? What, in fact, are people to do with all that knowledge that they are going to acquire? What use will it be to them?

FOUCAULT   One of the main functions of teaching was that the training of the individual should be accompanied by his being situated in society. We should now see teaching in such a way that it allows the individual to change at will, which is possible only on condition that teaching is a possibility always being offered.

C.D.   Are you in fact for a society of scholars?

FOUCAULT   I'm saying that people must be constantly able to plug into culture and in as many ways as possible. There ought not to be, on the one hand, this education to which one is subjected and, on the other, this information one is fed.

C.D.   What becomes of the eternal questions of philosophy in this learned society? . . . Do we still need them, these unanswerable questions, these silences before the unknowable?

FOUCAULT   What is philosophy if not a way of reflecting, not so much on what is true and what is false, as on our relationship to truth? People sometimes complain that there is no dominant philosophy in France. So much the better for that! There is no sovereign philosophy, it's true, but a philosophy or rather philosophy in activity. The movement by which, not without effort and uncertainty, dreams and illusions, one detaches oneself from what is accepted as true and seeks other rules — that is philosophy. The displacement and transformation of frameworks of thinking, the changing of received values and all the work that has been done to think otherwise, to do something else, to become other than what one is — that, too, is philosophy. From this point of view, the last thirty years or so have been a period of intense philosophical activity. The interaction between analysis, research, "learned" or "theoretical" criticism, and changes in behavior, in people's real conduct, their way of being, their relation to themselves and to others has been constant and considerable.

I was saying just now that philosophy was a way of reflecting on our relationship to truth. It should also be added that it is a way of interrogating ourselves: if this is the relationship that we have with truth, how must we behave? I believe that a considerable and varied amount of work has been done and is still being done that alters both our relation to truth and our way of behaving. And this has taken place in a complex situation, between a whole series of investigations and a whole set of social movements. It's the very life of philosophy.

It is understandable that some people should weep over the present void and hanker instead, in the world of ideas, after a little monarchy. But those who, for once in their lives, have found a new tone, a new way of looking, a new way of doing, those people, I believe, will never feel the need to lament that the world is error, that history is filled with people of no consequence, and that it is time for others to keep quiet so that at last the sound of their disapproval may be heard . . .